C000070194

SOUTHWARK LIBRARIES

SK 1393679 4

Shadow Warrior

Shadow Warrior

**THE AUTOBIOGRAPHY
OF GREENPEACE INTERNATIONAL
FOUNDER DAVID McTAGGART**

David McTaggart

with Helen Slinger

ORION

To my children
Lisa, Kerin, Tamra, Julia and George –
and to all the children of the world.

Copyright © Boussac Limited & Helen Slinger 2002

All rights reserved

The right of Helen Slinger to be identified as the author of this work
has been asserted by her in accordance with the
Copyright, Designs and Patents Act 1988.

First published in Great Britain in 2002 by
Orion Books
An imprint of the Orion Publishing Group Ltd
Orion House, 5 Upper St Martin's Lane, London WC2H 9EA

A CIP catalogue record for this book is available
from the British Library

ISBN: 0 75285 247 7

Pictures supplied by kind permission of Katz Pictures Ltd, Sipa Press/REX Features,
Gamma, Kerin McTaggart, Greenpeace, *Vancouver Sun* and Steve Rendall.

Every effort has been made to trace the copyright holders, but if any
have been inadvertently overlooked, the publishers will be pleased to
make the necessary arrangements at the first opportunity.

Printed in Great Britain by
Butler & Tanner Ltd, Frome and London

Acknowledgements

Dozens of friends and colleagues contributed to these memoirs. It would be perilous to attempt to thank them all – some would certainly get missed. But a few gave particularly generously of their time and their (sometimes personal) papers. Special thanks then to Erik Amfitheatrof, Leslie Busby, Brian Fitzgerald, Lennart Forsufhvud, Sidney Holt, Anna Horne, Bob Hunter, Myrna McTaggart, John May, David Newman, Michael Nielsen, Jenny Stannard and Pete Wilkinson. Grazie!

Nobody should be afraid of the dark side of his nature. It's there. Why disavow it? You try not to misuse it, y'know? You release it mostly in your work if you can. It's certainly there in mine ... If I got rid of my demons I'd lose my angels. *Tennessee Williams*

Foreword

I stared at David in disbelief from across the room. 'You want me to go all the way to the Antarctic as part of a million-dollar campaign, which took the organization months to approve, which has taken the best part of a year to organize, just so that I can provoke the American Base Commander to punch me on the jaw?' David's eyebrows arched in bewilderment at my inability to grasp such a simple concept. 'You bet your sweet ass that's what I want. If those guys try to force you out of McMurdo, they'll be admitting that they see Antarctica as their territory. It's not theirs; it's ours. It belongs to all the peoples of the world. That *is* the campaign. So get him to take a swing at you, make sure he connects and for crissakes get it on film.' I had just been initiated to the million-dollar punch campaign to which only three people were ever privy. This was David McTaggart at his obscure best. Amid the freneticism of a massive campaign initiative, he saw the fastest and most direct route to success. And the fact that it involved me getting a right-hander seemed not to concern him one jot.

David Fraser McTaggart was the father of the modern, active and outspoken genre of green organizations. While he could not claim to be the founder of Greenpeace per se, he was certainly the founder of the movement as we know it today. It was he who took the small, embryonic organisation of the early 1970s and worked it, empowered it and gave it the confidence to grow into a global force which came to strike fear into the largest of corporations. He recognized the jaw-dropping potential of an organization prepared to carry out unheard-of acts of heroic direct action from deep in the open ocean in defence of the environment. The combination of excitement, drama and crusading self-sacrifice was a heady and volatile mix, and David's philosophy was simple and compelling: reach tens of millions globally with the irresistible, dramatic images created by direct action and turn that exposure into a political force for environmental reform. It was revolutionary, innovative and it damn near worked.

McTaggart believed so strongly in this approach that he would sometimes enrage fellow Greenpeace activists by demanding that a direct action be terminated to allow valuable film footage to be transported ashore and screened as early as possible. He would argue with a cold, detached and incontrovertible logic that direct action does not stop an environmental abuse. Public opinion does.

He was a pragmatist as well as a realist. He believed that campaigns should maximize results while demanding the minimum of effort – a simple but sadly underemployed principle these days. If a phone call to the appropriate high-level contact in a company or indeed in a government could prevent a problem developing or stop an abuse, he would make it. Should that fail, the next level of campaigning methodology would be employed and so on until non-violent direct action became the last resort. This approach was carved into the Greenpeace campaign handbook and was elaborated upon to create the beginnings of a strategic approach to campaigning, an approach which was honed by the Greenpeace campaign organizations of the 1980s. The golden rule adopted universally by any pressure group worthy of its name is: be sure of your case and your facts before you act and make sure you have exhausted all other avenues. David could curl your toes with his naïvety, but his clarity of vision and incisiveness would often be so powerful that it would arrive like a punch on the nose.

Greenpeace would never have reached the heights of international notoriety it enjoys today without David driving it forward. He fused North American and European culture into a sometimes fragile Greenpeace alliance after having settled the feud between the Canadian and American groups over money. He cut and slashed his way through a rapidly expanding Greenpeace organization as he relentlessly pursued his vision of internationalism while vilifying those around him if they dared voice an opinion that smacked of national interest.

This sculpting of Greenpeace into a viable and credible international force demanded the steady hand of a cold, calculating and often Machiavellian personality ready to ride roughshod over even those who believed – correctly or mistakenly – that they had formed a friendship with this impossibly mercurial and enigmatic character. And in David McTaggart, the organization was lucky enough to have the seemingly insatiable enthusiasm of the one person who combined the vision, the energy, the determination and the sheer cussedness to get such a gargantuan job completed.

I first met David in 1976. He came to see my football team play at The Den in the shabby southeast London district of Deptford. After a dismal game, we chatted Greenpeace over a few pints. When I asked why he wanted me in particular for the embryonic Greenpeace, his reply was typically forthright: 'I asked Friends of the Earth [which I had helped to establish five years before] who was the most ornery sonofabitch they had ever had working for them and they kept mentioning you. I need ornery sonsofbitches.' And, believe me, after the pseudo intellectual atmosphere of FoE which I had endured for the previous five years with increasing despair, this sort of language was right up my street, even if David didn't exactly charm me off the trees with a nice fat salary: 'Twenty-five pounds a week to start then probably decreasing.'

Looking back, it is hard to believe that he had friends. For of all the people I have met, David was the hardest person to get to know

– by a country mile. In place of friends in the accepted sense of the word, in my experience, he had contacts, colleagues and associates and he manipulated them all mercilessly not for his own aggrandizement but to aid the realization of his plans for environmental salvation. I certainly never felt close enough to David to consider myself a friend for he lived in a protective, impenetrable shell. Everything David did or said was either related to work or was presentational. He was for ever working out the angles, cajoling, jockeying, suggesting or posturing. His death hit so many people so hard – me included – because they knew intuitively that there was so much more to come from David, that they had only scratched the surface of this man's deep and unfathomable personality. That the experience of finally getting to know him would be so pleasurable and rewarding. But there was never enough time and then the bastard died anyway – always one jump ahead was David.

David oozed appeal, charisma and mystery. His smile lit up the entire room, his face creased like a sheet of well-used greaseproof paper. But then his expression would change into a lowering, troubled mask, thin-lipped, ashen and intimidating as with a spittle-flecked mouth he delivered a statement with a finality that defied riposte. Normally he would end with: 'And I'm fuckin' serious', or, 'You bet your sweet ass'. He was a lethal, invigorating and intoxicating cocktail of venom and charm. He used moral blackmail as liberally and as cheerfully as salt on chips and he was not slow at delivering a withering character assassination across a crowded meeting room.

Despite it all, I truly loved David. I cried uncontrollably when I heard the news of his death. There is a vast empty void in my life which he once occupied, and I think and even dream of him often and deeply, such was his impact on my life. Without him, I doubt if I would have seen the world, taken part in some incredible campaigns or have made my own, inadequate contribution to environmental improvement in quite the same public way as I have been privileged to do. He was a man of incredible contrasts. Yet, within the time it takes to roll one's eyes in exasperation, he could display almost unbridled accommodation, bonhomie and empathy. He invoked in people a level of emotion most never knew they possessed.

It is frequently said that the organization outgrew David, that he became surplus to requirements, stuck in the past and overtaken by new methodologies and attitudes to campaigning. In fact, the reverse is true; David McTaggart outgrew Greenpeace. In his later years, while his professionalism and loyalty would never allow him to publicly criticize the organization he had catapulted onto the world in the 1970s, he would privately and with genuine sadness, question what he saw as the excesses of Greenpeace, the missed opportunities, the myopia and the bureaucracy. After his retirement from active work with Greenpeace in the mid-eighties, he tried twice to influence – from without – the organization he held so dear and both times he failed.

He found solace and new challenges in his Third Millennium Foundation and in his ceaseless work to protect the marine environment. And if he influenced, infuriated, enriched and enhanced the lives of those in his immediate sphere, his impact went far, far beyond. The fact is that the world owes David McTaggart an enormous debt of gratitude. While he can lay claim to specific environmental campaign victories, some of which are discussed in this book, he has a greater claim to fame even than being the originator, architect and guardian of the campaign that saved an entire continent and another which protected thousands of children in the South Pacific from radioactive fallout. He, along with only two or three others of his generation created the conditions that popularized the environmental cause to a degree that environmentalism was able to move from the fringes to centre stage. The Rio de Janeiro Earth Summit in 1992 legitimized, in a few days, what had taken David and the movement decades to construct and to recommend to a sceptical world.

He was a person of wildly varying contrasts. In turns generous and miserly, kind yet unthinkingly rude, witty yet woefully inarticulate. He was flawed like the rest of us but he was a visionary with the guts and the tenacity to force governments and corporations of the world to listen to the voice of ordinary people which has grown from a murmur of dissent into an insistent and global demand for change.

Pete Wilkinson
Former Director of Greenpeace UK
and Greenpeace International

Prologue

'NA ZDOROVYA!' SAYS Konstantin Masyk as he tosses back another shot of vodka.

'Na zdorovya!' I say, following his lead, and simultaneously pretty much exhausting my grasp of the Ukrainian language.

It's 21 August 1991, and I'm sitting in the office of the Deputy Prime Minister of Ukraine whacking vodka and trying my damnedest to protect the stake we've claimed here. There's a coup underway. Three days ago Mikhail Gorbachev was taken hostage at his Crimean dacha.

I was on my olive farm in Italy, taking it easy in the August heat when the news got out. It took about one second to know I'd be among the very few people trying to get *into* the Soviet Union this week. The world as we know it had just been tossed into the air and when the pieces landed, I didn't want them to wipe out the years I'd spent convincing the Soviets – and my own people – that there's a place for Greenpeace behind the Iron Curtain.

'Na zdorovya, to your health,' and the vodka burns my throat as we take another hit.

Masyk and I understand each other. There's a respect in this country for a man who can hold his liquor, and we've shared a bottle before. We've also shed a tear together, over the children of Chernobyl. Masyk's been asking the West to help the young ones who were caught in the fall-out when the nuclear reactor blew. I brought in a team of doctors, and we established a clinic to examine the children.

By the time the bottle's half-empty, I've got what I came here for – a promise from my good friend Masyk that we won't lose the buildings out of which we're operating, at least not if he's got anything to do with it. Which right now is a reasonably large 'if', as the world order shifts around us.

The phone rings and I can tell by Masyk's tone that it's not his wife calling. The conversation gets pretty intense before he hangs up.

'That was Yeltsin,' he says through his translator, 'the coup leaders are on their way down to see Gorbachev. They'll be flying over Ukrainian territory in a few minutes, and Yeltsin wants me to shoot them down.'

'Whoofff,' I felt the breath leave my body in a rush. The next few minutes will alter the course of history. I like to be close to the action, and this is certainly a good seat.

Masyk whacks another vodka, and so do I, and it occurs to me that maybe I'm not normal but I haven't enjoyed an afternoon so much in years.

Chapter One

NOW THAT I'M growing old – and not very gracefully – I'm trying to figure myself out, and it's not easy. I haven't exactly led what you'd call an 'examined life' – pretty much the opposite. One of my friends says I don't think in words, and maybe she's right. For sure I don't so much *think* about what direction to go, as *see* the path and take it. Instinct.

I've spent my whole life in motion and now, at 68, I've got emphysema and a heart condition, and as much as I hate it, I can feel myself slowing down. Life's been a bit complicated, so there are five kids by four different women and they deserve to know something about their old man. Which brings me here, trying to understand, trying to write it down, and it's all very uncomfortable because I haven't always been the kindest of men, and I've never been able to sit still long enough to be much of a parent. But I want my children to know that, even though I was driven forward as much by demons as I was guided by angels, I took the only path I could see.

Off the west coast of Canada, there's a place I always head for when the world has got me down, or somebody's beaten me up. I spent summers at the family camp on Buccaneer Bay from when I was about four months old until I was a teenager, and I don't know another place so close to heaven.

To get there you take a big car ferry out of Vancouver, British Columbia, across Georgia Strait to Vancouver Island and what they call the Sunshine Coast, proving that – contrary to our reputation – Canadians do have a sense of humour, because there's nowhere in these parts where it doesn't seriously rain much of the year. After about a half-hour's drive along the coast you come to Secret Cove marina from where, if you know somebody, you can catch a boat ride across to Buccaneer Bay. As you leave the Cove behind, look over to your right and you'll see an island – Vancouver Island the size of a small country – shimmering through the distant mist. A few minutes more and the Bay reaches out to enfold you. It's a long, long bay, very sheltered, and just before you reach the sandy beach where it concludes, there's a little shingle cabin with a red roof – the McTaggart Place. It's not far, maybe ten minutes by motorboat, but for me it's a journey back to the most idyllic boyhood you could imagine.

Maybe it's partly because we were so safe there that I grew up to take such risks with my life. I know it's because of this place, and my summers there, that I came to feel so much respect for the natural world, and so at home on the ocean.

I come back to Buccaneer Bay always with a sense of gratitude that I was born into this time, this place, this family.

If the tide's in, I slip the boat up to the family dock at the foot of a rocky cliff, and climb the path to the porch that circumscribes the cabin. From there I watch the eagles soaring across the bay, and landing in the two-hundred-foot fir trees that stand between our place and the distant islands. When the sun slides into the ocean before me, I head inside and get a blaze roaring in the rough stone fireplace, made out of rocks found along the beach. By the firelight I see on the wall the picture of my childhood.

There are four boys in a little handmade rowboat; two of them are me and my older brother Drew. He's second from the back, looking down, looking serious. I'm at the front, and I have a pole in my hand, ready to push us away to our next adventure. I've got a grin on my face that I can see now is the look of a rascal. How Drew and I grew to be so different and still stayed so close is one of the enduring mysteries of my life.

We share a kind of toughness, though, and we come by it honestly from our parents.

My mother, Mary Baker, was born in North Dakota, USA, the sixth of nine kids. The family trekked north across the border to Canada by horse and cart not long after the turn of the last century. For a while, they lived in a sod house near a place called Seven Persons Creek, where the winters are legendary for their ferocity. In 1920 they moved again, west to Vancouver where Mom would eventually meet George McTaggart.

George – Dad – was born on the island of Mull, off the west coast of Scotland. There were three kids in his family – Dad and two older sisters – and their life was quite middle-class compared to Mom's. Grandpa McTaggart owned a bakery, but if you're picturing a sweet old guy with flour dust on his apron, that wasn't my grandfather. He was one tough son-of-a-gun, and when the First World War started my dad saw the opportunity to get away. He took off and joined the Canadian navy. George ended up making a life on the west coast of Canada, in Vancouver, and funny thing was, Grandpa ended up following, and opening another bakery there. By the time I came along, Grandpa *was* a sweet old guy, or at least so he seemed to his grandchildren. But as a boy, my father knew a different man entirely.

They say that all happy families are the same, and while I don't know about that, it's probably true that those of us from happy families all like to remember how our parents met. Perhaps everybody feels it, the compulsion to call up the moment that without which, you wouldn't be. I know my brother and sister and I always liked to recollect the moment when George McTaggart stepped into the elevator of an office building in downtown Vancouver, saw a slim dark-haired beauty, and fell much further than the elevator was meant to take him. She looked into his bright blue eyes and instantly joined him on a journey that was to last their lifetimes. Whether or not it was really love at first sight or just a good story to tell your kids, by the time they got off the elevator George McTaggart had a date with Mary Baker, and I was on my way into being.

When I was born in 1932, Drew was three and our sister, Bunty, was ten. Every family has its legends, and one of ours is that I got special treatment in the family, and not just from being the youngest. As a small child, my sister almost died of a ruptured appendix, and since this was the 1920s – no antibiotics – even after they got it out it took a long time for Bunty to get better. My parents were understandably anxious about her health, and it was a while before they had another child. Bunty was seven when my brother Drew was born, and he was as healthy as they come, so the family focus stayed on our sister. By the time I came along, three years after Drew, it was clear Bunty was okay, and so was Drew, and everybody could just relax and enjoy the new baby. Ta-da! That was me.

I'm told I was a really beautiful baby, and that everybody spoiled me. I don't know about all the child psychology theories, but I do know that I always felt totally loved, and more than a little bit special. You can never really know how other people feel, so it's hard to compare, but I grew up knowing they'd adore me no matter what. And if I'm really honest I have to admit, I thought they loved me best.

Every summer, my mother would move us kids up to Buccaneer Bay, and my father would join us on weekends. Grandpa McTaggart had acquired land there for a song when it was pretty much unin-habited. The family built a little cabin and it became the McTaggart summer retreat.

I'm not exaggerating when I tell you it was paradise. Nothing fancy, you understand – there's still no indoor toilet at our original place – but it was absolute freedom. My brother and I would get up shortly after the sun rose behind the cottage. We'd eat our oatmeal out on the porch, watching the light spread across the water in much the same way as the day rolled out before us. We could do anything, and we did. We swam and rowed and fished and sailed, and explored the acres of tall timber behind the beach. It was a wild place, and we could be wild in it. I don't think it gets any better for a boy, and I carry that place and that feeling of freedom with me always.

It was at Buc Bay, too, that I learned to make my body strong, and to trust its strength. It was a lesson learned, not entirely intentionally on my part, with the help of my brother. Even though I didn't like fish, and still don't, Drew and I loved catching them for the rest of the family and that involved a lot of rowing out to where the salmon ran. Drew came up with a plan. We'd each row for half an hour, and he'd keep track of the time by the sun. It was a summer or two before I caught on: he'd row for 15 minutes and say it was half an hour. And I'd row for an hour, and he'd say it was half. But I sure got in shape.

And a good thing, too, because Drew and I had the kind of relationship that either makes you stronger or kills you. We were always fighting, and it was usually my fault. Maybe I couldn't stand the fact that there was somebody in the family who didn't always bend to my wishes. Whatever the reason, I was always sticking the needle into my big brother. You'd think since he was three years bigger and stronger than me, I'd be a little more cautious, but no, not me. When we were a bit older, I can remember the overwhelming feeling of anticipation when our parents were going out at night and I knew I could have a go at my brother without interruption. He was always the studious type, so I could get a rise out of him by making it impossible for him to work. You know the kind of thing – poking at him until he was ready to snap, and then hightailing it for the door.

My mother used to tell a story about hearing a horrible row in the sunroom – thumps and thuds and then finally a huge crash. She scurried in to see an overturned sofa with one of us trapped under it and the other wielding a golf club like a weapon. Mom never remembered who was going to kill whom, and it doesn't really matter. We both could be murderous if we thought the other was winning the day. My brother was a pretty good amateur boxer at university, and I think I get part of the credit because I provided a live-in training partner. Yet for all the brawls, Drew became and remained my best friend and the first person I'd turn to throughout my life when the going got really rough.

You could probably tell even before we started school that Drew was going to fit in, and I wasn't. He'd grow up to be somebody serious in society – a child psychiatrist, as it turned out – and I was going to have to find another way. As a boy, Drew was organized and thoughtful and focused; and I just couldn't sit still. If I were in school today, they might just do a bunch of tests on me, to find out if I have one of those attention disorders. I sure have some of the symptoms: perpetually restless, easily bored. Yet I've got this ability to hyper-focus – really zoom in and understand issues structurally. I don't know how to explain it except to say I get flashes of insight, more than thoughts.

But from the beginning one thing that's never been hard for me is making money. At Buc Bay, I invented my first job. On Friday nights the men would come out from town to be with their families, but there was one little problem – the ferry didn't come into Buccaneer Bay, it went right past the mouth. So I got this bright idea. By this time I had the use of a little motorboat, and I'd tie two or three rowboats behind it and head out the Bay into Welcome Pass when the ferry was due. It would slow down as I pulled up alongside and the men would jump fast into my boats – they had about three seconds. I made 25 cents a person. Good money for a kid in the early 1940s. And years later, when the

French navy came after me, I'd find a more serious use for the skill gained manoeuvring a little boat in tight quarters.

If we had lived year-round at Buccaneer Bay, if I'd been born before every Westerner had the 'privilege' of school, I would have been a much happier boy. My natural element was not the class-room, but the outdoors. My natural state was, and is, motion. I couldn't study; it bored me to tears. I learned by doing. It was inevitable that from the time I started school until I was finally kicked out, it'd be trouble for me – and I'd be trouble for it.

As I grew towards my teens, leaving Buccaneer Bay at the end of each summer would seem more and more like paradise lost.

Chapter Two

TO A NORMAL person, the home in Vancouver where we spent the winters would seem like its own piece of heaven. Of course I never thought about it at the time, but I can see now that I really grew up in the lap of luxury. We had a big three-storey house on a curving tree-lined road called South West Marine Drive. The house was surrounded by an English garden with lawns and flowers, and even a little pond. The whole bit. It was a really white Anglo-Saxon neighbourhood, and the McTaggarts lived almost as if we were still in the UK – or Great Britain, as we would have called it then. It was like movies you see of upper-class Brits living in colonial Africa but still using the good china. I'm exaggerating. But not that much. I've got pictures of us at Sunday dinner in the late 1940s, when I was in the full throes of adolescence, not that you'd ever guess that by the photos. My sister's not in them, I think she was married by then, but you see my parents and my brother and I all sitting around a dark polished-wood dining-room table with – you got it – the good china and silver, and the 'men' all in jackets and ties. Just about as far as you can get from how I live today.

My dad liked good cars, so we had a Packard, and even a Jaguar for a while. We weren't millionaires or anything, but Dad did well at the insurance and real estate business, and I sure didn't mind being reasonably well-off. Who would? But I did mind all the rules that went along with that upper middle-class life. My parents were always really good to me, and hardly ever said no, but still there were unspoken expectations about who I was supposed to grow up to be, how I was supposed to behave, and I just couldn't – or wouldn't – live up to them. I know I pushed my parents' patience to the limit many times.

My parents belonged to a fundamentalist church called the Plymouth Brethren. When I think about it now, it seems like a radical choice of a religion. The Brethren didn't believe in priests. They believed that only the Holy Spirit could show the way, so everybody had an equal crack at leading the congregation. They even took turns giving communion. They also believed in the Second Coming of Jesus Christ. As much as I loved and respected my parents, I thought it was a bunch of nonsense. My brother and I both stopped going to church as soon as we got old enough to refuse. I'm sure that hurt my parents, but they never said anything. They respected our right to make our own decisions.

By about age 13, I'd had enough of the dress regulations at school, so I organized something called National Bums' Day. You can probably imagine what it was like. Instead of coming to school in good trousers and shirts, we all dressed like bums, in the dirtiest, most ripped-up clothes we could find. I don't know if I really cared that much about the dress code or if I was mostly just bored to tears and saw a rule worth breaking. Rules have that effect on me. At any rate, it was my first political action! Got caned and sent home for the day, which again didn't please my parents much, but it maybe helped prepare them for the years to come.

Esse Quam Videri. That's the motto of my old high school, and whether or not I knew it at the time, I sure lived up to it. It means 'to be rather than to seem', and during those years from 14 or so on, I was busy *being* just as hard as I could, and sometimes my actions didn't *seem* so good, especially in comparison to those of my older brother. Drew graduated from Magee High School a year before I got there. Thank God. Our worlds were so different it was as if we barely breathed the same air. He was just so bloody perfect. Drew was athletic enough, but where he really excelled was at academics. He aced everything. And Drew always, always knew what he wanted to do and stayed focused on it. Beside his graduation picture it says, 'Intends to study at Montreal Neurological Institute', which he did. Imagine. Imagine knowing at 18 exactly who you want to be. That sure wasn't me. I hated – still do – making plans beyond this afternoon, and there was my big brother with the rest of his life lined up. I think he saw me as a bit of a lost cause. Really, we couldn't have been more different. I'll never know how much of that was the consequence of how our brains were wired or how much was due to the fact that Drew always had a sense of responsibility – maybe because of our big sister's illness – and I always had that feeling my parents loved me best, no matter what I did.

I hung around with a group of boys who shared my priorities – golf, booze and girls. Talk about a misspent youth. Actually, I think we spent it pretty well, if not very wisely. We played all kinds of sports, but I got obsessed with golf – I liked the control the game requires. My friends and I would fake doctors' appointments to get out of school, then head over to the Marine Drive Golf Club for the afternoon. We got to know the staff at the club quite well, which came in handy on Saturday nights when the cook would sell us a case of beer out of the backdoor. We'd drink it on the eighteenth tee, and then head for the Saturday Night Club.

The local United Church held regular Saturday night dances – that's all the club was. Of course, they were perfectly dry affairs in every sense of the word, but we'd arrive a few hours and a few beers into the evening. And there was nothing wrong with the music. They'd play old jazz tunes by people like the Inkspots and Fats Waller, songs like 'If You Can't Be Good, Be Careful'. I loved that stuff. Still do. We'd come in late and stand propping up the wall, listening to the music and watching the girls in their cashmere sweaters with their little strings of pearls. By the time the last dance rolled around, we'd each have picked out a good-looking girl, and we'd move in. Her partner wouldn't stand a chance. We'd cut in, 'Can I have this dance,' and he'd be cut out. We'd always ended up walking the best girls home. Not that much ever happened in those days – maybe you got a little snuggle and a kiss or two – but it was fun taking the girl away from the other guy.

I got really serious about a girl for the first time when I was about 16. Pat was a year younger, and I'd noticed her around the neighbourhood before, a tiny girl riding a big chestnut half-thoroughbred horse. Then one spring evening I was in my father's car, heading along Marine Drive, and there she was ahead of me, walking her dog. Wearing little white shorts, and bare feet, she looked like a million bucks. I asked her if she wanted a ride home, and she said yes.

We were so totally into each other that we didn't even notice we'd left the dog behind.

That was the beginning of a relationship that would last off and on for seven years. We used to pass each other notes in class. Mine were addressed to 'Bright Eyes'. We'd meet in the hall after school and walk home together, taking care that her father didn't see us. Pat's mother liked me, but her father really really didn't. He was a tough guy, a very successful businessman as well as a bit of a rogue. I think maybe he saw something of himself in me, and not the part he wanted for his beautiful daughter. He'd forbid her to see me, so she'd sneak out and that just added to the excitement, of course. We taught each other all the important things a boy and girl can – to go slowly and lovingly, to touch each other with respect and no shame.

Sixteen was a real coming-of-age year for me. That summer I went up north of Vancouver to a place called Bralorne, in the Coast Mountain range. I think my folks hoped it would straighten me out some. I had a job in a gold mine, bringing little railcars full of mineral-rich muck up out of the mine, and emptying them. It was hard work, so we'd get a one-dollar bonus for every ten cars, and some nights we'd manage more than 50 cars. I got to feeling pretty prosperous and very physically fit. One Friday near the end of July, I worked the night shift, 7 p.m. until 3 a.m., and then took off at dawn with a couple of mates to climb the eight-thousand-foot mountain behind camp.

Already high on sleep deprivation, we spent that long summer's day hiking 15 miles over brush and rock into the snow-belt. We'd been told about a derelict cluster of ski cabins where we might spend the night, but when we got there, we found they weren't all empty. An old prospector lived in one, or at least he seemed old to me at the time. In reality, Hugh Dailey was probably less than 50, but he had the grizzled and slightly suspicious look of a man who'd lived away from human company for a long time. I took to him immediately. He was just so unlike the middle-class world of south Vancouver – a total individual – and instinctively I wanted to know him. That night, I bunked in his cabin and we talked for a long time. When the rest of the fellows headed back to Bralorne in the morning, I wasn't going with them, but had decided to stay and prospect for gold alongside Hugh, to trade a weekly pay cheque for a bigger dream and a better adventure. It was one of those sudden sharp turns that were making me the black sheep of the family. I wrote my parents a rather chagrined letter, emphasizing the rich educational experience I'd be having.

And it really was an experience. We climbed up the mountain several hundred feet each day to the claim Hugh was working. We'd have to carry a rifle along with our gear, since there was all sorts of wildlife around, including grizzly bears; plus Hugh was always hoping to bag a deer. With a 15-mile walk to the nearest store, fresh meat was hard to come by. I missed my family, and weekends at Buccaneer Bay, but I got a certain satisfaction from having one up on my brother. He'd never had to take a rifle to work!

When I came back to Vancouver in September for what was supposed to be my second-last year of high school, I tried to settle down. I really did. But the world of school just seemed to be getting smaller and smaller and smaller. I felt as if I were suffocating. It all seemed so bloody pointless. So I got myself kicked out. At least, that's how it looks to me now. I frequently got into little scraps with authority, but it really blew up one afternoon when I was watching a school rugby game from the sidelines. A referee made a really bad call, and I told him so, and we got into a bit of a shoving match. Turned out he was a teacher, and he didn't think mere students should be standing up to him. The next day I got called into the principal's office and was expelled. Can't say it made me unhappy. I packed up my belongings, and said good riddance.

But of course my dad wasn't going to let me walk away from an education quite that easily. I wasn't allowed in to any of the government-funded high schools, but if Dad paid a fairly hefty tuition fee, he could get me a spot at St George's School for Boys. It was the kind of place where the rich sent their boys for a better and more genteel education – rowing and manners were big items on their curriculum. It was also the place where troublemakers went, if their parents could afford it. I was in the latter category, and knew it. Regular school had been confining enough, now this was like being in a cage. With my time in the mountains, I felt far too manly and experienced to sit poring over kids' textbooks with a bunch of upper-class twits. In hindsight, it was mostly the same old problem: I just couldn't sit still, period. I'd smelled freedom, and couldn't get enough of it. I should have told my father to save his money.

There was one good thing that came out of St George's, though, a lifelong friendship with one of the teachers. It's not as if he turned my life around – good luck trying – but Ingemar Gustafsson and his wife, Karin, would still end up with a major role to play in my story. Ingemar was the physical education teacher at St George's. He was a Swede teaching in Canada for a few months' adventure, and maybe that was one of the things I liked about him; he was somewhat exotic to me then, not another boring Canadian. He was a very good gymnast, and looked a bit like the actor Richard Widmark – dark and wiry with very chiselled features. Ingemar and Karin were probably ten or 15 years older than my girlfriend Pat and me, but we spent a lot of time together. I guess that'd be very unusual nowadays, and it probably was even then, but this was a man I could talk to, who treated me more like the man I thought I was than like the troublemaking boy everybody else seemed to see. When Ingemar told me I was screwing up – and he had reason to a little later – I had to listen.

It certainly helped our friendship that Ingemar was in charge of the only part of the school curriculum in which I had any real interest. Studying was an unnatural act to me, but athletics came as easily as breathing. Really. I'm not exaggerating and I don't want to sound boastful, because it doesn't have anything to do with me really – it's all in the genes – but any sport I took up I quickly got good at, very good.

I played football and tennis and squash, and I have already mentioned my obsession with golf, but I found a sport in my mid-teens that especially suited my character. Badminton requires you to stay in constant motion, to be hyper-focused in the moment. It's a game of instinct, and impossibly fast reflexes. And a reckless nature doesn't hurt. If you're willing to dive for shots and leave a little blood on the floor, you've got an advantage. I fell into the sport after hurting my shoulder in a football game. I couldn't play golf for quite a while, and couldn't sit still, so I started playing badminton. At first I didn't take it too seriously. One of my old friends remembers us partying all night before a big tournament.

He claims he had to throw me in a cold shower for 15 minutes before my first game. But I still won.

Pretty soon I was the best in the school and then the best in the city. So I was quite well known at the time of the accident, and that just made it worse for my parents.

This was one of those sharp turns, without which it's impossible to say how my life would have turned out. Maybe if it hadn't happened, I'd finally have settled down, changed from a rascally boy into a man who could fit into my parents' world. Maybe.

It was a sunny late afternoon. I was 17, and coming home from a big tournament, driving my old '32 Essex – not fast – along the wide boulevard that leads from the university. I was feeling very alive – winning's like that – relaxed, alert, not a care in the world. I noticed a city bus stopped along the side of the road – nothing unusual in that, there were lots of stops along this stretch leading away from the university.

Then suddenly from behind the bus, a shape appeared.

THWACK!!

It happened that fast!

Before I could even really take in what was happening, this young guy slammed into the windshield and flew up over the car.

He was pretty badly injured; a fractured skull, I think. I was in total shock, and sorry as hell of course, but I didn't really think it was my fault. My reflexes were so fast at this age that he really had to have come out of nowhere for me not to be able to stop in time.

Facing my parents with yet another screw-up wasn't the easiest thing in the world even though, as always, they took my side. This time that wasn't enough. The kid I'd hit was a university student. He'd be okay, but his father was a wealthy Italian surgeon who wanted compensation for his son's injuries. And it turned out we were considerably underinsured. While the insurance companies fought it out, I didn't see any alternative but to quit school and try to make some money.

This time my father let me go.

So, feeling battered and bruised and so much older than my 17 years, I set out for a labourer's job at Kennedy Lake Logging Camp on the west coast of Vancouver Island. It's about the most remote place you can imagine, especially in those days. To get there, I caught a big ferry that docked about a 30-minute drive from my parents' house. I sailed more than an hour and a half southwest across Georgia Strait to Vancouver Island, and then drove for most of a day across the island to the west side, where the breakers roll in across the Pacific all the way from Japan. It really feels like you're at the far edge of the continent – because you are – and it also felt to me at the time as if I was at the far edge of my life. Initially, it seemed like the right place to lick my wounds and get on with making some money, and making it right with my family.

I felt very alone. Ingemar was heading back to Sweden that spring, and he wrote me a tough letter from the ship. He said I was spoiled, and maybe this car accident, as hard as it was on my parents, would be the thing to open my eyes. He advised me to stay in the logging camp for as long as it took me to pay for my mistakes. He meant it more than just financially. As weather-beaten and old-beyond-my-years as I was, Ingemar knew I still had a lot to learn about facing my mistakes.

I wasn't ready yet.

When somebody told me that if I disappeared for seven years my father wouldn't have to pay up, I decided to go for it, disappear across the border into the USA and maybe from there make my way across to the east coast, and then on to Europe. I think my ill-formed plan was to make enough money to return home triumphant at 25.

So I snuck back into town from the logging camp and rented a room for the night in a seedy hotel in downtown Vancouver. I got my stuff together and in the morning called my girlfriend to come see me. 'It's important.' I wouldn't tell Pat what was going on, only that I had to go away for a while. I asked her to tell my parents, and Ingemar, that I'd be in touch. Then I slipped across the border, and was gone.

Chapter Three

I HITCHHIKED MY way south and east across the Rocky Mountains into the rolling ranch country of Montana – where the cattle outnumbered the people about six to one. My longest ride was with a rodeo cowboy heading home.

In the little city of Billings, Montana, the money ran out, and it became clear that this escape plan wasn't exactly foolproof. There I was, 19 years old, no money, no job – no immigration papers. I managed to land a job loading boxcars at a cannery for the princely sum of 90 cents an hour. There were two weeks to go until payday, two weeks to come up with a green card, two very hungry weeks during which I lived on corn and beans that I nicked from the company. Doesn't sound very good, I know, but I was hungry.

I was also very very depressed. I felt like a total failure. Too ashamed to even write Mom and Dad, I asked my girlfriend to call and tell them I was okay, and to write Ingemar and Karin in Sweden. 'You tell them all about me and how well I am getting along.' What a joke. I was barely surviving, scared and scrambling around like a lost little boy. Even using a fake name, Dave Exel. Exel was my brother-in-law's name, and he was a US resident at that time, so I figured I might be able to use his address and maybe get by for a while that way, without a green card.

For four months I managed to stay ahead of the immigration

authorities, moving from town to town, finally catching up with the realization that I was going nowhere fast. On Christmas Eve 1951, sick with pneumonia, I caught a bus back across the border to Vancouver – home to face the music.

As we waited for our day in court, two things kept me sane – badminton, and my fantastic family.

I always knew my parents would forgive me anything but while I was away I'd wondered if the same was true of my straight-as-an-arrow big brother. I didn't need to worry; Drew might have thought I was a wild card – I'm sure he did – but he didn't think I was at fault in the car accident and he planned to be right by my side no matter what the courts threw at us.

The waiting was the worst part. To keep myself from going right round the bend, I started playing badminton again.

I've mentioned that badminton's mostly about genetics, about the natural speed with which you can turn thought into action, how fast your muscles react to what your eye sees. Sometimes when I'm going on (and on) about this to friends in the bar, I demonstrate with a ten thousand lire note. The trick is to drop the note between a person's thumb and forefinger held one or two inches apart. The average person is unable to react quickly enough to stop the note from passing through their fingers. But not me. I catch it every time, and I don't say this to brag. It has nothing to do with me. It's all from my mother and father. Genetics. And that's most of what made me good at badminton.

The rest is psychological. To win at badminton, you have to stay totally focused, and totally cool. Never show the other guy you're tired, or down. And watch him like a hawk for signs of his feelings. Maybe you'll see that moment of doubt that tells you it's worth going on the offensive even though you're tired and he's a better player. Later on in my life, my old badminton lessons proved useful when the stakes were much higher – like going against the Japanese whaling lobby. People I've worked with say that's one of my greatest strengths; I think it's my only one – instinct. I watch, I see, and I act, almost in one motion.

On the badminton court in the spring of 1952, I was winning again and that never feels bad. So when the provincial championships rolled around in February, I thought what the hell, why not have a go.

The club was packed that Saturday night. Since one of the competitors was the Canadian men's singles champion Daryl Thompson, people knew they'd see an international calibre of play. I wanted to have a go at Thompson. I'd played him during a practice game and lost, but I'd felt strong, as if we belonged on the same court and – on the right night – I could take him.

By the time I'd played my way through the tournament to face Thompson in the final match, I could just about taste it. The first set was pretty even; he kept me moving from net to back boundary to recover his shots, but recover them I did, to take the set. The second set – well, it wouldn't be a game if you always won – I lost 15–10, but there was no bloody way I was going to lose the match. He might be the national champion, but nobody, *nobody* needed a win like I did. In the final set I just kept pounding. I was absolutely focused. One of the local newspapers would report that I 'made several recoveries bordering on the miraculous'. It was fantastic. I actually piled up an 11–0 lead before Thompson came back a bit. When the night ended, it was the first time in three years Thompson had lost a match in Canada. A little 19-year-old-Scots-Canadian boy had beaten the national champion!

Boy, it felt good. I'd go on to win the national men's singles championship three times, and to play in many international tournaments, but I don't think victory ever tasted much sweeter than it did that night.

I sent a telegram to Ingemar and Karin, feeling I had something good to tell them for the first time in a long while.

My dad was there to watch his black sheep make good, but he didn't stick around to share the victory celebration. As always,

George McTaggart quietly slipped out the back way, never one to seek the public eye.

Now that I was invited to the national championships, I decided to get serious. I even cut down – way down – on my smoking and drinking. I played badminton every day and spent many nights at home, trying to stay out of trouble. It made for a change. My dad wanted me to go back to school, but for now we didn't look much further ahead than the court case coming up in a month's time.

My brother Drew was training to be a doctor at this time, still very certain of who he was and what he wanted out of life. As different as we were, it sure felt good to have him beside me for the legal battle ahead.

Only there was to be no battle.

My quiet, conservative father couldn't stand the thought of all the publicity a court case would likely generate. I'll never forget the night he came home to tell his two combative sons that he'd decided not to fight. He came home late, dragging his feet. I noticed that the stress of the past few months had turned his hair white, and his face just about matched. There was no arguing with him, it was done.

Dad had settled out of court. The Italian medical student who'd run out in front of my car two years earlier would collect $18,500, an awful lot of money in those days. In one moment our privileged life had evaporated. My parents were, by this time, living in a luxurious apartment in a building they owned. The building had to be sold, and they moved into a rented flat. They lost everything, yet not one harsh word was ever spoken to me about it, not one ounce of blame laid on my shoulders. But of course I felt terrible. The best parents in the world, and through no fault of my own, I'd made their lives so bloody difficult. Try as he had, Dad couldn't even keep it out of the newspapers. The *Vancouver Sun* ran an article headlined, 'Badminton Champ Must Pay $18,500'.

One weekend morning at Buccaneer Bay, Dad got up at around

5 a.m. after a sleepless night and wrote me a tough letter, worrying about some of the habits I was forming – and about the ones I should have been forming, but wasn't. He told me that I should seriously consider night school, and that his money troubles were his own, not my concern. But I couldn't accept that. There was no question now of my going back for more education. My parents had done everything for me, and I felt I had a huge debt to pay back – emotional as well as financial. After raising their family, earning the right to a little peace and tranquillity, my parents were almost starting over, so vulnerable. And I'd learned the hard way, a lesson they don't teach you in school – the world revolves around the almighty dollar. If it is money that makes the system work – then I would make money! I'd pay back my parents, help them regain their security, and I'd never, *ever* be so vulnerable myself.

One of the elders in my parents' church owned a big construction company, C.J. Oliver. Jack Oliver knew I needed a job, and he knew I'd like nothing better than to get out of town, so he hired me as a general labourer working at his operation in a town called Cranbrook, some 250 miles east of Vancouver. In one way, it was just what the doctor ordered. We worked hard, I mean really hard – unloading railcars, breaking up cement with a jackhammer, mixing mortar for the bricklayers, digging ditches, wheeling cement. You could certainly say I learned the construction business from the ground up.

At night, we'd have a meal and go to a movie, or go out for beers. Sometimes way too many beers. Then I'd go back to the rough little cabin I shared with two other guys, listen to Duke Ellington playing 'Solitude' on the record-player, and write sad letters to my girlfriend. Pat and I were engaged – again – about this time. We even talked about saving money to build our own house. I don't know how many times the diamond ring went back and forth until it eventually ended the way it always seems to – me getting restless and a good woman getting hurt. I just can't settle down. One half of me was planning a honeymoon at Buc Bay with Pat, but the other half was stepping out on her with the best-looking girl in Cranbrook. I don't know what's the matter with me. Seriously. I don't know enough to stop when I'm ahead.

My restlessness invades every relationship I've ever had, and I think it's fair to say it's cost me every romance. Pat put up with a lot from me, but when she found out I'd also been seeing a top female badminton player, a married woman, that was it. In the mid-1950s in North America, sleeping with a married woman really was considered a cardinal sin. My engagement ended in a somewhat noisy scene in Pat's parents' driveway – her old man must have been delighted finally to be rid of me. She threw the ring back in my face, the whole bit. If the women after her had all had the brains to do the same thing, life would have been a lot more simple.

By this time Jack Oliver had transferred me back to head office in Vancouver and, although my romantic life was chaos, I was really starting to get it together professionally. I liked the construction industry, and it liked me. It's a tough, competitive business – a good fit. I spent what were for me some pretty uneventful years, working my way up the company and playing some serious badminton. I made Canada's international Thomas Cup team and became a bit of a celebrity for my, I guess you'd call it uninhibited, style of play. In the rather posh world of badminton, I seemed brassy and flamboyant. I sometimes talked to myself – quite loudly – during a match, occasionally even swearing, if you call saying 'Judas!' out loud swearing, and I guess it was in 1955. I was to badminton what John McEnroe was to tennis in the 1980s – a top player, but just a little too brash. I was someone people came to watch play, but whose behaviour was often the subject of a little self-righteous gossip. I couldn't have cared less, as long as I was winning.

And I was doing pretty well off the court, too. My family was slowly recovering from the financial beating we'd taken over my car accident. Jack Oliver liked having a minor celebrity in his company, and I think he liked the fact that I wasn't afraid to make decisions. I started taking on more and more responsibility in the company, until I was putting together the bids for big projects. Now that was interesting. You work for months on a big project figuring out how much money it'll take to build it, and then your profit comes out of what's really a high-stakes poker game with your competitors. The object is to bring a job in at just one per cent lower than the other guys. Then you get the job, and make the most possible profit. It's a totally goal-oriented world – winning is the only thing that matters. And it's constantly changing – different projects, different prices, different players. It's a fast game with real-life consequences. My favourite kind.

In my mid-twenties, I really felt on top of my game. It had been a rocky road to get here – what with getting kicked out of school and the car accident – but now the path seemed a little clearer and a whole lot smoother. I'd taken a different path, but I finally felt as if I'd caught up with my older brother professionally. My parents were pleased I seemed to have found my footing, and I knew my dad especially was quietly very proud of my badminton career.

It felt good not to be the black sheep for a while. Maybe that's why I did it.

I met Shirley at the badminton club. She was drop-dead gorgeous in her badminton whites – small and blonde and athletic-looking. Shirley was a nurse who'd become a flight attendant, in the days when you had to be a nurse first, and when being a 'stewardess' was a very glamorous profession. On top of all that she was smart, and a really good person. That would almost certainly have been enough, but there was one more thing. She was from Montreal and had dated my brother when Drew was in medical school there. Drew was married by now, and he and Shirley were friends, but I think knowing they'd gone out added a little something, a bit of competition maybe.

So I started taking Shirley out, and before very long I began pressuring her to get married. What was I thinking? At 24, I was not at all ready to settle down. She was a lovely lady, but marriage? I don't know how much was the Drew factor, and how much was the fact that I was genuinely trying to lead a 'straight' life. We met in the summer and by mid-autumn she'd said yes, but not for a year. Well I've never liked to wait, so I kept at it, told her we should get married by the end of the year for tax purposes, and so our honeymoon could be a European badminton tour that was scheduled for early in the new year.

She finally gave in.

My first wedding was in a greystone church near my parents' place. The pictures are hilarious – me in a tuxedo! Even had hair then. But Shirley looked beautiful, in her long white dress.

What the pictures don't show is what happened the night before, what a bastard the bridegroom was, and how utterly unready to marry. I'd stayed at a hotel the night before the ceremony and had a visit from an old girlfriend. I know at the time I made some kind of cockeyed rationalization about this being a final goodbye and all that nonsense that people tell themselves to justify their bad behaviour. Bottom line is the old girlfriend snuck out as the cleaning staff started work in the morning, and I went to say my vows at the first of too many wrong-headed weddings.

What *was* I thinking. Me a happily married man is about as likely as a vegetarian wolf.

Shirley and I had some good times, but our marriage was predictably rocky from the start. I'd always gone to the bar of the old Hotel Georgia for a few drinks after work on a Friday night. I didn't see why marriage should change that, and if I didn't come home some nights, well, I wasn't about to have anybody tell me what to do. We fought. We made up. We fought. She gave me an ultimatum. I tried for a while.

She got pregnant.

Growing up in my loving family, I had the idea I wanted a family myself, but always some time off in the future. It took me a while to adjust to the idea of having a baby right now, and I guess I never really did fully adjust.

My daughter Lisa was nine months old when I left. I've never been a good father, but with Lisa I think I was at my worst. I barely saw her for years after I split and although that wasn't so unusual in those days, it's not something I'm proud of. I can only hope she now understands that it was my problem, not hers. She was a wonderful baby, I just couldn't – can't – get past this unremitting restlessness.

Around the time my marriage broke up, I went to Mexico for a big Latin American badminton tournament. I played well – won, in fact – and made a lot of new friends even without speaking more than two words of their language. Venezuela had a team there; I think it was their first international tournament, and they were blown away by the level of play. There was the usual big bash when it was over, and I was both drowning my sorrows and celebrating my victory. I recall there was a particularly lovely young woman involved; I think the niece of the President of Venezuela. Anyway, we were dancing to a hot Mexican band, generally enjoying ourselves, when the army colonel who'd led the Venezuelan delegation stood up and made an announcement, which I, of course, couldn't understand but which led to a lot of people coming up to hug me and pat me on the back.

I had no idea what was going on.

The lovely niece leaned over and whispered in my ear, 'You're leaving for Caracas in the morning.'

The Colonel and I had been joking earlier about me going to Venezuela to teach his officers badminton. Or at least I'd been joking. Turned out he was quite serious.

I was flattered as hell, but told him I had a business to run in Vancouver and family responsibilities. No go. We had several more rounds of drinks before they deposited me, a little worse for wear, at the airport for the flight home.

In Vancouver, I went back to work but I was restless and depressed. Work was fairly slow just then. My marriage was in tatters, and although my long-suffering parents were supportive as always, I felt like the black sheep again. The Colonel's offer just kept playing on my mind. How many people get a chance like that? The Venezuelan consulate was quite near my offices downtown, and one day I just happened to drop in – no real intentions, just following my nose – and I asked them if they knew the Colonel. Turned out he was a big man in Venezuela. Everybody knew who he was.

When I walked out of the consulate, my depression had lifted, and my mind was dancing with the possibilities of an adventure ahead, and of leaving my troubles behind.

Chapter Four

WITHIN A COUPLE of days I caught a freighter to Curaçao, the duty-free island just north of Venezuela. My plan had been to fly into Caracas from there but I got a little distracted by the turquoise water and the white sand, and the girl lying on it. I spent a few idyllic days soaking up the sun and enjoying being single again. Every afternoon I'd go down and watch the fishing boats take off over the horizon. At least I thought they were fishing boats, but one of the locals quickly set me straight, 'C'mon, this is Curaçao. Duty-free. A watch that costs a hundred dollars in Caracas costs ten here. They're smugglers.'

Well, that didn't bother me. In fact, I saw the possibility of a cheap ride the 50 miles or so to the mainland, a helluva lot more interesting than hopping a plane with a bunch of tourists. So I packed away the bit of cash I'd brought, along with the little handgun that my host the Colonel had suggested might be a good idea. That would very shortly prove to be excellent advice. As the sun fell into the Caribbean, it became apparent that the smugglers weren't looking for second careers as tour operators; they were far more interested in quick cash and I had the feeling that if separating me from my money meant heaving me overboard, that wasn't too big a deal. As they came towards me, I pulled out the gun and said, 'No way!' I don't think they understood English, but the presence of a firearm made it across the language barrier nicely. Even then I believed in non-violence, but there's a limit.

It was a very strange night. I hunkered down into a corner of the boat and kept the gun out, of course, and the smugglers didn't seem too uptight about it all. Their attitude seemed to be win some, lose some. Not a big deal. Not a big deal to toss me overboard; not a big deal if they didn't succeed. Sometime overnight they met up with another boat and I guess they passed over the goods they were smuggling. Then we continued on to their home-port on the mainland. Their families were out on the wharf to greet the boat as we pulled into the harbour. My reception wasn't quite so welcoming. When I climbed up onto the dock, I was staring into the barrels of two machine-guns. Maybe the captain was getting his own back, passing the word that I was illegal.

They took me up to the police station in the village above the docks and there I faced off against a man who seemed to be the chief of police, sitting with his feet up on the desk, looking like he enjoyed his little bit of power way too much. Remember, I don't speak the language, so didn't really have a clue what was going on, except that this big bastard probably wanted a bribe. But I thought, bugger it, after all this I'm not giving it away. This seemed like the perfect time to find out just how important my friend the Colonel was, so I mentioned who'd invited me to Venezuela. Well, the attitude changed quite quickly. Suddenly they couldn't do enough for me. I was whisked off to the airport, still in my grubby jeans, and badly needing a shave.

That's how I looked stepping out of the plane onto a red carpet in Caracas not an hour later. No kidding, there really was a carpet; and the Colonel and a uniformed guard were standing at the end of it waiting to greet me and begin probably the most luxurious months of my life. A limousine whisked me off to the Circulo de las Fuerzas Armadas, which was more like a fancy resort than a military centre, with apartments and good restaurants clustered around an artificial lake in this perfect tropical climate – high enough up not to be too hot. I was taken to my own apartment with a sundeck on both sides where I could look out at the mountains under which Caracas sits. I had a smoke and a rum, and thanked my lucky stars.

My only duties were to play badminton, squash and tennis with the Venezuelan army officers who were stationed there. Not too painful. But it wasn't many weeks before it started to get a little boring, and the Colonel helped me get started on a couple of business ventures.

I was beginning to do okay when the Colonel's world exploded.

Now this was at the end of a long period of political unrest in Venezuela – successive military dictatorships toppling in coup after coup. They'd finally actually elected a leader, Romulo Betancourt, a few months before. But old habits die hard, and neither the right nor the left wing was entirely satisfied with Betancourt, so every now and again there'd be an uprising. My friend got caught in the middle of one of these aftershocks.

One morning just before lunch, he sent someone to warn me. 'Run! Car front door! Run.' I ran. I didn't know much about Venezuelan politics, but I knew it was serious. I had a pair of jeans and a sweater, my passport and sixty dollars. I jumped into the car and it took off down the highway to where a little plane was waiting for me.

I was dropped back in Curaçao, on a dirt road. Again it felt like one step forward and two steps back. At least I had my passport, but sixty bucks wasn't going to get me far, and I didn't want to go home again with my tail between my legs. Then I remembered the beautiful young woman I'd met on the beach in Curaçao on my way into Venezuela a few months earlier. Dorsey lived in Pittsburgh, she was a good soul, and right now I felt like I needed an angel. I called and right out asked if she'd buy me a ticket to Pittsburgh. She did, and I landed in her arms a few days later, very relieved and very grateful.

I got in touch with my family and told them everything was okay, but not too many details. I was still hoping that things would settle down in Venezuela and I could get back to my business there, but I think I knew it was over. Still, it seemed easier to let my parents down a bit gently – just a bump in the road, not another failure. I didn't realize how transparent it all was, and how worried they were, until years later, when I saw a letter from Drew to Mom and Dad:

I am sorry to hear that you are upset about David. I can understand how that may be. I talked to him on the phone, he was in good spirits and health. His plan involves an arrangement for selling wholesale oil motor products in Caracas … Apparently he is in the States to arrange details of the set-up. Now it did not sound scatter-brained at all to me and I frankly would rather see him in this mood than defeated. One of these times he may make out alright. Unfortunately he is one of those people who cannot be content with a run-of-the-mill job and is only happy if the stakes seem enticing. This brings heart-aches to the ones who are personally involved with him. Anyhow I hope it works out because only if and when this happens will be begin to feel content and appreciate the better values in life. My own opinion is that his chances are good. I am sorry that I cannot give more specific details, but frankly I couldn't care less. He is old enough and battered enough to make his own life.

That's my brother. Tough son-of-a-gun. It's got to be life-threatening before Drew gets too worried. I'd put my life in his hands anytime, without hesitation, but you don't trouble him with little things, like a failed marriage or a lost job.

I actually made a living in Pittsburgh for a few months, travelling around taking pictures of little babies, before I gave up entirely on the idea of going back to Venezuela and decided to head home to Canada where I could restart my construction career. I took Dorsey up to my brother's place in Montreal as a new bride, but didn't tell my parents I'd married again. I knew it would be too soon for my dad, and didn't want to face the music until I was firmly resettled. When my parents found out second-hand about my marriage, I felt like a real shit, but asked them to look at the change in me before they jumped to any conclusions. I got a job quite soon, with a big international construction outfit, Perini General Contractors, assigned to their Toronto office. I'd miss the summers in Vancouver, but felt I had to settle down once and for all and wouldn't get a better opportunity than with Perini.

Dorsey and I were in Toronto for about a year before I started feeling a little too settled, so when Perini decided to open an office in San Francisco, I asked to go. We'd had our first child by then. Kerin was born in October 1960; her sister Tamra would follow a year later.

Dorsey and I were more or less okay. She'd had a very strict Catholic upbringing, so I know she found me a little wild, but she had the kids, and a nice house on a golf course, and even a black collie pup we called Angus – after some Scots relative, I think. I had work.

There were two of us in charge of all Perini's projects west of the Mississippi River. The jewel in the crown was the Golden Gateway Redevelopment Project, a mostly residential complex that covered three city blocks right in the heart of San Francisco. There were four high-rise apartment buildings, luxury townhouses, landscaped gardens and plazas and a shopping centre. This was a very big project – $120 million wasn't chickenfeed in those days – and I was under a lot of pressure, sometimes working just about round the clock.

I was enjoying the hell out of life, but wasn't giving my marriage much attention, and it started to bend under the strain. And about now you're probably thinking this guy sounds like a real bastard, and maybe you're right. I'd begin a romance with the best of intentions. I really meant it when writing to Mom and Dad about how much I'd changed with Dorsey, and how nothing was to be desired in our personal feelings for each other. But then that bloody restlessness would come. I know it sounds hopelessly old-fashioned, and probably sexist to some, but to me the greatest work of art in the world is a woman. Throughout my life, I've tried to be good, but – especially when I was young – it seemed as if everywhere I turned there was another work of art I had to have. I've never learned to accept the word no. Nobody said it to me much as a child, and I'm not good at taking it for an answer – can't even hear it from myself. Self-denial is not one of my strengths.

At the same time, I can't have been a complete bastard, because – almost without exception – the women I've been involved with remain friends, good friends. Dorsey is one of the exceptions.

Early in 1964, 31 years old, I divorced for the second time. My daughters were still pre-schoolers, but – unlike the situation with my Vancouver daughter – we'd been together long enough for me to know them, and so be determined not to lose them from my life. I tried to do the weekend father thing, although just my appearance at the door would provoke some awful fights with their mother.

By now I'd moved on professionally, too, to a construction company that specialized in building hotels, and we were scouting around for possible hotel sites in the new ski areas opening up around San Francisco. One of my contacts told me about a rancher who was working on a development some 125 miles north and mostly east of the city. The rancher owned the land, it had been in his family for five generations. So there'd be no problems with government bureaucracy – I thought! I decided to take a case of beer and go meet the guy.

It was late autumn, a beautiful crisp day as I drove up into the Sierra Mountains. I found the rancher, Bruce Orvis, out burning old piles of slash timber to clear a road into the nearby lake area. Pretty down to earth for a guy who owned half the county. Well I pulled my old clothes out of the car and set to work right alongside him.

It felt really good to get out of the city and to be doing something physical for a change. By the end of the day we were covered in dirt and ash, and very satisfied to be sitting together by the fire sharing that case of beer. Bruce was about my age and had also been an athlete – a very competitive American football player at the university level. So we had a lot in common, including the desire to build something unique in this high mountain country. We wanted to put together a very high-end ski resort, aesthetically and environmentally sound, and we wanted it to be a destination resort – people would stay for a week or two. That doesn't sound very radical now, I know, but not many people were doing it in those days. We were both crystal clear on one thing: we didn't want to make just a real estate deal; we wanted to make a project we could both be really proud of.

I know it's strange to anyone who met me first as an environmentalist, in the second half of my life, but for years I was motivated by the pursuit of the dollar, the possibility of a *big* deal. Psychologically, I have no idea how much this had to do with my parents' losing everything, and my role in that, and how much it was just that competitor's instinct to win – whether it's a badminton game, or a deal, or an environmental victory.

But with Bruce Orvis, I knew I had a true partner – somebody who dreamed big and competed hard.

I stayed a week with Bruce, and by the end of it, my life had taken another turn. I would become the vice president and general manager of the Bear Valley Development Corporation and, together with Bruce, would build our dream, a complete recreational community in the heart of the Sierras. We'd build a lodge and commercial area, and then 600 home-sites, all nestled as compatibly as possible in amongst the pines. We were essentially building an extremely classy small town.

I moved in with Bruce and his wife, Roma, for a while at their ranch in the foothills, while I was building a little house at Bear

Valley. They liked my sometimes-crazy energy, and I sure liked the feeling of deep calm I got from them. They were solid. Bruce taught me to ride horseback and even took me out for a night-time cattle round-up. I'll never forget that – not feeling entirely secure on the beast moving beneath me, and then seeing, out of the dark, the sudden shapes of cattle coming over the hill towards the corral. I used to like to borrow Bruce's sweaty old cowboy hat. I wonder if I thought it would make me a better rider, or a better person.

We were a good combination business-wise. I had the push and Bruce had the pull. The community knew and trusted him, whereas they thought I was a bit much. The locals saw me as the big-city developer, raking in the dollars. Not so. Bruce paid me twenty thousand dollars a year to manage the development, and then a commission on any sites I sold. So I might make fifty thousand. Very good money in those days, but hardly a king's ransom. It was years before people realized that Bruce and I might not act the same, but about Bear Valley, we really thought alike.

We faced a lot of bureaucratic battles during the next few years, for which I have no patience, but we managed to get a beautiful lodge built, and sales were pretty good on the home-sites. We were getting people who'd sold their old inherited homes at Lake Tahoe to build at Bear Valley, because they didn't like the gambling atmosphere at Tahoe, and they wanted the quiet class we were offering at Bear.

I managed to get the National Alpine Championships signed up for Bear the year before we even opened. And we started up our own ski team. I thought it'd be great publicity, and it was. Our guys were just a step below Olympic calibre. One of the team – Spider Sabich – did go on to make the US national team. Strangely enough, he was shot and killed some years later, by a woman he'd met at Bear Valley.

By now it won't surprise you to know that I met a woman there, too. She never aimed a gun at me, although I bet sometimes she wanted to. Betty's mom owned a place on Lake Alpine, about four miles above Bear. Mom was a PhD and a medical doctor, if I remember correctly. Her daughter was no slouch in the brains department, either, although that wasn't what I first noticed. Betty was about six feet tall, and blonde and stunning. She was the perfect California girl. Really a work of art. By now you're thinking I must know better. Wrong. We got married. My mom came down to the wedding, but Dad didn't. He had nothing against Betty; I think he'd just lost his illusions about me and marriage.

Betty became the focus of one of our publicity campaigns. I mean that quite literally. I took a very tasteful nude photograph of her, on skis, with a pine bough strategically placed across her bottom. We turned that into a postcard that said, 'Ski Bare'. It was fantastic! North America was so uptight at the time that this sweet little photo caused quite a stir. I know for a fact that it became a bit of a collector's item among the ranchers up there. I think you can still find it on a few tackroom walls.

While I was working for Bruce, I spotted a property about four miles below Bear Valley that I thought I might buy and develop myself, as more of a night spot. That was fine with Bruce – if we were going to draw people to the area for extended periods of time, the more action, the better. So I bought Tamarack – a little lodge with a few rooms, with the emphasis on dining and dancing. In January 1969, I resigned from Bear Valley to concentrate full time on Tamarack.

God, how I wish I'd never seen the place.

We were just a few days away from the official opening, and expecting some of the national ski team the next day, so we were a bit tense about getting everything done on time. To add to the pressure, one of the guys had smelled gas the day before – the main generator was in a little adjacent building out back. We'd had the gas inspector out, and everything was supposed to be fine. Supposed to be.

I was standing at the front of the main building, in the restaurant area, talking over last minute details with my foreman when – KABOOM!! The back of the building blew off. I raced round and – sure enough, my worst fear – my mechanic had been at work inside when the thing went up. It was awful. He was alive, but it was clear that one leg was very badly injured.

I felt terrible. I wanted to look after the guy, but didn't have the money. Every penny was tied up in Tamarack, which was now worth about ten cents.

I decided to take the gas company to court. While I waited for the case to be heard, I took a job developing a big ski resort just north-west of Aspen, Colorado. It was 8,300 acres, bigger than Aspen itself. The owners were easterners who didn't know much about the ski-resort industry, but were eager to make a buck off it. They wanted 10,000 beds in seven years, so we started fast, with big bucks on the line. I was going a mile a minute between Aspen and New York.

My third marriage got left behind somewhere in the jet-stream.

I was always better at work than relationships, and now I really threw myself into my work. I had all sorts of development deals on the go. It was looking as if I might end up a lonely old man, but at least I would be a rich one. Then the bottom fell out of the money markets.

Suddenly the fat-cat easterners were very over-extended at Aspen. When we were sitting pretty, they'd loved my style and my ambitious vision. But it was a different movie now. I could see that Aspen would be worth a fortune, and we should just hang in there, but they weren't interested in vision anymore.

I resigned at the beginning of June 1970.

A week and a half later I had my day in court over the Tamarack explosion. I couldn't believe it. They decided against me. I wrote in my diary for 10 June: 'All is lost – court threw out my case. Other lawyers and insurance people couldn't believe it. Jesus, to lose

$125,000 in one day is a bit of a shock. Well, this seems to be my lucky year. First job, then Betty, then this ... well, will try to pay all small people back, afraid the bank is in trouble.'

The bank wasn't the only one in trouble. I was about as far down as it's possible to get, and still be breathing. George and Mary McTaggart's favourite son, full of promise, and full of promises – and screwing up, again. It didn't matter that it wasn't my fault; somehow that made it even worse. I'd been a good boy, I'd played inside the system, and still I'd lost everything.

To quiet the noise in my head, I drove up into the mountains to Bear Valley and spent a lonely and desperately depressed few days in the little lodge there, trying to see a way to make it right. I turned it all over and over and over – my marriages, my kids, my financial mess. I couldn't see a way out. Or maybe it's more accurate to say that the only way I could see was *all* the way out. Leave the country. Screw money, screw love, screw responsibility.

Erase the old Dave McTaggart; he's not doing anybody any good. Forget him. Start over.

Chapter Five

ONE WEEK TO the day before my thirty-eighth birthday, I boarded a plane bound from Los Angeles to Tahiti. I'd called my parents and my kids, just to hear their voices, but didn't tell them I was leaving. It was just too hard, since I didn't have a clue when – or if – I'd be back.

To be honest, and with the benefit of hindsight, I guess I was pretty close to free-fall here. And I had a horrible sense of *déjà vu*. After the first big accident of my life, I'd dedicated myself to making money. Money was the answer. It was going to keep me and my family safe – and maybe, as a bonus, show my parents that I was just as special as they'd always thought. So I made a fortune, and still my world blew up, almost literally in my face. Now what? Well money clearly wasn't the answer. I'd have to find a new god, and at the moment nothing was coming to me.

But one thing has always made me feel better, call it my drug – motion. So I ran as fast and as far as I could.

I'm not sure why I chose the South Pacific, perhaps because of some contacts at the Club Med down there. And, honestly, if a guy's going to be broke and lonely, he might as well be warm. I had maybe enough money to buy a little sailboat, and then just bum around, leading the exact opposite life to what I'd left behind. It'd be simple and free and not concerned with the almighty dollar. After twenty years in the construction business, I'd got pretty close to the top of the heap, and it had brought me nothing but grief. Now I just wanted to keep my head down.

No way did I have a clue that I was turning onto a path that would find me sticking my head up about as far as it could possibly go. It would take me a while to get there, a couple more turns, but I was heading for a collision course with the world's nuclear powers.

But at that time I wouldn't have believed even my own grandmother if she'd told me that – I was far too busy licking my wounds, and finding lots of good company to help. It seemed trying to be a good family man hadn't worked out any better than the construction business, so I might as well just enjoy myself. When I look back at my diaries now, I can see that I was as depressed as hell, but I was sure doing a good job of hiding it.

A very nice Pan Am flight attendant who'd worked the flight from LA got me through the first couple of days in Tahiti, then I left the main island for Moorea, a quieter island about 12 miles away. Moorea's one of the most beautiful places on earth. It's all jagged volcanic peaks, covered in lush green and surrounded by the soft turquoise Pacific. There was a Club Med there, and I thought maybe my contact could find me some work, but I found François Ravalo instead. He was a fantastic artist who lived on Moorea full-time and did oil paintings of Polynesian people that were reminiscent of Gaugin. He cooked just about as well as he painted, and for about two weeks Ravalo looked after me. When he was working, I'd wander along the white sand to the Club Med and get into all sorts of trouble with the American girls there.

I did my very best to lose myself, or at least to lose my past, but it was always there. Late on a sleepless night, home from some 'date' or another, with a belly full of booze, it would still be there. I would still be there, and desperately lonely. I couldn't figure out if my life was over or just beginning. I wanted another chance, with no woman this time. Women maybe, but no woman. Or so I told myself.

After a couple of weeks, I got myself to Auckland, New Zealand, and started looking for a little sailboat to live aboard. I thought maybe I could survive by taking tourists out deep-sea diving, and perhaps make it more interesting by having an all-woman crew. So much for avoiding the opposite sex.

Meanwhile, I lived in a ratty little room and did odd jobs at the boatyard. The guy who ran the place, a serious sailor named Harry Pope, was helping me find my boat. He recommended a 38-foot ketch called *Vega*. She wasn't my first choice, but luckily she was my last.

I made an offer on *Vega* and in the meantime went sailing. Harry was delivering another boat from Auckland to Melbourne, across the Tasman Sea, a two-week trip, and he needed crew. I needed a challenge after a couple of months of not doing much. Well, I got my wish.

The wet, stormy season in that part of the world is more or less November to April, so in August we thought we were pretty safe heading the 1,600 miles from New Zealand to Australia. We thought wrong. The week before we left, man was it blowing and raining. It was as if the heavens were saying, 'McTaggart, try me!'

It was raining like hell as *Windrush* sailed out of Auckland Harbour. The rolling swells were calm as we headed round the North Cape into the Tasman Sea, followed for about one hour by a school of dolphins. That's supposed to be a good omen. I was on watch, at 1 a.m. under a bright moon as we began to move, pushed by a fresh easterly breeze.

The next day the breeze turned into some serious wind. We were now bowling along at ten knots on a heavy broken sea, and the weather was deteriorating. The wind kept increasing, and the sea was getting wild. We dropped the mainsail and ran with just a storm jib. The waves were now roaring down the sides of the swells, like skiing down a mountain.

At dawn, it was clear skies and the wind dropped. We had already logged 653 miles, more than a third of the way to Melbourne. That night, the radio bleated out a gale warning. Jesus, another one.

We headed right into the mouth of the storm. Soon we were doing 15 knots, with just the storm jib. Sheet lightning struck right in front of us, as we flew along in the darkness. God, it was beautiful.

In the morning the wind eased and then died, leaving us thrashing around on big seas.

The next few days were pretty calm, except for something that now strikes me as pretty funny. I thought we were going to be attacked by a whale.

Six o'clock one morning, we were moving along at six or seven knots, when I spotted a big whale port amidships at 50 yards. Well this had never happened to me before, and I remembered hearing a story in the pub about a whale hitting a boat like ours and sinking her in a few minutes. Looking back, I'm sure it was just a good yarn, but then – whoofff, my heart went up into my throat. I was more afraid of the whale than I had been of the storm. What a joke.

We sailed into Melbourne on 5 September, after the physically toughest 13 days of my life – to date. It was a Saturday, and what a Saturday night! We were very tired, very dirty, and very turned on by having fought the sea for our lives, and won.

We flew back to Auckland a few days later to find we were celebrities. The newspapers loved the story of our voyage. I told them my name was David Fraser. My middle name is Fraser, and I was still very uncertain if I ever wanted to reclaim my identity as David McTaggart, the man whose world blew up in his face.

I moved into a cheaper hotel while waiting to move aboard *Vega*. My offer had been accepted, but then the owner had turned round and sold the boat to somebody else, for a thousand dollars more. *Vega* might have been only my second choice, but now I was bloody well going to have her.

My little hotel room was cold and damp and pretty much matched my mood. The excitement of the *Windrush* crossing behind me, I felt very alone again. Too much time to think, and my thoughts weren't pleasant. I missed my parents, and my three daughters. I wrote letters for the girls to open on their eighteenth birthdays, figuring that by then they might be able to understand and forgive their old man. But I couldn't bring myself to mail them, and I didn't even try to write my mom and dad, didn't know how to explain myself. I kept calculating and recalculating the total amount of money I'd lost. It came to almost half a million dollars, a huge amount in those days. And while I'd almost convinced myself I wanted a simpler life, I couldn't shake the feeling of loss.

Oh, to just get aboard that bloody boat and be moving forward again.

After weeks of lawyers' wrangling, I'd had enough. I 'borrowed' a small boat and rowed out to *Vega*. I cut through the chain that held her, climbed on board, and sailed away. A day or two later I called my lawyer and instructed him to phone the owner and tell him we'd meet in court. We did, and a judge upheld my right to *Vega*.

I had myself a boat. And it might have started slowly, but this was one love affair that would last my lifetime.

Vega is a 38-foot double-ended ketch. For you earthbound souls, that means she has two masts, the forward one being the tallest, the mainmast. She's not fancy, just exquisite – the kind of boat that real sailors drool over when you put in to port. Built from an old Norwegian design, out of native New Zealand wood, *Vega* was crafted by a Kiwi who knew what he was doing and loved to do it. He refitted the old girl for me, and in early February 1971, I launched the boat that would carry me into a war to save the world.

I was one man when I first stepped aboard her, and quite another when I stepped off after our first serious voyage together. *Vega* would be my home during my transformation from a self-centred hedonist into a reluctant warrior.

But I wasn't done with the good life quite yet.

I sailed *Vega* to Fiji and spent several contented months living aboard, chartering the old girl out to tourists, but always with me at the helm. *Vega* and I got to know and respect each other. Maybe that was what gave me the strength finally to get back in touch with my family, after dropping off the face of the earth for a year and a half. I told Mom and Dad that I was earning the same amount per week as I'd made per hour in California, but that I was healthy and relatively happy, although heartsick at causing them so much worry. I promised to keep in touch from now on, acknowledged what a pity it was that I'd wasted so much energy chasing women, and said I didn't know why I couldn't be satisfied with any of the great women in my life. I assured Mom and Dad that I was alone, and planning to stay that way.

As always, they sent their forgiveness, and their love. But at the end of 1971, they had sad news for me, too. My oldest daughter was now 13. Her mother had remarried, to a very fine gentleman, and he wanted to adopt Lisa. I had barely laid eyes on the girl since she was nine months old, and yet it hurt to know that my eldest child would carry another name. It felt as if I was being stripped of an important connection with the world, but I knew I had to give permission in order to make her life easier. I certainly hadn't done much else in that regard.

In December, feeling a little sorry for myself, I headed on up to the Bay of Islands north of Auckland. I was spending most of my leisure time now with other cruising yachtsmen. As they began to play their Christmas music, I felt homesick, and increasingly certain that I was born to be alone.

New Year's Eve 1971 was a quiet one for me. I rowed ashore and lit a fire. A group of 'yachties' joined me with their children. We sang a bit, but mostly sat with the fire between us and the Pacific Ocean, deep in our own thoughts. I was puzzling over whether it was time to move on, maybe to the Mediterranean. Or perhaps I should have another go at settling down, this time in New Zealand.

A few days later, I decided on New Zealand, or maybe it decided on me.

Vega and I were anchored off a place called Russell, in the Bay of Islands. On a sparkling summer morning in early January, I rowed the dinghy in to treat myself to lunch at the Duke of Marlborough, one of the Bay's hotspots. There was this rather beautiful young lady serving tables, a small, blonde, sun-kissed Kiwi. I went back to the boat, but she played on my mind through the afternoon. So that night I went back just as they finished serving and – to make a not very long story every shorter – I convinced her to come back to *Vega* with me for a drink. She was a college student, working during the summer holidays before her final year, and she told me later that she'd promised herself she wouldn't go with strange men onto their boats, 'but somehow this chap was a bit different'. By this time, *Vega* was shipshape, a real bachelor's paradise with every-thing neat and tidy and polished and pleasant. She was impressed. I put on some nice music, poured her a rum, and – in her words, again – 'it was the beginning of the end'. Within a few days, I'd effectively kidnapped her from her job, and her boyfriend. She packed her bags, and we went sailing for the next six weeks.

Ann-Marie Horne and I would be lovers for years, and friends for a lifetime. Without her, without that meeting, very likely none of it would have happened. No voyages against the nuclear machine, no Greenpeace International, no transformation of a pleasure-seeking failed capitalist into an environmental activist. Through her, and her family, I would get a chance to use my restless obsessive nature to do some good for a change.

Ann-Marie's parents weren't much older than me, and initially they were a bit horrified that she'd taken up with a man twice her age. But the Hornes were a very tolerant family, and they trusted their daughter. Eventually they even got used to the idea of Ann-Marie and I exploring the world together on *Vega* after she finished school.

As usual, things got a little more complicated.

Unlike me at the time, Gene Horne paid attention – a lot – to what was going on in the world. One day the two of us were sitting in his front room, just quietly listening to music together, when Gene told me that some Canadian group was looking for a boat and crew to protest against French nuclear testing in the South Pacific. Well, it caught my attention because the organization was from my hometown, Vancouver.

I'd never heard of this Greenpeace group. Turned out it had been founded in Vancouver a couple of years earlier, to protest against American nuclear testing off the southern coast of Alaska. This small group based itself on the Quaker philosophy of 'bearing witness' – a kind of passive resistance that involved simply placing oneself at the scene of some social or environmental horror. Your presence was your protest. Simple enough to appeal to me.

But the testing site was at Mururoa, an atoll in the middle of nowhere, halfway between Australia and South America. It was 3,500 miles from New Zealand, and the test was scheduled for 1 June, six weeks away. To prepare for such a voyage, and get there within six weeks, well it just couldn't be done.

And I was about as apolitical as a person can be. I was against nuclear testing, sure, but mine was the softest of positions. I hadn't thought about it really, or about anything else much recently, other than the pursuit of my own pleasure.

But like a dog with a bone, I started chewing over the idea of such an unthinkable voyage. And the more I thought it couldn't be done, the more I wanted to do it. If it was impossible, it just might be worth having a go.

Chapter Six

MY MOM AND dad must have thought that I'd completely lost my mind. I finally made contact after a year and a half to tell them I'm safe – if sorry and broke – and then six months later, I wrote: 'Well, when you receive this letter you will probably have heard from Mr Ben Metcalfe, chairman of Greenpeace, a nuclear disarmament group in Canada. I have decided to sail *Vega* to the Mururoa Atoll, approximately 800 miles S.E. of Tahiti ... I realize you might worry, well Mom and Dad, there is nothing to worry about, really.'

I couldn't have really believed that, could I?

It had been seven years since the USA, Russia and the UK had signed the Atmospheric Test Ban Treaty to put a stop to testing nuclear weapons above ground, and here was France just casually continuing to explode their hideous weapons above Mururoa, scattering clouds of radioactivity across Polynesia. I was planning to put myself and my little boat directly in the path of the radio-active fall-out – in the hope of stopping the test – and I was telling my folks not to worry. Ya, right.

There were two things about the protest that really intrigued me.

One, I've mentioned: I thought it was damned near impossible.

Two: France was trying to limit my personal freedom. I'm sure that sounds egotistical, but it's no joke. To set up their test zone so that they didn't irradiate anybody who might be travelling through the area – they seemed to have a blind spot about what was happening to the Polynesians – France had declared a huge exclusion zone – a hundred thousand square miles around Mururoa. Well, they just couldn't do that. International law says that a nation's territorial rights end 12 miles offshore. Beyond the 12-mile limit is the only place on this globe where a person is truly free.

I don't like limits on my personal freedom, don't like anybody telling me what I can and cannot do. So somewhere right around this point my personal rights and the planet's, my outlaw self and this quite righteous crusade, came slamming together, and held fast.

That's how a guy like me got hooked up with a bunch of hippies from Vancouver, calling themselves Greenpeace. I called them to say that *Vega* and I were willing to make the trip to Mururoa. We'd fly their colours if they'd pay expenses and supply a long-range radio and an inflatable liferaft.

The strategy was mine.

If I could get to Mururoa in time – and this was a big if – I'd sail right into France's ridiculous exclusion zone, and up to the 12-mile limit, but then stay just outside it, and down wind from any test. They'd be breaking international law if they tried to tow us out of there, and I'd be betting our lives that they wouldn't set off a bomb with us in its path. It was a good bet, but the stakes were high enough that it would never be a comfortable one. Within 15 miles of a nuclear blast, I was told, we'd receive third-degree burns. Our flesh would be charred, and *Vega* could ignite.

I needed to find crew who would play with such high stakes.

Even if everything went well, we'd still spend a month on the open seas to get there, who knows how long trying to maintain our position at the 12-mile limit, and then there was the thirty-day return trip to look forward to. All in all, not really a pleasure-cruise.

I thought first of Nigel Ingram. I'd met him down at the boatyard when I was finishing up a painting contract on a big steel-hulled ketch called *Bluebird of Thorn*. I looked up and saw a dark-haired young guy in his twenties, equally paint-spattered, heading for the showers. We talked about work for a while, and that inevitably led to beers at the Leopard Tavern across the way, the boaters' favourite watering-hole. I found out Nigel had a degree from Oxford, had spent time in the Royal Navy, and had since then been making a living cruising and racing boats all over the world. He was quiet and solid, and I took to him instantly.

When I first told him what I was planning, Nigel said no – for about two minutes. He was supposed to take a yacht from New Zealand to the Caribbean and he'd promised his lady the trip. She'd have to wait.

We had ten days to get *Vega* ready to go, and it was a crazy time. We needed everything! *Vega* was in beautiful shape, but she wasn't prepared for an offshore voyage of this magnitude. She needed a complete going-over from bow to stern, including the somewhat temperamental diesel engine.

Oh, and we needed food and water for four months. And enough cigarettes, or things were going to get really ugly.

Vega was temporarily renamed *Greenpeace III*. The numbers *I* and *II* belonged to a couple of ships that had, the year before, sailed north from Vancouver towards Amchitka Island off the coast of Alaska, where the Americans were testing nuclear weapons.

As we got closer to our departure date, small miracles began to bloom around us. Dozens of people made their way to the docks and down to *Vega* offering their help. It lightened our load, and our hearts. Someone even offered us the back-up generator we needed for emergencies, gratis. We found out much later, when 'our' generator was confiscated by customs, that it had been smuggled in from Fiji. Hilarious.

We had current problems with customs, too, brought about by my playing a little fast and loose with the rules. In Fiji some months earlier, as the US dollar was diving, I got rid of my American currency by buying more than a hundred watches. Thought I could sell them as and when I needed a little cash. When my Fiji visa ran out, I took off for New Zealand, not declaring the watches at customs when I got there. I don't think I'd really planned to stay in New Zealand long enough for it to matter, but then I met Ann-Marie and took one of my left turns.

Anyway, it was little more than a week before our departure date, and we were hard at work on the boat. I was below, just about to grab a quick bite to eat, when I heard the thump of somebody landing heavily in the cockpit. One after the other, five burly men squeezed through the hatch and into the galley. They were not dressed for a day's sail.

They had a search warrant, and started ripping everything apart. I had the feeling they were looking for any excuse to stop the voyage, at least that was my guess. I'd been tied up to this dock for months, and now that we were days away from sailing against the French, they came with a search warrant! We were making too many waves.

Eventually they found a few watches, and I ended up downtown in the office of the customs inspector. What a trip that was. You'd think I'd had *Vega* stuffed full of opium, the cold way he treated me. The bill of sale with the watches had tipped him to the fact that there were a few more somewhere – like a hundred. He wasn't letting me go anywhere until he saw those watches. It was everything I owned, except for *Vega*, but there was no choice. All I wanted now was to get away from bloody Auckland, and get driving towards Mururoa and the French.

I took a customs officer to the bank where the watches were stowed in a safety deposit box, and turned them over. He rewarded me with an indictment, for smuggling. In court, my lawyer tried to explain that it was more of a misunderstanding than anything, but the magistrate was having none of that. I was found guilty and fined $800, payable immediately or I was going to jail for four months.

Well of course I didn't have the money. As the jail door clanged shut behind me, all I could think of was *Vega*. How the hell were we going to get out of here.

Two o'clock in the morning, down to my last few cigarettes, when the guard told me to pack up my stuff and come with him. My lawyer paid my bail, in exchange for a promissory note. Throughout my life, I've found angels in the strangest places.

But that wasn't the end of the bureaucratic barriers we faced trying to get away. We jumped through major hoops over whether or not *Vega* had to be surveyed again, to be declared seaworthy. If she was a Canadian yacht – which she was – she didn't have to be re-surveyed. But try convincing them of that. I think it was just another stalling tactic, maybe on behalf of a conservative government or petty bureaucrats who found us too much of a challenge to the status quo.

We were scheduled for a bit of a send-off on 29 April at eleven in the morning, and we still didn't have the survey thing resolved.

I decided it was prudent to forget the publicity and sneak away the night before. We all left *Vega* in the late afternoon, as was our custom, and headed for the Leopard. I figured whoever was keeping an eye on us would think we'd just called it a day. Shortly after five o'clock we reassembled at the boat. It was getting dark, and the overcast winter sky nicely reflected our mood. We could hear the clatter of rush-hour traffic on Harbour Bridge, as *Vega* motored out of Westhaven Harbour.

We dropped anchor 15 miles and two hours later in Matiatia Bay on Waiheke Island, still in the mouth of the big Gulf on which Auckland sits. We were making dinner, Radio Hauraki playing quietly in the background, when lights began to flash across us. Someone was trying to attract our attention. We heard shouting, but couldn't make it out. The radio soon supplied the answer. They'd announced that we'd dropped anchor in the bay, and the islanders had come to wish us a safe voyage. After all the hassles leaving Auckland, it was quite a moment. Those car lights dancing across *Vega*'s hull were the last friendly contact we'd have for months.

The next day we finished stowing everything safely before we really got underway. And we had to figure out what the hell to do about our radio.

Greenpeace in Vancouver had come through with a long-range radio, but it came with what turned out to be a price tag. Their chairman, Ben Metcalfe, wanted to come along. It seemed like a good idea at the time, but the moment he stepped off the plane, I knew it wasn't. He looked middle-aged, out-of-shape, and just a little too gentrified for what we were heading into. Before we'd even left port, it was obvious we'd never exactly become close friends. It's funny looking back to see that our relationship then mirrored what my relationship with Greenpeace in my homeland would always be – a marriage of necessity, without a natural affinity.

Greenpeace in Vancouver grew out of the 'Don't Make A Wave Committee', a little organization started by a handful of serious anti-nuclear activists who believed in the Quaker philosophy of protesting simply by being present at a bad scene, by 'bearing witness'. By 1972, they were attracting scores of hippies, and the organization was beginning to take on that tone. These were easy-going flower children wanting to rock the world political scene without ever offending their comrades. Nice people, with good intentions, and with a worthy desire to work collectively. Well, by now you probably know that isn't me. I'm not easy-going, I'm not nice, and I think more gets done when someone is in charge. And in 1972, we were aboard *my* boat, and the skipper's word is law. Metcalfe didn't quite see it that way. Maybe he figured I'd steer the boat and he'd run the campaign. Not bloody likely.

Ben was supposed to be in charge of the marine radio. Very critical, since it would keep the world informed of our whereabouts, and might just keep us alive. Well, it seemed Ben was a different kind of communications guy – press releases and all that – not a technician. He didn't know much about ham radios, and the radio he'd supplied wasn't working.

We got a real radio man out to the boat. He showed us all how the thing operated, but also dropped his own little bomb. The ham radio drew so much power that it would drain *Vega*'s engine batteries in minutes. We'd have to rewire the boat completely to make it work, and there was no time for that.

Oh boy. Now we had the choice of turning back or going forward against the French nuclear machine without a reliable communications system. One little boat sailing against a fleet of warships, in a conflict hidden from the world. Chilling thought. But the thought of turning back was actually worse.

On Sunday morning 30 April 1972, we hoisted *Vega*'s sails and were outward bound on a broad reach across the dark green seas of the Hauraki Gulf, heading for the open Pacific. Mururoa is about 2,750 nautical miles west of New Zealand, and 750 miles north. Just 3,500 nautical miles to go. Our plan was to stay south most of the way, where the prevailing southeasterly winds would carry us to the atoll. On the way back, we'd stay north in the prevailing southwesterlies. Good theory. Nigel and I knew we were bound to run into some storms, and just hoped our green crew could weather them.

'We' consisted of me and Nigel, Ben, Roger Haddleton – an ex-British navy man with a good knowledge of diesel engines – and a young Aussie named Grant Davidson who was along because he was willing and funny and brave enough to say yes.

Nigel and I used the first few days out to establish our own 'house rules'.

On watch, every man did three hours in daylight and two at night. The cockpit's a cold and lonely place to be at night, so there were absolutely no excuses for being even two minutes late for your shift. The man on watch would wake the next guy by shining a flashlight in his eyes through the hatch, that way the rest of the crew could sleep on. When coming off watch, you'd make a hot drink for the guy you'd just woken up, and stand in the hatch and talk to him for a few minutes before you turned in. Just a way to make the dark a little less lonely.

For this to work, we had to teach Ben and Grant to navigate by the stars. Not complicated, really, you just use a flashlight to make sure you're on the right compass heading and then choose a bright star you can see through the rigging. Then make damn sure it stays put.

Grant caught on. Ben was having trouble, and he and I were really getting on each other's nerves. We weren't exactly coming together as a crew the way we needed to if we were going to have a go at the French.

I decided to alter course for an island called Rarotonga, to give us all a little rest before the big push to Mururoa.

The next few days were okay. Steady wind, calm seas and clear blue skies. As we sailed towards the Tropic of Capricorn, we quite suddenly left the dark green seas of the colder latitudes behind us, and *Vega* was gliding along an aquamarine ocean sparkling under the warm tropical sun. That was okay, too, after the tension of the last few weeks.

We'd been at sea 13 days, when shortly after 5 a.m. on 13 May Grant woke me to show me Rarotonga off in the distant dawn light. After two weeks of seeing nothing but different shades of blue on the horizon, it looked beautiful, lying there in its green cloak of jungle. We had logged 2001 miles, and I was proud of my *Vega*. She knew what she was doing on the open ocean.

Once we were ashore, Ben hitched a ride into town, two miles away, without a word to the rest of us. We sweated our way in on foot a little later, and set up camp in the Banana Court, an open-air bar, while we sorted out fresh provisions and arranged phone calls home. Ben had a lot of calls to make, and he was very secretive about it.

A couple of days later I was sitting sipping a rum and coke on the verandah that wrapped around the little hotel, when Nigel came barrelling up the street, looking ready to kill.

'We're a bloody hoax,' he roared. 'Our friends are right pissed off!'

There was a story running in the Auckland papers claiming that *Vega* was a decoy to distract the French while another boat slipped into Mururoa, coming from Canada or South America. The article pointed at Ben Metcalfe as the chief source for the story. Suddenly all those hush-hush phone calls made sense. Pardon my French, but shit! we were mad.

We confronted Ben in his hotel room and couldn't get a direct answer. Metcalfe kept talking about the need for secrecy and how he'd handle the plan, if I handled the boat. Well, give me a break. There we were prepared to risk our lives for the cause, and we weren't to be trusted with the truth.

I made the decision that Ben wasn't getting back on *Vega*, and he made it easy. The next morning, he taxied down to the dock to tell us that he had to leave for Peru at once – apparently the protest captain there was being thrown in jail. We watched with relief as a twin-engined plane took off over the bay, carrying the one and only official representative of Greenpeace.

To this day I don't know for sure what was going on with him. There was never any protest boat from Peru, and Ben and I haven't talked since.

As *Vega* sailed away from Rarotonga on the morning of 21 May, there were three of us – Nigel, Grant and me. Roger had come down with a bad case of tropical fever.

Ahead of us the Pacific endlessly rose and fell, indifferent to our hopes, and to our fears, and certainly indifferent to petty human politics. It brought our lives down to the simplest common denominator – survival. Now Nigel, Grant and I could put our whole selves into doing what we'd come for – demonstrating that one little boat can make a big difference.

Eleven days and 1,500 nautical miles to go before the French nuclear test, scheduled for 1 June.

Chapter Seven

IT'S HARD TO describe the size of the South Pacific, the magnitude of our journey, even forgetting what was waiting for us at the other end. I think a globe probably shows it best; as it spins past New Zealand, there's an *awful* lot of blue before South America rolls by.

And we're right in the middle of it.

We look out the ten or so miles to the horizon, and sail across the empty blue sea to get there. And then we keep sailing, another horizon, another ten miles. Blue. Endless blue. *Vega* moves beneath us as if she were alive, absorbing the repeated pounding of the sea, and gliding over it, gliding over submarine mountains perhaps two and a half miles beneath in the darkness.

We are alone, and we are fragile. If bad weather hits, there is nowhere to shelter. We'll take whatever the sea and sky throw at us.

For the first four days out of Rarotonga, Grant, Nigel and I have fine weather, but the southeasterlies force us north, off course. We begin to worry that we won't make Mururoa by 1 June. And we have other worries. None of us is an engine expert, *Vega*'s diesel is a cantankerous old thing, and we need the engine batteries charged to use our power-hungry ham radio, our lifeline back to our friends and supporters. Each evening, I get edgy with anticipation as we approach the time to start the engine. But so far, so good.

We broadcast false positions, the idea being that the French will look for us in the wrong place as we slip over the cordon line into their stupid exclusion zone. The danger is obvious. If anything goes wrong, our friends won't have a clue where to look for us, but it seems the best strategy. Before each transmission, Nigel and I pore over the chart and work out a position that's believable. Occasionally we actually raise Radio Rarotonga, but most of the time we don't hear anyone on the other end. All we hear is crackling and squawking. I come to hate the bright tuning eye on the radio.

We feel especially alone knowing that only we three know our true position.

We have a little portable radio receiver that brings us some comfort, and has indelibly burned the Australian national anthem into my brain. Each morning Grant turns on the receiver, so we can see if anyone out there cares. (They don't seem to, so far; there's no mention of us on the newscast.) And we hear this zany morning radio ritual – Radio Australia signs on with the sustained screeching of a cockatoo, followed by the anthem, 'Waltzing Matilda'.

Many years later, the American singer Tom Waits will record a blues version that takes me right back to that wonderful, terrible time, and tells more about how it felt than I've ever been able to:

> And it's a battered old suitcase
> to a hotel some place,
> and a wound that will never heal.
> And no prima donna,
> the perfume is on
> an old shirt that is stained with blood
> and with whisky.
> We'll go waltzing Matilda...

God, I love that tune. I hear it and I'm right back on *Vega*, tacking towards Mururoa.

Lying in my damp bunk between watches, I can hear the boat

straining as she ploughs through the water. In my half-sleep, it begins to sound like somebody grumbling, and maybe she is. I'm getting a little depressed myself. That's not entirely unusual for me. I can't stand it when I'm stuck in one place, and can't stand it when things are screwing up. And that's what it feels like. We're moving, but not fast enough, and if the wind doesn't change soon, we're screwed.

The good news is that the three of us are jelling nicely, into a very compatible and competent crew. Nigel is just so level, so quiet and confident. And Grant's a bit of a joker, which really helps keep the black dogs of depression at bay.

I don't know if it's the fatigue from the long watches imposed by our small numbers, or the depression playing tricks on my mind, but I start to get a strong, almost supernatural feeling that maybe some force above – or below – is trying to tell me something. We're not supposed to go to Mururoa. Tahiti is not far ahead, and it's really tempting to put in there, and say we tried. I can't help but remember the rather delicious times spent on the beach at the Club Med when I first came to these parts. A re-enactment looks a lot more appetizing – and sane – than fighting an uncooperative ocean for the right to try to stare down a nuclear navy.

I'm reading *Mutiny on the Bounty* and identifying way too strongly with the main character who leaves Tahiti to clear his name, and when he returns his wife has died and he's all alone. It's obviously getting to me, being so far out here. It's hard to explain, but usually when you go someplace on a boat, you look forward to getting there, so as you get closer to the end of the voyage you start to perk up a bit. I'm getting just the opposite feeling on this trip. When we get to Mururoa, we have no idea what's going to happen, and even if we do get away safely, we have another 1,500 miles to sail just to get back to Rarotonga. No question I've got to get some sleep because we should be in better shape than we are now when we meet the French. I really hope my depression isn't affecting Nigel and Grant.

The heat's certainly affecting all of us. It must be 120°F in the cabin. When we finally get some rain, Nigel and Grant go out and dance around in their first freshwater shower since Rarotonga. And Grant again practises his pirate act – running up and down the boat, sweeping an imaginary cloak behind him while he spears Frenchmen over the side of the boat with the imaginary cutlass he pulls from between his teeth. At least his teeth are real. And his sense of humour.

On the morning of 28 May, four days from the scheduled test, Nigel's at the helm and I'm pouring buckets of saltwater over myself to cool off from the prickly heat of the cabin. We still have 700 miles of Pacific Ocean between us and Mururoa. And there it is. Temptation. Tahiti's Mount Orohena rising over the edge of the horizon, 75 miles off the port beam. Settle down, David. Be good.

For once in my life, I stay on course.

I'm in my cabin about midnight that night, struggling to make radio contact with anybody out there, when the storm hits. It howls force 9 for the rest of the night. With Grant at the helm, *Vega* screams on through the darkness.

The next morning, the wind drops a little – force 7. Our world is white and grey now. Foaming seas, and a low, dark sky. We spend the day skiing over twenty-foot swells. Nigel is below, trying to get through on the ham radio, when there's a small explosion; I can just hear it over the wind noise. I fight my way through the hatch to see a disconsolate first mate sitting in front of a smoking radio. That's that. We still have our marine-band, so we're not totally dead in the water – you should excuse the expression – but we won't be making contact with anybody on shore.

The gale blows force 9 again that night. *Vega*'s moving like a train, which is the good news, but the wind direction means we're approaching Mururoa indirectly. After all this, it's not looking as if we'll make it in time. Then we cross the international dateline.

I know this sounds really stupid, with all we'd been through, but only at this moment do we realize we've got another day.

It's 30 May in this part of the Pacific.

That night the storm abates. Le Chef Nigel cooks us a decent dinner of macaroni and cheese before I head for my berth and a few hours' sleep. When he wakes me at midnight for our shift rotation, the wind has changed. It's coming now from the southwest, just what we need to set a direct course for Mururoa. And it's a good breeze, too; we're doing about 7.5 knots. Maybe somebody up there likes me after all. On watch that night, under a full moon, it sure feels like it. I can almost hear a voice whisper, 'Go for it, McTaggart. Now!'

My depression's gone. It's like playing badminton, or business, or anything else; all of a sudden you smell the end and your heart comes back and you start driving.

But the next day, the last before the test, the wind dies and we forge ahead with the engines. It's going to be touch and go.

As the sun sets, an almost holy calm falls upon the water. No kidding. It's like nothing Nigel or I have ever seen before, in all our sailing experience. Absolutely still. There's no horizon. It's like we're in the twilight zone. The sea's a mirror, reflecting the blanket of stars above us. The phosphorescence in the water is amazing, and when Grant and Nigel go for a swim, it's as if their motion is churning up the heavens. We don't know whether we're being blessed or warned.

Sitting on deck that night, the usually jovial Grant is very subdued. He says something about when he eventually has kids and tells them about this, they'll never believe it. And then we all get quiet, realizing that this is it. Nigel and Grant may not have kids, and I may never see mine again. I suddenly miss my three daughters like crazy, and wonder if that's what they think I am – crazy. And I see myself as a child in a little handmade boat on Buccaneer Bay, my brother beside me, and not a care in the world.

There's been a lot of water under a lot of bridges since then. Big successes and big failures, and ceaseless motion, all to get me to this moment of complete stillness. This moment before my next life begins.

At 10.45 that night, we cross the line. In an hour it'll be 1 June, the date of the first scheduled test. Really, you can't cut it too much closer on an ocean voyage. We pop the bottle of champagne we'd begun to think we'd never get to drink, and toast the 3,500 miles we've come together.

Before us in the darkness is Mururoa, and the French naval base. Somewhere out there is an atomic bomb. We'd spent weeks getting used to absolute aloneness, and now that feeling is rapidly replaced by the sensation of being watched. We know *Vega* has company – naval warships – and we have no idea when they'll be coming to call.

The next day we're up and down, watching the horizon for the first sign of the French navy. We figure we're about a hundred miles from Mururoa, and we need the French to know that. If our false radio communications worked, the French are thinking we're quite a way northwest, and they've got no reason to delay their test. We don't relish getting blown out of the water. We raise our radar reflector and hope for the best.

Our immediate priorities are to work our way into position downwind of the test site – and just outside Mururoa's 12-mile limit – and to get a message to our friends in New Zealand, again with our real location. But like so many days, the radio emits nothing but squawks.

We're busily hammering holes in a fuel drum so it'll sink when we jettison it overboard, when a roar drowns us out. A French aircraft banks 300 feet above us. Whew! At least they know we're here. And I'm really hoping they took some pictures. All of us bearded and scruffy. Grant and Nigel naked as the day they were born, pounding on a metal drum as if they're at some pagan feast. We're tougher than we look, fellas.

Late afternoon, we decide to heave-to for the night, which just means manoeuvring *Vega* broadside to the wind and waves. That way she'll stay fairly stationary. In calm weather it can even be fairly comfortable. Now that we've stopped the boat, Grant decides he needs to get off for a while. He pumps up our little inflatable and rows away. Sitting out there all alone, he calls back over the water to tell us how small *Vega* looks with the empty sweep of the horizon behind us. As if we need reminding.

Overnight the wind comes up. At 5 a.m., tired and irritable, I stumble above decks to relieve myself, and just about lose it. Through the rainy mist I can see watery yellow lights flashing. Hell! If we've drifted that close to Mururoa, we're about to run aground on the coral! It's all hands on deck, and as we hoist the sails, I take a look through the binoculars. The mist clears just enough to get a better look at the 'town' off our starboard. It's a bloody big ship, maybe two or three hundred feet long. Company's coming. We get the hell out of there.

Late that afternoon, the weather clears enough for Nigel to get an accurate sighting. We're about 27 miles from Mururoa, which means we must have been damn close to the 12-mile limit when we saw that ship. In all likelihood, it was waiting to pounce the moment we broke international law.

Now days pass in the same monotonous way. Each night the wind pushes us away from the atoll. Each morning, we sail back in.

We focus obsessively on our little radio receiver, hoping to hear any word that we exist, and that somebody out there cares. We work out a listening schedule, based on the relative strengths of the different stations' signals throughout the day. We're often late to bed, talking endlessly. Every morsel of news is thoroughly digested, discussed over and over. Every aspect, every possibility, past and present. On 5 June, we hear that the Stockholm Environmental Conference has just started. Maybe that means the French will delay the test. We don't know if we think that's good or bad; two more weeks out here will just about finish us.

But by noon on 7 June, we're not bored anymore. The barometer drops from 1013 to 1007 and I know there's some serious weather coming.

By mid-afternoon the waves are 25-feet high. I'm at the tiller when the wind blows up to force 11. One moment we're in a trough looking up at a wall of water, and the next we shoot the wave, as canyons of water hiss beneath us. We've got no sails up, we're bare poles all the way, and the wind is driving my brave little *Vega* forward at about seven knots. We throw out every extra rope we've got as sea anchors to slow us down, and still the wind carries us sixty miles in the next ten hours. It's bloody impossible to stay in position fighting this weather. But thank God *Vega*'s a tough old girl, who doesn't mind a little breeze.

That night I become completely consumed with the need to make contact with the world I've left so far behind. When the storm abates, I write a letter to Ann-Marie and put it in an empty wine bottle. I say some kind of goofy blessing and set the bottle adrift on heavy seas.

During these long days, our only human contact off the boat is with a radio operator on a Belgian ship that sounds to be near the island of Tubai. The radio picks up his faint signal very occasionally, drifting in and out. It's not much, but it's our only hope that the world knows where we are.

As far as we can tell from our little receiver, the Stockholm Conference is still going on, but there's no mention of us. The French have done the smartest thing possible: ignore us. We hear that they're still planning to go ahead with the test, and now the skies are clear and the wind is in the right direction for them to commence.

We almost wish they would.

The constant tension of trying to maintain our position is starting to get to us. Just imagine sitting in a very small room with a low ceiling for days on end. And that room is rolling back and forth, back and forth, 24 hours a day. Even when you're sitting down, you have to wedge yourself against something or you'll be thrown to the floor. After a while, it drives you bloody crazy.

On 16 June, the last rays of sun are gilding the sky as I go up on deck to check for our companions. The French have been paying us distant visits by boat, and by plane. Something catches my eye over west, in the direction of Mururoa. It's a reddish mass of some kind, maybe a helicopter. No, it couldn't be, it's not moving. I grab the binoculars. Oh my god.

I shout at Nigel and Grant, 'It's a balloon! A damn bloody great balloon! They're getting ready to blow off the bomb!'

We know that before the nuclear test, the bomb will be raised over the atoll, suspended under a large dirigible-type balloon. As the light of day fades, we wonder if we're looking at our last sunset. We decide that at dawn we'll sail toward the atoll, stand 15 miles or so out, and pray.

We don't think the French really want to blow us out of the water – not very politic – but we can't be sure. We go about the gruesome task of placing wooden plugs near all the air vents on *Vega*, so we can quickly hammer them into place and seal off the interior. If we survive the initial blast, two of us will stay below and the man who draws the short straw will start the engine and steer the yacht out of the danger zone. We know it's not much of a plan, but we have to do something.

We send out a message, hoping our Belgian friend is picking it up: 'Balloon raised over Mururoa last night STOP Greenpeace Three 16 miles northeast STOP Situation frightening please pray.'

Nothing that day – later we'd calculate that we'd probably delayed the test – and nothing the next. And on the evening of 18 June, we pick up a Radio Australia broadcast that says the French government would 'take all necessary measures to protect anyone likely to be in the vicinity of Mururoa atoll in French Polynesia where a projected nuclear test is to be held. This assurance was given by the government to the Australian embassy in Paris, in reply to a request. A young Australian, Grant Davidson, is believed to be in the area in the ketch *Greenpeace III*. The French foreign minister said he has noted the Australian government's concern and France would take all necessary measures to ensure that they would not be affected by the nuclear blast.'

Hallelujah! Somebody – besides the French – knows we're out here.

That night a French ship is sitting about a mile off our bow as we turn in for the night. It's almost reassuring. But as I'm drifting off to sleep, I start thinking about what 'all necessary measures' might mean. It doesn't sound that comforting.

Now we have constant companions, in the form of one French warship or another. We slow, it slows. We increase speed and, with a belch of smoke, so does the warship. It starts to get a little irritating, a new form of torture. But our spirits lift when we hear on the portable receiver that there are anti-nuclear demonstrations in Australia and New Zealand, as well as dock-workers refusing to work on French vessels. Maybe we're getting to them.

At six in the morning on 21 June, we wake to a booming voice over a megaphone, 'Greenpeace III! Greenpeace III!' That's followed by three deafening roars from a ship's horn. We stumble up the hatchway into a wall of grey steel, the minesweeper *La Bayonnaise* is sitting a few yards away. The man with the megaphone leans over a rail high above and says he's got a letter for us. They lower an inflatable into the swells and drop our mailman into it for a short but extremely hair-raising ride to *Vega*. He looks very relieved to deliver his message and get back to his big steel home.

We read the message. And, frankly, he shouldn't have bothered. It's just a standard-issue warning that there'll be nuclear experiments happening in the area, and all mariners should keep away.

We decide to send them back a long legal opinion we'd had

drafted at the University of Auckland, which outlines our position that they have no business trying to push us, or any boat, around in international waters. As long as we stay 12 miles offshore, we can do as we bloody well please.

We put up a flag signalling that we have a letter for them, and *La Bayonnaise* comes back. The little inflatable again lurches and crashes over to us, and this time we exchange messages. Turns out they've got a personal letter for us from the Admiral commanding the nuclear tests force: 'You are still in danger area defined in the notice to mariners you received this morning STOP You are requested to keep off the area or at least sail immediately and join position 15 nautical miles west of Tureia where I will ensure your safety against nuclear effects.'

Well that's a bit chilling. So they're not guaranteeing our safety where we are.

We stay put, and decide that, in the morning, we'll head a little closer to test their reaction to our communiqué about international waters. We don't have to wait for it.

At five o'clock I wake to shouts from Grant that there's a ship heading right for us, and it makes yesterday's minesweeper look like a baby. We decide it would be good to get underway, and as the mainsail with its peace symbol shakes out into the air, I can see we've got more company – two smaller ships and one of them looks like *La Bayonnaise*.

Throughout the morning, the three warships harass little *Vega*. They come close. And stop in our path. We tack away to open water, only to be chased by another ship. The big cruiser, *DeGrasse*, looks about six storeys high, with a massive radio tower on her afterdeck, and heavy gun turrets forward. She gets so close I can see the Admiral on the bridge, watching us through his binoculars. It's terrifying.

Finally the *DeGrasse* moves off away from us. We come about and put our bow again towards Mururoa. Whew. We've got a good stiff breeze behind us and are making some headway, but there's still the matter of the two ships astern. *La Bayonnaise* and *Hippotame* are rapidly gaining on us, their bows crashing through the heavy seas. Sixty yards, thirty, fifteen. What the hell are they up to?

La Bayonnaise starts to come in tight on our port quarter, with *Hippotame* slightly back, to our starboard. They move in together, their huge grey hulls churning the bit of water now between us. My heart's pounding as we three crash along together at eight knots.

I can see the bridge of *La Bayonnaise* as the Commander gives an order to the helmsman. They move in closer. I steer slightly to starboard, but can go no further or we'll fall off the wind and right under the bow of *Hippotame*.

Grant screams at *La Bayonnaise*, 'Get away you fuckers! You'll kill us all!'

As if that were an invitation, *La Bayonnaise* moves closer.

We begin to fall off the wind, directly into the path of *Hippotame* on the other side. Just as it looks like we're going under her bow, *Hippotame* swings sharply to port, missing our stern by less than 15 yards.

They fall away.

We set our course again for Mururoa. And the bastards do it again! This time I lower the sails. If they're going to put us out of commission, they'll have to bear down on a stationary vessel. They've broken God knows how many rules of the sea, but this is too much even for them. For the rest of the day they stay close; keeping track of our whereabouts is obviously their main assignment.

It's 24 June, my fortieth birthday, and I'm really feeling my age. *Vega* and I are quite a pair. Her sails are ripped, her decks are cracked, the white exterior paint is wearing away and the varnish everywhere is thin. I know just how she feels.

That night it blows again, and in the morning our constant companions take off over the horizon. We decide to move in closer to Mururoa. Ten o'clock, and we're still under sail when we get a new visitor. A large plane begins to make a series of passes over our masthead. It's an eerie feeling in the darkness. We can just make out the plane's silhouette, as a floodlight under its nose sweeps across the whitecaps. Two flares float down to starboard of us and catch *Vega* in a ghostly light. The plane stays with us for about two hours.

By the end of June – four weeks since we crossed into the exclusion zone – our food and water are getting low, but our little threesome, well foursome, really, if you include *Vega*, is hanging together very well.

A couple of days after the plane incident, the weather's calm enough to open my birthday champagne. We haven't been drinking much, and after a couple of swallows, we even start to feel warmly towards the French. Someone suggests we invite them over for a drink. Yachts often have a flag to signal, 'Come aboard for a drink', but that wasn't one of the things we'd thought necessary to pack for this particular voyage. So we make one. I rip up my pillowcase, and Nigel cuts the shape of a cocktail glass out of his brand-new red shorts. We march up on deck, attach the flag to the halyard on the mainmast and – singing 'La Marseillaise' – we raise the flag. We sing 'Oh Canada' and 'Waltzing Matilda', too. Our constant companions come to have a look, but they don't join us.

The next morning Radio Australia broadcasts sickening news. The French had successfully set off a nuclear device three days before, on 26 June. Now we know why we were buzzed so often that day. They wanted to be sure of our position, and maybe even camouflage the noise, since we had been only 30 miles away from the explosion.

Oddly enough, the news only makes us more determined to fight our way back into position downwind of ground zero and try to prevent the next explosion. Well, the French are equally deter-mined. Throughout the night, as we make for Mururoa, a warship called *La Paimpolaise* is right on our stern. When we come about onto a new tack, *Vega* slows, and *La Paimpolaise* almost thunders right over us. Over and over.

On 1 July, coincidentally Canada's national holiday, we hear a radio report that we'd sailed out of the area on 21 June and not been seen since. If they want to get rid of us without causing a ripple, now's the time.

At 9.30 we hoist *Vega*'s tattered sails and head southeast towards Mururoa. Within ten minutes, *La Paimpolaise* is running alongside us. We've got a good force 6 northeasterly blowing, so we set the self-steering and go below. I'm enjoying the thought that *Vega* must look a proud old girl, sailing along on her own, when I notice that the warship is flying a signal flag, MY2. We look through our international flagbook, but it's not there. (Much later, we'll discover that it means 'Do not continue on present course.')

We don't know what the hell's going on, but when *La Paimpolaise* gets about fifty yards away, I decide we'd better go above and give *Vega* a hand.

The warship draws close on our starboard quarter, running parallel to us. If she wants to force us to turn, she should be on the other side where she can block the wind from our sails, forcing us to fall off fairly safely to starboard. If we have to turn to port and into the wind, we'll lose speed momentarily and could have a minesweeper over our deck. The French skipper doesn't seem to know anything about sailing.

Nigel takes *Vega*'s tiller in his capable hands.

Frantically I try to signal *La Paimpolaise*, and for a moment it looks like they understand. The ship slows up and we slip ahead.

But now she's back, on our starboard quarter, and this time comes even closer. I can see the commander waving at us from up on the bridge. I feel a cold shock run through me as I realize he's actually laughing.

They're now so close that I can't see the men on the bridge anymore.

Twenty yards off and still coming.

I yell at Nigel, 'Hard over!!!'

He desperately tries to bring *Vega* up into the wind and to port, to carry us away from the massive grey hull bearing down on us.

Vega struggles for our lives, but begins to hesitate. The wind is out of the mainsail.

We are losing way, and *La Paimpolaise* is still coming.

Now she is ten yards away. Her bow nearly over our heads.

Vega is caught in the pressure from the minesweeper's bow wave, and skids sideways.

The huge bow looms over our head. For a moment we see nothing but grey.

And then, CRASH! The bow smashes down on us.

For a moment, I think we'll be sliced in half, and my mind races with the problem of which way to jump to clear the minesweeper's propellers. But she's just caught *Vega*'s edge ... and now the warship's bow is tangled in our rigging.

The water is boiling with foam. *La Paimpolaise* is in full reverse, with our rigging still snagged on her bow. Instinctively, Nigel grabs a knife and slashes us free. The line explodes, and we roll back upright.

It takes a long moment to realize what's just happened, and that we are still standing upright on the deck of my brave and beautiful *Vega*.

Chapter Eight

MIRACULOUSLY, *VEGA'S* HULL is in one piece, but her rigging is badly damaged, and she's taking on water. We're not going anywhere without repairs.

Our supporters think we left the zone a week ago, we're 1,600 miles from the nearest neutral port, and the only people near enough to help us don't really seem to have our best interests in mind. We wonder if they'll just leave us adrift out here.

We're scared, but we're also proud. *Vega* bobs helplessly on the Pacific for hours as we discuss the possibility of trying to limp back to Rarotonga without help. Finally, good sense prevails, and we negotiate a tow into the naval base at Mururoa for repairs.

Shortly after dawn on 3 July, my poor *Vega* is pulled into Mururoa by a tug called *Courageux*! What a joke. The atoll is very low, just sand and a few palm trees. As we pass into the lagoon, there's a short chop kicked up by the breeze. We see the *DeGrasse* sitting off our starboard bow. Beyond her there are at least 30 ships of all sizes and kinds, from minesweepers to passenger liners, that have been converted into barracks. On land, cars move to and fro between the buildings along the two-mile curve of main beach. It looks like what it is – a place dedicated to war.

Hundreds of sailors line the decks of the *DeGrasse* as we pass by, our Canadian flag flying aft. We wave somewhat cheekily, and to our immense surprise, some of the French sailors wave back. We get the feeling we've earned their respect.

As we complete a more thorough survey of the damage to *Vega*, and try to negotiate communication out to our governments and our families, one of the officers asks if we'd like to join him for lunch. What the hell. We haven't had a decent meal for weeks. We go in his launch round to a coral beach, away from the harbour, and it's another world. It's clean and white, dotted with palm trees and little huts. Polynesia again, instead of French nuclear navy!

We walk – on very wobbly sea legs – to a clearing where ten or so men stand talking. One looks particularly distinguished – about 55 with short-cropped grey hair, not tall but in very good shape with a distinct presence. He's wearing dark glasses, and he could be a film star playing a French admiral. Of course, it turns out he's Admiral Claviere, in charge of the nuclear fleet at Mururoa. When we're introduced, I find myself disappointed that he doesn't speak any more English than I do French. Basically, none. One of his officers interprets for us, and I think as I listen that he'd be a good father – strict, but fair.

The Admiral invites us to go for a swim in the lagoon. No thanks. I can just see the headlines, 'Protesters find no radioactivity at bomb site.' Drinks are served, and he congratulates us on our sailing before we sit down to a meal that's *almost* worth the trouble it causes.

We're at a long table set in the shade of the palm trees. There's a white tablecloth, and clean dishes, and shiny cutlery. And wine. And salad. And pizza. And roast beef. Even fresh bread and cheese.

Our sensation-starved tastebuds are working overtime, but our brains aren't. As we talk and eat and eat and eat, our glasses are kept full of wine. The Admiral and I engage in a real conversation about nuclear weapons; real enough that I wonder if different circumstances might have put him in my shoes. Girls walk by on the beach. Everything's so nice, and so normal. (Later I wondered if the

Admiral knew enough about me to think I might just have followed one of the beauties into town. That would have made for great headlines!)

I'm not paying much attention to the fact that there are photographers with long lenses standing beside the palms, busily snapping our pictures. I see them, but I don't really focus on them. It doesn't seem important.

When I'm wrong, I'm really wrong.

Two days later, *Vega*'s in good enough shape – we hope – to make it back to Rarotonga, and we're ready to go, except for one big problem. We still haven't been allowed to communicate with the outside world. *Courageux* (ha!) tows us out to the mouth of the lagoon under protest. We let the tow line go, and hoist *Vega*'s sails up into a brisk southwesterly, but we're not happy. We don't want to leave until somebody knows our whereabouts. Admiral Claviere assures us we'll hear something on the radio before the day ends.

And, boy, do we.

At six o'clock that evening, we pick up the news on Radio Australia. The French have released a report that says *we caused the collision*. I'm not kidding. They say the collision was the result of a faulty manoeuvre on our part. Bloody hell!! I guess we're naïve, but we didn't expect bald-faced lies!

A little while later, Radio New Zealand runs the story with a juicy little update about us joining the Admiral for a friendly lunch, after they rescued us from our own stupidity.

It's my first experience with government propaganda, and it's a helluva way to lose your virginity. I really didn't believe a democratic government would lie through its teeth. Now I know better.

We're seething with frustration and rage, and there isn't a bloody thing we can do about it without a functioning radio.

When *Vega* finally hobbles into Rarotonga, we're exhausted and penniless, and we have to deal with getting on the phone to our disappointed friends and lovers. They'd bought the story that we screwed up. Who'd ever believe the French could be so damn dishonest.

While it's relatively easy to set the record straight with the people close to us in New Zealand and Australia, the French spin machine has been quite effective with the press. By now the cosy-looking pictures of our lunch with the Admiral have made their way around the world. We look like screw-ups.

I don't know if I'm more angry or depressed as I board a plane for Vancouver to see if I can convince my government to go after the French. It'll be the first time in three years that I've seen my family, and I'm not exactly returning the conquering hero. I've just finished the most difficult task of my life, and it looks like yet another failure.

It's a pretty subdued homecoming, not helped by the fact that the Canadian government isn't exactly eager to take up my case.

But at least I'm back for a while in the shelter of Buccaneer Bay.

It's a beautiful Saturday morning in August, with our funny little annual sports day going on down on the meadow behind the bay. I've been enjoying my role as the lovable – if notorious – uncle, but I've had enough of my brother's kids for the moment. So I'm up at the cottage, sitting on the verandah, smoking and staring out at the water. And I'm thinking about the big yacht that's moored in front of me.

On board is the Prime Minister of Canada. His wife is from Vancouver, and they're taking a boating holiday with their new baby. The rumours that have been circulating all week about their being in our vicinity have come true. The evening before my nieces had spotted Pierre Trudeau swimming off our little beach. He's doing what I'm doing – taking a break from it all. I'd sure like to talk to him about my case, but even prime ministers deserve a day off. I smoke another cigarette, and then, what the hell.

Still deeply tanned from the Pacific, still thin, and tired and very scruffy, I row out to the yacht. I honestly don't want to be rude –

hate being intruded upon myself – but there's just never going to be a better chance. I politely lay off about twenty yards until Pierre Trudeau comes on deck with his very young – and very lovely – wife. I row over, and we engage in a spirited forty-minute conversation about my case. All the while, I'm sitting in the dinghy, staring up at him. He's a man who knows how to maintain his advantage.

Trudeau says he'd understood we were not flying a Canadian flag at Mururoa. I assure him we were. It goes back and forth like a championship badminton game, until finally I ask him outright what he'll do to help.

My heart sinks as he delivers an answer I'll never forget: 'Mr McTaggart, I'm not prepared to go to war over your little boat.'

Well, at least that's cleared up. Rowing away from the yacht, I know where Canada stands: not on my side.

Without my government's help, I don't know how the hell I'm going to go after the French. I don't even have the money to repair *Vega* properly – she's still in the South Pacific with Nigel – let alone take on a court case of this magnitude.

Christmas 1972 is approaching, and I'm about as low as you can get when I call Ann-Marie in New Zealand and ask her to come over to Canada, to help put her old man back together.

The two of us get the use of a rough little seaside cabin for the winter, where I plan to raise some money writing a book (titled *Outrage! the Ordeal of Greenpeace III*) about the voyage, which winds up getting published by a company in West Vancouver. But it's not a very happy time. Ann-Marie is a young girl in love, and I'm a selfish old bastard, obsessed with setting the record straight, getting the French to tell the truth about the one really good thing I've ever done.

We have very little money. For Christmas we spend five dollars on treats for each other and end the day on the beach, watching a driftwood log burn, starting out at the Pacific Ocean. *Déjà vu.* Exactly a year before I'd been sitting staring at a log burn on a beach in the Bay of Islands, trying to decide whether to move on to the Mediterranean or settle in New Zealand. I'm essentially asking myself the same question – what next? But the choices are a lot more serious. I'm not the same man anymore. Those days of just catching the next breeze to the next beautiful bay feel very long ago.

To add insult to injury, Greenpeace in Vancouver gets into a squabble with me about the bloody ham radio that didn't work. I got myself back to Canada by selling it, and they're none too pleased about that. They've got to be kidding.

By February – six months after my costly lunch with the Admiral – the French have announced that they're going to do it again. More bombs over Mururoa in six months' time. Nigel and I begin exchanging letters about the possibility of undertaking another voyage. Now *we've* got to be kidding. We're broke, *Vega's* in no shape, and we've barely recovered from our last go.

Then in the middle of May, France denies the authority of the International Court of Justice at The Hague to rule on France's right to test nuclear weapons. Oh, great, so now any nation that wants can blow off bombs without censure? Is that what France is saying? That seems to be the implication, and it just doesn't sit right.

It had begun a year ago as an intriguingly impossible sailing challenge. Then I got focused on my freedom to sail in international waters. And now I find myself in the middle of an international political war to stop the nuclear madness, and it's a war where there are way too many politicians and too few warriors on the ground. Or on the sea, as the case may be.

I'm starting to feel extremely political, in spite of myself. And, personally, I'm still mad as hell.

I call Greenpeace and ask if they'll work with me to raise money for a second voyage. The guy on the other end of the phone is a friend of mine, Bob Hunter, and he responds the way my family has, 'It's too dangerous, McTaggart, they'll be laying for you.' But they help, anyway.

On 23 July 1972, *Vega* heads seaward, away from the coast of New Zealand. Even with the desperate rush to complete repairs on the boat, it's been a smooth departure, compared to the year before. There's been a change of government in New Zealand. The new guys are opposed to the French tests so the bureaucrats are no longer interested in holding us back.

My crew is Nigel again, thank God, along with his girlfriend Mary Lornie and my Ann-Marie. We'd reasoned that females on board may make the French navy think twice about getting rough. Both women are good, experienced sailors, but I still can't shake that old protective feeling. You never know how people will react at sea until you're there. This year there are several boats trying to make the journey to Mururoa, and we've heard lousy reports back: men overboard, serious fighting amongst crew, even an attempted suicide.

And assuming we get there, I don't think the Admiral will be rolling out the welcome mat. I imagine he's taken some heat over the events of last year, and over my faltering attempts to bring a case against his government for the damages to *Vega*.

The tests have already begun. In fact, an atomic bomb mushrooms over Mururoa on the day of our departure. But we don't know that as *Vega* glides over the whitecaps followed by a school of porpoise. Sailors believe porpoise playing around a boat are a good omen, an indication of a successful journey.

And if last year I'd had the feeling somebody up there was warning me away, this year it's just the opposite. From the start we have a strong southwesterly wind at our backs. It's a little tough on the girls, but we make more than 1,300 miles in ten days. *Vega* is flying – maybe she's as mad as me. We log 150 miles one day, 178 the next. Ann-Marie notes in her log that the hardest thing to get used to is the fact that the boat sails for 24 hours a day. The motion never stops.

It's a good thing it isn't going to take us for ever to get to Mururoa this time, since the four of us aren't exactly coming together into the perfect crew. Ann-Marie is feeling a little jealous – more of *Vega* than of me. She's having trouble sharing the boat, and every now and again we have one of those ridiculous arguments over nothing that make me crazy – like should she do the laundry now or not. Mary's okay, but she doesn't seem to understand why we're out here, at least she doesn't share our passionate commitment. And while the women get along well enough at the beginning, their differences show more and more the further we get from shore. Ann-Marie is quite an innocent girl, deeply religious. Mary's more worldly. They like each other okay, but okay isn't quite enough in such tight quarters. There's always a little tension in the air.

Somehow the chemistry has changed between Nigel and me, too, in little and big ways. He cooks with a lot more garlic than I can tolerate, and that bugs me more than it should. Probably because of my nagging paranoia. You see, there'd been a rumour circulating, just before we left, that Nigel's a French agent. Quite likely there's absolutely nothing to it – except maybe the French trying to set the crew against each other. And with some success. When Nigel makes a – rare – error in navigation which takes us too far north, I start to wonder if it's intentional.

I don't think there's anything to it, except that we are all just too stressed, and depressed.

We lose voice contact with the outside world. Nigel uses Morse code to signal our position, as I sit by the radio hour after hour, trying to raise one of the protest boats that we believe may be close to Mururoa. During May and June a large number of boats had left New Zealand to protest the French tests. Most had turned back, but two have reached the test area – the *Fri* and the *Spirit of Peace*. Still, it feels like we're all alone, and it turns out we are – both boats had been forced to leave the zone.

As we get closer, there is a constant sense of urgency and danger, as Nigel and I prepare for the confrontation that most certainly lies ahead.

Late on the night of 12 August, we cross the cordon line into France's illegal testing zone. There's no champagne this year, but there is a deep feeling of satisfaction that the French won't be expecting us. Twenty-one days from New Zealand to Mururoa is one hell of a fast run.

We heave-to for the night, and raise our radar reflector to announce that *Vega* is back. Repeated attempts to raise another friendly vessel on the radio fail.

The next morning is a fine one. We're sitting about 35 miles off Mururoa, and we're all on deck trying to hide our fears from one another. Mary's on the foredeck washing her hair. Nigel's reading, as he does whenever he gets a spare moment. Ann-Marie and I are mending sails. We hear the unmistakable drone of a military air-craft, banking two hundred feet overhead. They know we're here. What are they going to do about it?

At noon they deliver the familiar warning that 'the following area has been declared dangerous.' Blah, blah, blah. Now what?

Mary's a little insulted that the French message includes our navigational position, 'as if we didn't know where we are'. With a swat of his hand, Nigel squashes a fly that seems to have come over with the French messengers. 'Filthy French flies!'

Ann-Marie tells me she's a little nervous, and maybe that's why we have words over how she's handling the helm. It'll be the last of our silly little arguments. The small things are about to come into very clear perspective.

During the early hours of the morning, 14 August, the weather deteriorates. A force 7 wind coming out of the east is forcing us away from Mururoa. Damn. That's what happened last year. And the French set off a bomb when a storm blew us out of position. Throughout the day, we tack back and forth, fighting to stay put, always under the eye of a French warship. Ann-Marie manages to scrawl in her log: 'Everything is moving. Have to be always bracing oneself. Wind howling non-stop. Water sloshing and crashing. One bruise after another … It's exactly like being on a Ferris Wheel or an Octopus ride at a show – only this is 24 hours a day. Exhausting.'

But we're determined that this time we won't be driven away from the test zone.

Through the night, and through the storm, we actually manage to work our way north of Mururoa and slip into a position on the west side of the atoll, squarely down range from the test. If the French blow off a bomb, the fall-out lands right on our civilian heads. Sounds crazy, but we're delighted with ourselves.

As the skies clear the next day, I look towards Mururoa, and there it is – that big bloody balloon, with the bomb suspended beneath. Good morning, McTaggart. Well, the good news is they haven't blown it off yet.

Throughout the day, there's a lot of action around us. Big planes going and coming from Mururoa. It feels like the test is at hand, and if it is, what are they going to do about *Vega*?

At four that afternoon, we find out.

Three French vessels converge on us – a fifty-foot vedette, a minesweeper and our old enemy, *Hippotame*. We set sails and start south, slightly away from Mururoa, hoping it'll be harder to board a moving vessel.

The minesweeper is crashing along a hundred yards from our port side and *Hippotame* is coming in starboard – a variation on last year's squeeze play. And that's when I notice that the little vedette is towing a dinghy full of men, almost certainly a boarding party. That unsettled feeling in the pit of my stomach finally names itself: fear.

The vedette is about a quarter of a mile to our starboard, when it releases the inflatable. I tell the girls to grab their cameras, and Nigel to go below and send out an SOS.

We're trying to outrun them, but they're gaining fast.

I put the helm hard to port and try to turn into them, hoping to go by them in the opposite direction. No luck.

Before I'm halfway about, the inflatable bumps against *Vega*'s starboard side – just about exactly where they'd rammed her the year before!

I let go of the tiller and rush over to the rail, and that's when I get a good look at these bastards. There are at least a half-dozen of them, and several are carrying some kind of weapon that looks like a piece of black pipe. They sure don't look like ordinary sailors. More like commandos from hell.

One of them is in the bow of the inflatable, trying to secure it to *Vega*. As I approach, two more men stand up. I shout at them to stay the hell off my boat.

One man lunges for my arms. Two others come over the rail and grab me from behind. My shirt is pulled over my head and I'm yanked off my feet into the inflatable.

With no one at the helm, everything on the boat is crashing around, and I can hear screaming – Mary, I think – as they start to beat the shit out of me.

They hit me over and over with those black truncheons. And they're thorough – they don't miss my kidneys or my head. I'm fighting for my life, when suddenly something drives into my right eye with incredible force. I'm out like a light.

I've lost the battle, but we are about to win the war.

Ann-Marie has it all on film. She slips below decks and hides the camera. When she comes topside a couple of minutes later, Nigel is lying semi-conscious in the cockpit and I'm coming to in the inflatable, covered in blood.

When I put my hand up to my eye, it feels like there's nothing there but a bloody hole. I can feel the lid, jammed closed, but there doesn't seem to be an eye behind it. When the commandos head the inflatable, with me still in it, back to their mother ship, I'm too weak and too dazed to resist.

I'm also too out of it to know if our plan has worked. The commandos have found a camera and taken the film. I don't know

1934. I'm about two years old here, which makes my big brother Drew about five. As boys, we were fierce competitors, but we would grow up to be best friends. Throughout our lives, Drew was the person I turned to when things got desperate – but not before!

A boy's paradise – Buccaneer Bay. I'm standing in the front, and Drew's second from the back. At around this age – five and eight – my brother would trick me into taking *much* longer shifts on the oars than him.

1942. By the time I was ten years old, I knew just how precious the summers were at Buccaneer Bay. I was in the natural world, I could move at will, I was free.

This is Drew (right) and me in our late teens. I've no idea what occasion required the 'fancy dress', but it wasn't so unusual for me in those days. That sure changed!

This picture was taken in about 1950 and still hangs on the Wall of Champions at the Vancouver Lawn, Tennis and Badminton Club. McTaggart matches used to draw crowds because of my blood-on-the-floor style of play.

With my feisty second daughter, Kerin, in 1961. She's still got the kind of personality evident in this picture. The silverware in the background is badminton trophies.

SKI BEAR

South Pacific 1970. A photo taken during the lull before the storm, the idyllic time after I'd fled from my Bear Valley life, and before I'd heard the word 'Mururoa'.

This sweet little photograph of my third wife, Betty, was considered quite controversial in the mid-1960s. I'm told it still adorns some ranchers' walls in the Sierra Mountains.

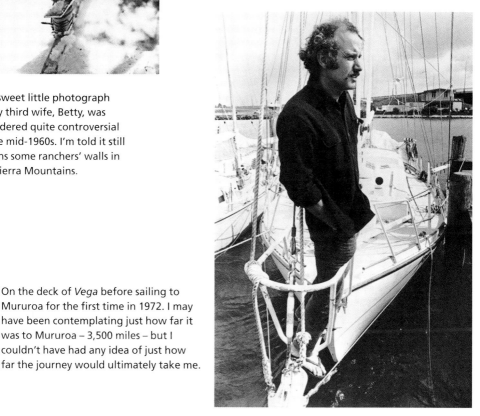

On the deck of *Vega* before sailing to Mururoa for the first time in 1972. I may have been contemplating just how far it was to Mururoa – 3,500 miles – but I couldn't have had any idea of just how far the journey would ultimately take me.

A big mistake! Lunch with the French Admiral in 1972 turns out to be a brutal lesson in government propaganda. The public would *not* see the French ramming *Vega* at sea, but *would* see photos of them being so bloody nice to us.

French commandos head for *Vega*, 15 August 1973. One of the pictures taken by Ann-Marie just before they boarded the boat and beat the stuffing out of Nigel and me.

Late August 1973. The press conference at Vancouver airport after being discharged from the French military hospital in Papeete. This was the night that I realized it was working – one little boat *could* make a difference.

Outside the Palais de Justice in Paris, showing a truncheon almost identical to the one the French commandos rammed into my eye.

1974. With Ann-Marie Horne in Paris, grabbing a moment away from the court case. We parted not long after this, but she remains one of my truest friends.

Brigitte Bardot at a conference to end seal culling. She was a joy to work with when we brought her to the east coast of Canada, protesting the Newfoundland seal hunt.

This awful picture shows what Greenpeace was protesting – the large-scale and inhumane slaughter of seals.

Rainbow Warrior's maiden voyage in 1978, to protest Icelandic whaling. A very green crew takes on the men who won the Cod War!

1979, after the tumultuous meeting that resolved the problems between Greenpeace Vancouver and Greenpeace San Francisco, and ultimately ended up with me in the executive director's chair at Greenpeace International. From left to right, lawyer Pete Ballem, me, Paul Watson, Patrick Moore and Bob Hunter.

Rainbow Warrior, free at last! After our midnight dash from El Ferrol, with the Spanish navy in hot pursuit. From left to right, Pierre Gleizes, Tony Marriner, Athel von Koettlitz, me, John Castle, Tim Mark and Chris Robinson.

Greenpeace protesters keep the pressure
on the Norwegian whaling fleet.

if it's the Nikon with which Ann-Marie was shooting, or a decoy that we had deliberately partially hidden before the festivities got underway.

On the minesweeper, I rally enough to stick the needle into the captain. 'We were in international waters,' I say. 'You know that as well as I do.' He nods, but says nothing.

They take me to Mururoa. Same time next year. Only this time it's me, not *Vega* who's hurting. A French officer loudly recites to me some bullshit about me being arrested in territorial waters. Ya, sure.

I ask to speak to Admiral Claviere. Request denied.

I finally agree to go to hospital in Papeete, Tahiti, as long as I can phone Canada the moment I get there. They bring me in an ambulance down to the wharf where my crew is waiting. Ann-Marie has brought my passport and a few toiletries. As she hands them to me, she bends down and whispers something in my ear that I can't quite catch. She's trying to tell me that the film is safe.

In hospital in Papeete, I feel totally vulnerable. My eye's still in there somewhere, and they want to give me drugs to prevent acute glaucoma. I'm too confused to really understand, and more to the point, it's a French military hospital. I'm supposed to be willing to swallow drugs handed to me by the same guys who ram me one year and beat me the next? I don't think so.

I won't swallow anything until they let me talk to my brother in Vancouver. Drew's a doctor, and he'll know what's okay. When I finally get him on the phone, Drew tells me to take the bloody drugs or I'll lose my eye. Okay, that's good enough for me. And he tells me he's sending an eye specialist from Canada to look at me. Hang in there.

That's the thing about my brother. Don't bother him with the little stuff, but when you really need him, he'll send in the marines.

The French try to float the story that we were in territorial waters, and that I hurt myself falling. Unbelievable. But Ann-Marie gets the pictures out to Drew, and suddenly it's a whole different ball game.

They're exposed as looking like liars, and I've just become a martyr.

Flying into Vancouver airport a few days later, it's quite a scene, and quite a contrast to the year before. It's night-time and I can see the twinkling lights on Grouse Mountain below. I take off the bandage over my eye, so I don't look too dramatic. But I have to leave my dark glasses on – the eye's extraordinarily light sensitive, and it looks ugly as hell. I'm in my old jeans, and a scruffy dark-coloured turtleneck as I descend down the stairs of the plane into the arms of my very relieved family.

I'm the prodigal son returned home, the black sheep who finally grew up. And I'm bloody glad to be alive.

Behind Mom and Dad and Drew – and Nigel, what a great surprise – is a battalion of press. I say a few words to the assembled reporters, and as I head home with my folks, it suddenly occurs to me that it's working. The world now knows we were at Mururoa, and why.

Not bad, for one little boat.

Chapter Nine

MY BROTHER HAD released the pictures to the press as soon as he knew I was safely on the plane, out of French custody. The headlines scream around the world: 'France told outright lie, vessel seizure illegal, France has to explain.' Nobody's buying the French navy's story that the boarding party was unarmed and hadn't struck a single blow, that I must have fallen and hit my head on a cleat!

Vega's not the first, and won't be the last, protest boat to sail to Mururoa, but somehow it's me and my old girl who got under their skin. She's the boat the French boarded. I'm the skipper they assaulted. And we've got the pictures to prove it.

I'm worried as hell about my eye – the doctor's say it'll be six weeks before we know if I'll lose it. (I don't lose it in the end, but it's months before I can see properly, and even then the doctors warn me that I remain at risk of acute glaucoma. I'm supposed to live the rest of my life close to medical help, just in case. Not likely.)

Initially I'm not really worried about getting *Vega* back. The French must be bloody embarrassed. Surely apologies, and the boat, will be along in short order.

Well I hadn't counted on national character. The French really don't like to lose face. And the Canadians – my countrymen – can just be so damn polite.

I keep thinking about Prime Minister Trudeau saying he's 'not prepared to go to war over my little boat.' I think I know why. Canada exports uranium and is deep into nuclear technology, with international sales of the Candu reactor. And then there's the Quebec problem. Canada's francophone province is becoming increasingly separatist, and I suspect the national government doesn't want to piss them off by getting into a big brawl with Quebec's motherland.

Canada's external affairs minister sends a 'firm note of protest' to France and asks for an investigation into the incident. Gee, thanks.

The press pushes for Canada to take the case to the world court at The Hague, but France has already ignored a court ruling that the cordoning off of international waters makes their nuclear testing programme illegal. So The Hague doesn't look like a very good bet, and my government's clearly only got the balls to bet on the sure things. Wouldn't want to make a fuss. Well, excuse me, but that's the point.

I want my government to do *something*, something strong. It's absolutely outrageous to me that the navy of one country could beat up a private citizen of another, and the respective governments discuss it oh so very politely, through diplomatic channels. Outrageous.

I'm starting to feel as alone as if I was still in the middle of the blue Pacific.

Ann-Marie writes me a letter from New Zealand – she's back there after a week held incommunicado at a French Polynesian military base: 'Do you know what I really want to do most? Go to Whangarei, this time completely free, make love in every one of those flower-filled fields, sleep under the stars, listen to the oysters popping at night and the sound of water licking round the boat.' It sounds so good, the life I had before I got swept up into this political game. A big part of me wants that back.

At the beginning of September, ignoring my doctor's orders, I borrow my sister-in-law's Thunderbird and drive across the border to Seattle to collect Ann-Marie off a cheap flight from New

Zealand. It's wonderful to see her again, still very blonde and tanned from the voyage, although she can't resist teasing me about the sunglasses I have to wear all the time to protect my eye. She calls me 'Playboy McTaggart', which I guess is an improvement on what she usually calls me – 'Pops'.

With *Vega* still in French custody, we have absolutely nothing, but I'm determined it won't stay that way for long. One thing I know how to do is make money. Ann-Marie drives the return leg to Vancouver – I'm in serious pain with my eye – while I tell her the plan. She'll find some kind of job in Vancouver and I'll get back into land development. It's going to take a while, but we'll get back on our feet, back to enjoying life. Forget politics.

I find a good-looking piece of land across the channel from my parents' place at Buccaneer Bay, and I scrape together the down payment by selling a lot adjacent to the old family cabin. If I can get it built, I'm betting that a marina will turn a nice profit. Ann-Marie finds a job as a dental assistant on the mainland. During the weekends she takes the little ferry across to Secret Cove and helps me clear brush with our bare hands.

It's a funny autumn. I spend most of my time in dirty dungarees, working on the land. But we also do a round of press interviews. Canadian journalists are hot for the story, and it's an easy way to draw attention to nuclear testing, while keeping the pressure on the French to return my boat. One television show flies us across the country to Toronto for an interview, and ends up providing Ann-Marie with what she says is her first real date with the old man. After the show, I take her up to a bar on the twentieth floor of our hotel and we have a drink and listen to some jazz, looking out over the lights of the city.

My parents are fiercely proud when, on that same trip, we're presented to the Canadian Parliament. They give us a big round of applause, but I think it must have been a real trip for the parliamentarians! Straightest-looking bunch of guys you ever saw, applauding the ageing hippie in his suede jacket and sunglasses with his very young blonde girlfriend in her tight pink sweater. Not the typical Canadian couple of the day, I'll tell you.

At the beginning of November, France announces that it's moving its nuclear testing programme underground. The *Vancouver Sun* newspaper calls it 'a considerable victory for world opinion; and the skipper of the *Greenpeace* and his supporters at home and abroad can take credit for their part in that victory.'

Three days later, France says I can have *Vega* back. I fly to Papeete to sign for the boat and finalize shipping arrangements. It hurts to see my valiant *Vega* tied down on the foredeck of a military ship, looking rather like a neglected toy. If boats could talk, she'd be telling me to get her the hell out of there. I discharge the French navy from my ship and get her aboard a freighter bound for Vancouver. It still looks bloody unnatural – seaworthy *Vega* travelling on deck as freight – but at least I no longer have the image that she's in chains.

On the second day of the new year, 1974, I watch dockside in Vancouver as *Vega*'s lowered off the freighter. I'll take her to Secret Cove for a well-earned rest, and a well-needed refit.

And that might have been the end of it. I just might have faded away, back into happy capitalism, if only the French had been a little more reasonable. They still hadn't paid me the $7,000 it took to repair the damage to *Vega* the year before. And it doesn't sound like they're ever going to learn how to say sorry.

The two-year statute of limitations is just about up on my case for damages in the 1972 ramming of *Vega*. I want to forget it and get on with my life, but it just doesn't sit right.

If my government won't take on France, I might have to.

It seems a wild idea. I'd be one person against a national government. And I don't speak a word of French. But I can't let it go, either. So I borrow $300 from Ann-Marie and fly to Paris, on the last day of May 1974.

It's the kind of Parisian spring they write songs about, but the city of love doesn't look so good when you're broke, and your sweetheart's half the world away. I walk the streets of Paris until I find a place to stay for twenty francs, with breakfast. It's pretty dismal, lying there in that dirty windowless room, overwhelmed by the enormity of the city, and of the choice before me.

A representative from Canadian external affairs will try once more to settle the matter between governments. Which won't work. Then I'll have to decide whether to direct Canada to espouse my case officially – as they've now agreed. If they formally take over a negotiated settlement and screw it up, I've lost my chance to go to court. The question is: do I bet on the polite diplomatic route, for which I don't have to pay, or do I bang a writ into court as fast as I can and figure out later how to pay for it?

While I'm trying to decide, I get a little help. India detonates their first nuclear bomb, with help from Canadian reactor technology. It looks as if Israel might follow in a few months. I'm just not sure my government knows which side to stand on.

Luckily for me, this is a politically vibrant time in France. Pompidou has just died, and Mitterand on the left and Giscard on the right are engaged in a political dogfight that'll go on for years. Mitterand says, if he's elected, he'll halt the nuclear programme. And the politicians are feeling the pressure of street protests, organized by a growing ecology movement. I sniff around for allies.

Les Amis de la Terre – Friends of the Earth to me – operates out of a beautiful old house at 16 Rue de l'Université. It's just a few blocks from the Seine, on the Right Bank, not too far from the dive where I'm staying. I go through the gate into a beautiful little courtyard, and then up to the second floor to meet the man who will become my closest ally in France, the co-founder of Les Amis, Brice Lalonde. He's twenty years younger than me – like pretty much everybody in the environmental movement – tall and lanky, with a moustache and soulful blue eyes. He's got that understated

French elegance going for him. I find out later he comes from a wealthy family, which probably helps. And he's also got a very elegant lady, Lison de Caunes, long legs and long dark hair and a proud attitude. They run Les Amis from the second floor of this six-storey house, and live one floor up. And they both speak very good English. Whew.

Through Brice I connect with a lawyer, Thierry Garby-Lacrouts. Not your typical lawyer, Thierry's got long hair and the proverbial 1970s moustache. He smokes almost as much as I do, has an eye for a good-looking woman, and is into what he calls 'the beauty of my case'. He's been practising law for only four or five years, but he's smart, and not afraid to take on his own government on behalf of a Canadian sailor.

Thierry's got a day job with a big legal firm, but most nights and every weekend, we meet at his flat and go to work. I love his place. He's got an apartment in a seventeenth-century building with slanted roofs and big timbers running through it. It's a little like being on a boat, maybe that's why I'm so comfortable there. Saturday mornings, I stop at the café on the corner and buy coffee and croissants. Thierry still laughs at my accent. He claims I call them 'croy-settes'. Anyway, he eats them.

We talk strategy. Thierry convinces me that if we proceed, it should be in civil court. Sounds a little weird to me. Normally a case against the government in France would go to the other judicial branch, the administrative court. And that sounds right to me, given that we're going after the national government. But Thierry says we'll lose for sure if we do that. He says the administrative court is not permitted to make a judgment when the facts concern a decision of the government in foreign affairs. The civil courts, Thierry thinks, are our best bet. He just has to find arguments for each case, 1972 and 1973, to turn what are pretty obviously governmental affairs into civil matters.

Even then, it's a real crapshoot. No private citizen, of another country no less, has ever taken the French nation to court. I am in foreign territory, in every sense of the phrase.

I decide to go for it.

At the beginning of June we deliver the assignation – drop the writ – on the French government. Thierry will present both cases together. For the first year, he'll keep it to a simple traffic accident on the sea, since an accident involving a government motor vehicle belongs in civil court. The second year is a little more complicated. We'll go after them for restraining my freedom, and for seizing the boat. Restraints on freedom of the individual, or on property, are also considered civil matters.

While we wait for a court date, I have lots of time to worry about how I'm going to pay for it.

Back to Vancouver, and my land. It's next to miraculous that I got my hands on ten acres of prime real estate, when I came home from the South Pacific without a penny to my name, but the property's still a long way from being ready to sell for a profit. I'm going to hang on to it until then, no matter what. I've started from scratch one too many times.

I try to convince Greenpeace in Vancouver to help out with the court case, but they can't see the movie. They don't have the energy or the will to raise the money for a long legal battle. I feel cut adrift. I sailed under their banner twice, risked my life, might lose the sight in one eye, and they can't make a commitment to me. Talk about a one-way street.

To outsiders, we look like comrades-in-arms, members of the same band of eco-warriors. The truth is, I'm not a *member* of anything. Greenpeace Vancouver and I are like separate countries. We're allies, and we sometimes fly the same flag into battle against the bad guys, but we still operate independently most of the time. And it's the 1970s – peace, love, and very little structure is the order of the day.

I decide I have as much right to the label as anybody, so I set up a bank account in West Vancouver under the name 'Greenpeace', and ordinary Canadians send in their ten- and twenty-dollar donations to help out with the court case. It's good to know my countrymen are with me, even if the government isn't, but these little private donations aren't going to pay too many legal bills.

There's only one other thing I own that's worth anything. *Vega*. She's tied to a little dock at the foot of my property in Secret Cove. As I walk down the new road towards the water, I can hear her halyards clanking in the Pacific breeze. Hello, old girl.

I find a pack of cigarettes stowed aboard – Player's Plain – and I realize that they were almost certainly there during the test. I smoke one, with a feeling of ceremony. Also find a few notes in my handwriting. Something about not badgering other people to explain their motivation, since I've never clearly understood my own.

I remember reading this book called *The Ulysses Factor* while I was between Mururoa voyages. It tries to explain why men – often in their forties – sometimes take up ridiculous challenges. It credits (or blames) 'the Ulysses factor' – made up in varying degrees of courage, selfishness, physical competence, imagination, self-discipline, endurance and competitiveness. Sounds about right, a complicated mix of the best qualities, which I got from the family, and the worst, which I managed to pick up in spite of them.

I've come too far on this voyage to turn back – not my favourite direction, anyway. And there seems to be only one way forward. I know there'll never be another boat like *Vega*, but with a heavy heart, I clean her up to sell.

She's gone the week before Christmas, sold to a nice guy who doesn't look much of a sailor. And I try not to think about that.

I send some of the money to Thierry, and hear back that we've got a court date in early April. That cheers me and Ann-Marie considerably. We make the best of a rainy Christmas week, sneaking out into the woods to cut down alders for firewood and nipping away before we're seen. We play darts in the local pub, go to two-for-one movie nights, and just generally act like kids on Christmas vacation. I think we both know that when the holiday's over, life's going to get serious again. Really serious.

On 8 April 1975, Ann-Marie and I find ourselves standing in a spring shower outside the black metal gates of the Palais de Justice in Paris. Thierry and I are having a last nervous smoke before we walk up the stone steps under the watchful eye of the three statues that stand along the Palais roof – liberté, égalité, fraternité. Somehow I don't think we're included in those noble sentiments.

As we walk in, I see our friends from Les Amis de la Terre. Thanks, Brice. I don't know how we'd have made it this far without your help. There's a television crew by the far entrance. We walk through clusters of black-robed lawyers, chattering in French. This is going to be hard. Thierry's warned me that the French legal system isn't what I'm used to. No witnesses will be called. He's prepared the case entirely on paper, delivered it to the judge and the defendant. Now he'll present it to the court, and I'm just going to have to sit on my hands and listen to my fate being decided in a language I don't understand. I can't stop fidgeting, cleaning my glasses on my tie, ducking out for another smoke.

It's almost three years since I first set sail for Mururoa. It seems so far away, in every sense. And I feel very out of my element. But as the court is about to convene, the April sun breaks through the clouds. No kidding. It streams through the tall windows and streaks down the wood-panelled wall. I can see blue sky. I decide I might as well take it as an omen.

The three judges sit high above us, and over to the right sits a guy called the Procurer: this is a new one on me. He's basically a second defendant, representing the government's interests in special cases of public policy. He gets to speak last, and we can't challenge him. I'm not liking this. Plus the guy looks like a rugby player from the south of France, a bit of a street-fighter.

But Thierry's tougher than he looks. He knows that the opposing lawyer's strong suit is political argument, not legal technicalities. So Thierry sticks to the facts, walking the judges methodically through the ramming in 1972 and the beating in 1973. He shows photos from both incidents, and produces a truncheon like the one used to beat me. Even just interpreting the body language, I can see he's impressive.

He ends his presentation by saying, 'The issue in the case is whether the seas are free: it is not one of French politics'.

The defence lawyer argues the story to which France has been clinging since the 1972 ramming – that *Vega* caused the collision. Ya, right, a 38-foot sailboat decides to take on a warship. But a question from the judge shows how well Thierry's nailed the events. The judge points out that *Vega* couldn't have rammed the French ship without sailing backwards!

The defence argument in the 1973 beating case is just as ludicrous. He ignores the photos, basically says they didn't do it, you can't trust McTaggart's friends, and French navy truncheons are white not black, anyway. Thierry says that if we can all agree that beating people isn't normal French naval practice, then perhaps we can agree that they wouldn't be required to use regulation truncheons.

The defence lawyer looks like a kid with chocolate all over his face, saying it wasn't him who'd finished the ice cream. Yet I know that what we're asking the judges to do is huge – deny their national government, affirm the rights of their nation's adversary. As the judges adjourn to consider the evidence, I know we're still running against the wind.

During the many weeks waiting for the court's decision, I have long conversations over the phone with Bob Hunter in Vancouver. He's one of the leaders of a Greenpeace contingent who've decided to go after the Russian whaling fleet off the west coast of North America. In the mid-1970s Greenpeace in Vancouver had all but disintegrated because of ongoing disagreement over whether to stay focused on anti-nuclear issues, or move into saving the whales. When one of the original anti-nuclear founders, Irving Stowe, died in 1974, that pretty much finished it. There wasn't much left of the organization but the anti-whaling committee, Project Ahab, run by Bob Hunter and a handful of like-minded folk.

From where I'm sitting, broke and absolutely focused on the anti-nuclear campaign, the organizational chaos is really unfortunate. There's nobody to support me morally, or financially. The little West Vancouver bank account Ann-Marie and I set up for contributions to the legal case against France never collected more than a few hundred dollars.

I get on well with Hunter, but Project Ahab is sucking up money that might potentially help me out, and it all seems pretty hippie-dippy. Here in Paris, we're talking about the nuclear annihilation of mankind. And they want to break the bank trying to save adorable marine mammals. Crazy! Well, as they say, hindsight is twenty-twenty. It'd turn out to be a good move after all, even if it looked pretty flaky to me at the time.

But I'm sure feeling all alone out here.

And to make it worse, my relationship with Ann-Marie is disintegrating under the pressure. Even before we'd left Vancouver, we had a couple of barneys – as she'd call them – about my inability to plan life as a couple. I blame it on the state of suspended animation the court case has me in, but I think it's just me. I hate making plans. Finally, we decide she should go home to New Zealand and get on with her life. I know it's the right choice, but its a bloody sad day. We share an omelette and go for a walk together. We sit beside the pond at the Tuileries, watching the toy sailboats – both sad, not wanting it to end, and wishing it were done. We decide to get it over with and part on a street corner. I think I'm just going to drive away, but something compels me to drive around the block and ask for one last kiss. She's such a fine lady. One of the best.

A month later Thierry and I head to the Palais de Justice for the court's decision. I think the odds are a thousand to one against me, and mostly I just want to get this over with and go home. Win or lose, let's just finish. But win would be better. For good luck, I take a gold Virgin Mary someone's given me, a cross, and shaman stones.

On 17 June 1975, exactly three years since I saw the balloon go up over Mururoa, we hear the verdict.

As hard as we fought, as tight as Thierry's arguments were, I still can't believe it when the court rules against France, and *for* us, in the ramming case. They tear to shreds the allegations that we caused the collision – the *Vega* sailing backwards argument – and award damages, the amount to be decided by a panel of experts.

But in the 1973 piracy case – illegally boarding my boat – the court says we haven't provided enough evidence. We can appeal if we want.

We have just won big time. A private citizen of a foreign nation has gone head to head with the government of France, and won. Never been done before. I should be euphoric, I would be euphoric, but we've also just been told that it's not over. We have to appeal the 1973 case, if we want to finish it. Who was it that said you can never go home again?

I don't know whether to laugh or cry.

Chapter Ten

DURING THE WEEKS leading up to my big day in court, Bob Hunter's band of merry men has been wandering around off the Canadian coast in a chartered trawler, looking for the Russian whaling fleet. If and when they find the whalers, their plan is to chase them in zodiacs, putting the inflatables between the whaler and the whale, making it impossible to get a clear shot. Even ignoring the huge financial cost to an organization that isn't exactly rolling in dollars, these guys sound a little flaky. I mean, Bob's a great guy, but he made the decision to pursue the issue on the basis of a throw of the *I Ching* while he was watching grey whales swim along the Canadian coastline. Apparently it told him to approach. 'Joint approach. Good fortune. Everything furthers.' Maybe it just meant he'll marry rich, if he smokes another joint. Really! Besides, they left Vancouver weeks before the whaling fleet was due to arrive, which means spending a pile of money that they don't have. I guess to pass the time before the fleet's arrival, they've been going out in the zodiacs to bond with the whales. Even playing music to a pod of greys. Apparently they like the saxophone best. It's all a bit much.

Well, I'll find out later that we're more alike than I thought. The flaky stuff and the terrible financial planning aside, these hippies do have a pretty good idea where they're going. Turns out they'd done some serious espionage the winter before. Supporting the group is a whale scientist, Paul Spong. He'd managed to get himself into the Bureau of International Whaling Statistics in Norway and had walked out with the locations and schedules of the fleet for the two previous years.

While I'm pacing the streets of Paris, waiting for the outcome of my court case, Hunter and company have put in to Winter Harbour, at the wild and remote north end of Vancouver Island. They'll refuel here before pushing south to the waters off northern California, where they expect to find the Russian whaling fleet. They're keenly aware that it's still a long shot.

The night before they're to set sail, the news comes through from Paris that we've won. The French will have to pay damages for ramming *Vega*. There's a big party in Winter Harbour that night – much booze, and more love-making, I'm told – and the next morning at 5 a.m. they set out to engage the whalers.

Hunter records that day's *I Ching* reading:

Political revolutions are extremely grave matters. They should be undertaken only under stress of direst necessity, when there is no other way out.

Times change, and with them their demands.

Fire below and the lake above combat and destroy each other. So too in the course of the year a combat takes place between the forces of light and the forces of darkness, eventuating in the revolution of the seasons.

The hour has come.

Okay, maybe there is something to that stuff.

This will be a wildly successful campaign, the first of many where little Greenpeace inflatables challenge giant whaling vessels, and win – at least in the court of world opinion. When David faces off against Goliath, it's not difficult to guess which side most people want to be on.

I'm not really an animal person, but I was starting to see the value of a warm and fuzzy issue that appeals to people emotionally. To me, nuclear disarmament is a *much* more important issue. But it's just too big to ponder for most people, and too political. Saving intelligent, lovable animals, now that's something *everybody* can embrace. The whales are a real people-magnet, and in democratic societies, if you've got the people behind you, you've got power. Maybe that's the way to tackle the big issues, like the annihilation of the human race.

But that's there. And I'm here, stuck in Paris, trying to figure out if it's worth giving another three years of my life to a point of principle. Should I appeal the 1973 case or not? I'm 43 years old, and I'm tired. I'd like to just sail away from it all. Really. But I feel like Gulliver in the land of the Lilliputians, hundreds of threads holding me down – the court case, my land, my obligations to my folks, and to my children.

And now there's another thread, that will prove stronger than any of them. Greenpeace in Europe is being quietly spun into existence out of the raw wool of the ecology movement in France and the UK, my own little act of defiance, and the allies that these two elements have brought together.

While Thierry and I are figuring out what – if any – our next legal moves should be, my two key allies at Les Amis de la Terre go at me relentlessly about broadening what they call my 'obsession' with French nuclear testing in the Pacific. They want to take on the world – through the Nuclear Test Ban Treaty.

Brice Lalonde, one of the founders of Les Amis, suggests I move into a little studio apartment on the sixth floor of his house on Rue de l'Université. I can stay rent-free while I'm pondering my next move. Brice and his beautiful Lison are on the third floor. Les Amis' offices are on the second.

My other ally is a slight, dark, intense young man named Remi Parmentier, who spends a lot of time hanging out at Les Amis. Remi's maybe twenty, looks a bit like Napoleon, and is just about as full of drive. Remi's fully engaged in the Parisian pastime of the 1970s – protesting against France's nuclear programme. He's finding Brice's group a little too respectable and wants me to stay in France and put together a radical group focused solely on anti-nuclear.

I decide to stay. Just for a while.

I'd like to say I immediately had this grand vision of an international organization with the power to change the world, and that I systemically set about putting it together. But that wouldn't be me. I'm not very systematic. I operate more on some weird combination of instinct and action.

I feel trapped in Paris, immobilized by the slow turnings of the legal system. A big part of me still wants to run away, at least as far as my property at Secret Cove, and retreat into what's for me an easy life – making money. But I can't go. Some instinct tells me that this is where the action is. Everything in my life, from my fantastic upbringing to my dramatic failures, brought me here and gave me the strength and stubbornness to win against France in court.

I'm starting to accept that George and Mary McTaggart's youngest son has a role to play in this world that's bigger than getting rich, and a helluva lot more important. They raised me to believe I could do anything. Let's see if that includes changing the world.

First I need to finish up with the government of France.

France is stalling on the money they owe me for damages to *Vega*, assessed at seven thousand dollars, hardly enough to break the national bank! But it makes me mad, which also diminishes my hedonistic inclination to drop the appeal and just get the hell out of here.

Also, I'm having these endless bloody conversations with my own Canadian government about taking a more active role in the appeal on the piracy charges. Now that I've won the collision case on my own, surely Canada realizes I might have a point, and maybe they should take a stand. Prime Minister Trudeau has written me a letter that fairly drips with condescension. He says some of the stuff he's been reading in the press leads him to believe I don't really understand what it means if Canada formally takes up the negotiation with France, the so-called espousal. Trudeau's advisers tell him that it's in my best interests to delay espousal until I've exhausted every possible legal remedy on my own. He says the government of Canada won't take over the lawsuit, or pay my legal bills: 'Espousal will simply mean that we continue actively and forcefully to press the French government for an <u>amicable</u> [my underlining] and reasonable out-of-court settlement.'

This is making me crazy. I don't have the money to 'exhaust every legal remedy'. I need my government's help. And it sounds like they're telling me they're happy to help *only if it doesn't cost them anything*, including their 'amicable' relationship with France. By the way, I should also be aware that if they do take up my case, they'll probably fail. And Trudeau wonders why I'm using the press to stick the needle in!

Late that autumn, 1975, I take Brice up on his offer and move into the little studio three floors above him and Lison. If I didn't feel so trapped in Paris, it would be quite nice. I look out over the rooftops of the city. When the grey winter skies clear, I can even catch a glimpse of the Eiffel Tower. I'm basically in the old servants' quarters, so I come and go as I please through the court-yard, but there's also an inside stairway that takes me down to Les Amis, or to Lison and Brice. We three become close. They're a bit sorry for the lonely old man and frequently have me down to dinner. We talk a lot of politics, smoke a little 'herb' and feel that special bond of comrades in arms.

I decide if I'm going to be stuck here, I should learn French. That's my New Year's resolution for 1976. I enrol in classes at a local school, but I'm hopeless. I tell myself that too many of the lessons conflict with my legal meetings. This is true, but mostly I'm hopeless at French. That's not just an excuse. Some people just aren't wired for it. And I can communicate a lot better in sign language than I'd ever be able to fumbling along in French or German. Thierry used to shake his head at how well his mother and I got along. We could talk for hours, and neither of us spoke more than two words of the other's language.

I think words are really overrated.

I can't sit still, so I take what action I can – talking to the press, haunting the Canadian embassy, writing letters to external affairs, meeting with anyone who might help advance my case, which is more and more becoming mixed up with the bigger cause of nuclear disarmament. When I look back now, I can see that I was unwittingly, and sometimes almost unwillingly, building the organization that would become Greenpeace International.

France never does have to face an appeal on the 1973 piracy charges, a fact that'll always bother me, but at least we got some other things done. If I hadn't been stuck in Paris, working on the appeal, I don't know if there'd be a Greenpeace International today.

In the middle of February 1976 I find out that my parents are both ill. Mom's got the flu, a bad one, and Dad's in hospital with what looks like a heart condition. I want to go home, but I'm flat broke. My parents gave me everything, and I can't even do this for them. I try to write what's in my heart: 'I hope the love I feel for both of you overcomes and dampens the sadness I have sometimes introduced into your lives. I know I have been a disappointment to you, but *never* have I intentionally tried to embarrass or hurt you. I want to say so much but I find the words so hard.'

My need to get home to see those two gentle and remarkable people is actually a big part of the reason why I decide to join Greenpeace Canada's anti-sealing campaign that March, off the coast of Newfoundland, on the country's east coast. To tell the truth, I never really buy it as a good cause. The seals aren't endangered, and the sealers are locals trying to scrape together a living, not multinational corporations raping the resource to keep their shareholders happy. But those Vancouver hippies really seem to like cute causes, and the baby seals sure are cute. Well, if they're determined to go for it, I might as well at least make sure they get some press in Europe. On the second go-around, we even get Brigitte Bardot there, the actress turned activist. That really helps with publicity; everybody's eager for pictures of the sex goddess who wants to save the seals. I get into a small scrap with the Vancouver group over making sure the French press corps gets helicopter access, and good visuals to take home and spread across the continent. I'm not sure Vancouver really understands how important that is. Canada has *no* clout internationally, but nobody wants to piss off the local press, even to make sure Europe gets the message. Sigh.

The French do get their pictures – which doesn't make me any more popular with Greenpeace in Vancouver – and as soft as the sealing issue is, it touches the hearts of people in Europe. They're starting to put it together – the funny little Canadian sailor who took the French to court, the hippies in North America who are running around saving the animals. Even though I'm still not totally sold on the soft campaigns, as somebody said, 'as long as they spell the name right'. People in Europe are beginning to know the name Greenpeace. I'll never be convinced about the seals, but whales really may be endangered, and an anti-whaling campaign in Europe would push the same 'soft' buttons and get people think-ing about this fragile planet. My heart's more with the nuclear issue, but maybe the way to pull people in is through this touchy-feely stuff.

And at least the seal campaign got me a ticket home to see my parents. They're getting old and frail, and I'm painfully aware that

I won't have them around for ever. But they still make me feel like their blue-eyed boy, loved beyond measure, my actions – no matter how unconventional – accepted without question.

Maybe that's why I don't live within the same boundaries as most people. I just don't know when to stop. Whether it's taking on the French navy, or going after the woman I want.

Which is my uncomfortable way of taking us to Christina.

In lots of ways I'd rather not tell this story. Some of it doesn't make me look very good. But she's too important to leave out, and I keep telling myself that I'll be as honest as I can on these pages. I owe that much to my children.

Remember Ingemar? The physical education teacher who was my last real connection with formal education, back when I was a teenager? Well, I see him again in Vancouver on this trip, and he has his teenage daughter with him, not a lot older than I was when Ingemar saved my sanity. Christina is breathtaking. Irresistible. She has the kind of wholesome blonde good looks for which Swedish women are rightly renowned.

But even I know that getting together with her is crossing some kind of invisible boundary. She's too young, and her father's my good friend. But she's so lovely, and sweet, and we genuinely like each other. We move slowly. Christina comes with me on a little holiday to Mexico, but it's strictly as friends. Well, not just friends, but you know what I mean.

I can't stop myself from falling.

By the time Christina goes home to Stockholm, we've decided she'll come sailing with me, on a protest voyage. It's important to me to get Ingemar's approval, even if I'm not entirely honest with him about my motives. From Paris I write him a letter, which I must admit emphasizes more the political and educational aspects of the voyage: 'I am working with three groups on a combined protest to the countries in the world that still kill whales, the object being to visit them and deliver a simple message asking for a moratorium ... I hope she comes with your blessing because she will make a great crew member.'

I'm really in some kind of altered state. I actually try to stop smoking and start working out again, using the Canadian military's fitness regime. I guess I want to be a whole new man for her.

I don't succeed.

And this is the really sensitive part.

While I'm waiting for Christina, and looking around for a boat, I spend time with Brice and Lison. As always we're talking ecology and political strategy, but they're also commiserating with me in my somewhat tormented state over Christina.

Then it's August in Paris, and the city's dead. Brice is on holiday in Brittany, but Lison has come back to her work. She's an artist, and a writer, and she's got a job correcting prints for a publisher. I'm in town for some meeting or another, and you've probably guessed the rest. Lison and I go for dinner – quite normal for two close friends – and then we talk and walk through the streets of St Germain de Pres. Something begins to happen between us. She comes up to the sixth floor for one last drink. And, hell, not smart, McTaggart.

I am now seriously involved with two very wonderful women, and I have betrayed a close ally. I don't know how I'll explain this to Brice, or to Christina. I don't know how to explain it to myself.

Lison and I are crazy about each other. We take off for a week to her parents' place, in a little village between Marseilles and Toulon. We lie in the sun in their luxuriant garden and talk and talk and talk – about our feelings for each other, about my feelings for Christina, and about Brice.

Lison wants too much from me; she's too demanding. She is a small woman, but she crackles with power and passionate energy. And then there is my Christina – quite and soft and not demanding. It even seems fitting that one is so fair and one dark. This is as tortured as I've ever been in romance.

When we are all – Lison, Brice and I – back in Paris, we don't talk about it, but it's in the air. Something is broken. Brice and I will remain allies, but I have betrayed his friendship.

Lison and I snatch hours together in my sixth-floor studio, listening to music – Cat Stevens, mostly. His song 'Lisa' always reminds me of my oldest daughter. We play a lot of chess, too, to distract us from the inevitably approaching pain.

Finally, I tell her I have to go. She knows it. She doesn't see me, anyway, as a man for the long run. But that doesn't diminish the feelings between us. We say goodbye in that little studio. She makes a grand gesture, gives me an expensive farewell gift, a beautiful brown leather bag.

It had lasted only two months, but the aftershock reverberates through my life for years. It was a beautiful mistake, but a very big one.

I move into an old Volkswagen van and camp out in it near the Quai de Seine. Christina comes to stay with me there for a while, but it very soon becomes evident that we're not ready for each other, and she goes back home to finish school.

A couple of months later, a book comes out in Paris, written by Lison de Caunes. It makes a pretty big splash, partly because her parents are both well-known writers, partly because she's Brice's lady, and partly because it's so passionately written. It's called *Les Jours d'Après*, The Days After, and it's about the end of a love affair. The cover shot is a rumpled bed. It's supposed to be a novel, but the lover's name is David, and when they part the woman gives him an expensive present, an exquisite brown leather bag. I am full of conflicting emotion. Anxious that Tina not be hurt. Mortified for Brice. Worried about our alliance. And, yes, proud to have been loved by such a brilliant and passionate woman. I still feel all those things.

I've retreated to Wales by this time, to try to write my own book. It won't be so intimate! But maybe the tale of my adventures in the

Pacific can make a little money to keep body and soul together until the French pay up.

I've told you that words aren't my natural language, so I ask my old friend Bob Hunter to join me. His first career – before environmentalism – was writing, mostly for newspapers. Bob knows my story, he's a good worker when he wants to be, and we get along really well. In our different ways, we both go at life pretty hard.

Actually, we don't so much retreat to Wales, as end up there. We were going to hole up in Ireland for couple of months. But when I pick up Bob from Heathrow in the van, his back is killing him. As a young reporter he'd gone skydiving for a story, landed badly, and ended up with his bottom two vertebrae fused together. By the time we get to Wales, he's in agony.

In a little village in the Welsh mountains, called Corwen, we see a wee house for rent. Bob stays in the van, suffering not entirely silently, while I make inquiries of the lord and lady at the manor house. Well, it's in our price range – eight pounds per week. The bathroom's outdoors, and it is winter. But there are three fireplaces, lots of coal to burn and, most importantly, the setting is lovely. We can see out across green fields, broken by the line of the River Dee passing close by. The mountains rise behind the river. A good place to write, and we get at it, although for the first few days, Bob's propped up in bed, typewriter on his lap. But eventually he's mobile again and we find a rhythm that includes heading down to the pub each night to take the village on at the only pool table in town. Hunter keeps trying to tell me we should lose once in a while, but I don't see the point.

About 15 miles away in another small town, called Llangollen, there's a sports club where I start playing squash several days a week. It feels really good to get on a court again – to move – but I do notice my age. Back when I played championship badminton, I never really worried about warming up, and never got hurt. Well, I'm 25 years older now, and my body reminds me. I pull a tendon.

But that's just physical. Inside, I'm feeling okay. It's good to be away from the noise of the city, from the politics of my case, and from the demands of the Greenpeace group forming around me in Paris. In a weird way, it's even good to be away from women. I can concentrate.

And we're really productive for a couple of months. But we're just a few chapters from the end when Bob can't stand it anymore and imports his lady. Work, predictably, grinds to a halt. I struggle to be patient, for a day or two, but this is horseshit. We're here to work. And the lady's got to go. I pretty much pack her off to London. I don't think Bob's too upset, really. He understands. But I'm not entirely sure his lady has ever forgiven me.

We wrap up the book, and I head to London and find a publisher for what will be called *Greenpeace III: Journey Into the Bomb*. I'm planning to go on from London to Vancouver for six months or so to finish the work on my property, and finally get some real money behind me again. The rest has done me good, and I'm ready for some simple hard work.

Around this time I ask my dad to send me one of those *I'd Rather Be Sailing* bumper stickers for the van. Well, they always say to be careful what you wish for.

On 17 January 1977, a letter catches up with me that has been sent on from Friends of the Earth in London. In rounded, feminine handwriting, it begins, 'I understand that you may be able to advise us on a project we are undertaking, namely to visit the Norwegians during their whaling operations in the North Sea/Arctic and to attempt to prevent them from killing whales.' It ends, 'We would welcome any advice you may offer (except Don't Go)!' Signed, 'Yours sincerely, Denise Bell (Miss) for the Whale Fund.'

Well, I've never heard of the Whale Fund. I strongly suspect this Denise Bell (Miss) is trying to sound a lot more official than she is.

She doesn't have a ship, she doesn't have any money, she doesn't seem to have any knowledge of the ocean. On the other hand, she does seem to have more important qualities – desire and will.

I have to be in London anyway. It couldn't hurt to meet.

Chapter Eleven

I GET ON the tube at Oxford Circus, near the Friends of the Earth offices on Poland Street. It's a 40-minute ride north from London to Harrow, where Denise Bell lives. The train clicks along past mile after mile of red brick terraced houses, through a series of short tunnels. By the time the city gives way to industrial land, I am feeling as grey as the day, and very shaky. Sick as a dog.

It's a 15-minute walk from Harrow station to Denise's flat, above a coin-operated laundrette. I barely make it.

Denise tucks me into bed to sweat it out, and when I wake some hours later I can't figure out why, in the dead of winter, I'm watching fluffy pollen balls drift by the window. In my weakened state, it takes a full minute to realize it must be fluff from the laundry below. And I'm in the bed of the woman who wants to take on the whalers.

Denise Bell is in her late twenties, a long-haired hippie, always in one of those Indian bedspread-type skirts that were the uniform of hippie women in the 1970s. She's a gentle soul, but she's got a bit of life experience. Her dad was a London taxi-driver, a fact about which she's quite proud. Like me, Denise hated school and dropped out early. She got a job at a scrap-metal yard and became involved with her boss, who I think was a bit of a gangster. But apparently he loved animals and they went on a safari together, which really turned Denise on to the natural world. Funny way to get involved with saving the planet, but no weirder than the path I took, I guess.

While I slurp soup, Denise tells me a little more of her plan, which isn't exactly fine-tuned. She wants to buy a ship, and she wants to stop the whalers. Period. I ask if she has a budget. No. I grab a piece of paper and rough out some numbers. It doesn't look practical, to say the least. Even if a miracle delivered the right boat, there'd still be enormous upkeep, and Denise doesn't want to lease, as Greenpeace has been doing in North America, because she thinks we should make more of a commitment, and that a ship is a good symbol. I have to give the woman a lot of credit. That commitment *made* Greenpeace in Europe. Without her, I don't know where – or if – the organization would be today.

This is another of those moments where I'd like to say that I grabbed on to the vision right away. But from where I was sitting, with the court case hanging over me, three kids I'd like to help educate, and *no* money, this looks like too much financial risk. But Denise is beyond keen; she's dead determined. So I suggest we set up a little Greenpeace office in London, and she can start fund-raising from there.

We move into a tiny office on the fifth floor of 47 Whitehall. If you know London, you'll probably recognize this as a hilariously 'good' address, along government row, a stone's throw from Trafalgar Square and Nelson's monument. We stumble into it because of another Canadian, a refugee from Greenpeace Vancouver named Allan Thornton. He's talked the Anti-Vivisectionist League into giving us a room. Thornton and I couldn't be much more different. He's quiet, and contained. Doesn't smoke, or drink much, doesn't eat meat. He does like to be in charge. I really like Allan, and respect his brain, but over the years we naturally have our moments.

Until this time, Greenpeace was a little like wild-flower seeds, scattered by the wind. The 1970s are fertile soil for the ecological movement, and wherever a seed lands, an organization springs up. They're not always connected, or even aware of each other. Greenpeace is officially registered in Vancouver, but as a Canadian foundation. I don't remember asking for permission to use the name Greenpeace in the UK. I felt the name belonged as much to me as to anyone, and as far as I know the Canadians felt the same way – we were a pretty 'organic' organization in those days. So I just did it – registered Greenpeace UK. Through me we're connected to Remi and Paris, and that handful of seeds begins to root and spread across Europe.

Our first board of directors includes pretty much the whole Greenpeace UK organization in 1977. There's Denise, Allan and me, along with Susi Newborn and Charles Hutchison. Susi is a diplomat's daughter, blessed with looks, brains, and a low boredom threshold. Charles Hutchison is a sincere young academic with a passion for whales.

Denise is really the heart and soul of the place, and – although she isn't yet 30 – she's our mother hen, pushing everybody to keep going. She scrounges together a few office supplies, gets us writing begging letters to everyone we can think of, organizes benefit concerts, and even begins making and selling T-shirts, the beginning of Greenpeace marketing! Lots of energy being generated, but not much money.

We get World Wildlife in Holland fund-raising for us, too. They're showing a film from Bob Hunter's adventure with the whaling fleet off the North American coast, and asking for donations for a Save the Whales voyage. Denise and the other youngsters are wildly enthusiastic, and I'm trying to keep my doubts to myself. I figure we need an absolute minimum of fifty thousand pounds, probably closer to a hundred thousand, and that's a lot of money in those days.

We are so broke it isn't funny. Denise stays with her sister in Harrow, and Susi with her diplomat dad, but the rest of us camp out in the office much of the time, sleeping on the floor. Charles and Allan head down to Soho market at the end of each day and nab the vegetables that are going to be tossed out – I think they actually pick them up off the ground – and that's dinner. Vegetable stew, with much too much soy sauce. This gets a little wearing, especially for an ageing carnivore.

But we have a bit of fun, too. Somebody makes a huge papier mâché whale, and we hang it out our fifth-floor window, along with speakers broadcasting whale sounds into the startled ears of Whitehall's prim and proper civil servants.

With the office more or less organized, I take off for Vancouver for what I hope will be the final push to finish – and sell – the marina at Secret Cove. I figure if I'm going to keep getting sucked into these environmental causes, I better be putting something away for the future. While I'm willing to live day-to-day on stale vegetables, my practical Scot's nature kicks in when it comes to looking after my kids, and my old age.

And I have to say it's nice just to be on my own again, doing physical work, and when I stop, the only noise is the sound of the ocean breeze in the hundred-foot trees that dot my property. But in my life, peace and quiet never seem to last.

This time it's broken by a phone call from Denise, 'David, we've put an offer down on a boat. Fifty thousand pounds. Allan thinks it's a good buy'.

Oh shit. Here I am 5,000 miles away, up to my knees in mud, and these two good souls – who know nothing about boats – have committed money we don't exactly have to buy a ship I haven't seen. It's suddenly quite clear to me why Greenpeace has always chartered in the past. For an organization with not much money, and an unstable future – to say the least – this is a helluva commitment. Back on the plane.

It's not exactly love at first sight with me and the *Sir William Hardy*. It's a rusty old trawler that had been used by the UK Ministry of Fisheries as a research ship. It was built in 1955, and retired after twenty years' hard labour. Not a pretty picture. And stepping aboard a dead ship is a very creepy experience. There's no power, of course, so it's dark below, and cold and very inhospitable. It's what someone in the business of selling houses would call 'a handyman's special' – everything needs work. But the ship has its good points. Fundamentally, it's a seaworthy design. And because it's been used as a research ship, there's a lot more crew accommodation below decks than you'd find in a regular trawler.

I decide if we can get it *really* cheap, we'll be able to fix it up. So I send Denise and Allan back to the Ministry of Fisheries to tell them we don't have the fifty thousand pounds, which is true. Technically.

Actually the response to World Wildlife's fund-raising campaign on our behalf has been fantastic. Close to a hundred thousand pounds. But we don't actually *have* that money yet. It's still in Holland. And I ask WWF to keep it there, until we finish negotiating.

We're in a good position. This is right after the Cod War; the Brits have been chucked out of Iceland, and many fishermen are getting out of the business. Lots of trawlers for sale, and I guess the Ministry doesn't have a long line-up to buy the *Sir William Hardy*. They tell us to make them an offer. I decide to low-ball it. Thirty-five thousand.

They go for it! And in a handshake Greenpeace has her first ship.

We bounce off the walls of our little office, reeling between euphoria and shell-shock. We've done it! Euphoria. Now what? Shell-shock.

Well, the first thing is clearly to celebrate. We pile into a little Italian restaurant near Leicester Square, buzzing with adrenaline. Over too much red wine, we search for a name for our new baby. *Sir William Hardy* is clearly not the right name for an ocean-going ecological warrior. I can't remember all the different ideas we have – wish I'd kept the napkins. But I do remember when Susi Newborn speaks up. She'd spent some time in North America, I think on the seal campaign, and had become acquainted with North American aboriginal legends. But I don't know that. All I know is that when she says she's got it, she sounds very serious. Unusual for Susi. And the next two words out of her mouth are absolutely right, and unforgettable. The *Rainbow Warrior*.

It sounds good, and then she explains it. Apparently in Native North American lore, when the tribes ignore natural law and begin over-hunting and over-fishing, the rainbow warriors descend from the sky to save the world. You know those rare moments in life when you're absolutely in the moment, and the background noise disappears? It seems as if the room goes silent for a second. This was one of those.

The old *Sir William Hardy* is dead. And the *Rainbow Warrior* begins her voyage into history.

The next thing is to find a skipper. That might be a bit of a challenge, since we obviously need somebody with commercial experience, and how many commercial captains are going to risk their reputations signing on with this motley crew of eco-freaks?

Denise puts an advertisement in the union newspaper, and we wait.

There's one response that looks hopeful, a guy who's had experience in the merchant navy, supplying British bases in the Antarctic. At least he won't be afraid of North Atlantic weather! But if he's sensible, he might be afraid of his crew. Everybody in the growing cluster of people around the office wants to be part of this voyage and nobody – other than me – has ever been offshore. So basically we're looking for a captain who's experienced and responsible enough to skipper a trawler in the wintry North Sea, and weird enough to want to do it with a crew that's green as grass.

Enter Nick Hill, up the grotty stairs at 47 Whitehall into a haze of smoke and an office that clearly doubles as a crash pad. He's about six foot four inches tall, with a strong but spare physique, and chiselled features. He looks straight as an arrow, and I'm more than a little concerned about how we look to him. Nick's very fair, and he seems a little paler since he walked in. But somehow I just have the feeling that this is the guy.

He listens to our half-hatched plan to find the Icelandic whaling fleet, somewhere in the North Sea, and stop them. Simple. High degree of difficulty, but simple. We'll send inflatables out to get between the harpoon and the whale.

He's pretty deadpan, but I can see a light flicker behind his eyes. He likes this idea! And when he tells us a little of his story, I understand why. On one of his trips to the Antarctic, Nick had seen a Norwegian whaling station in an advanced state of decay, mountains of bones stacked on the beach. It hit him hard, for some reason. As a seaman, he was well aware that no one had seen a blue whale for ages, and the idea of extinction began to haunt him. Then, when he got home, there was our ad in his union newspaper, waiting for him.

We take Nick down to the West India docks to have a look at the ship. When we step aboard into that dark deadness, I keep every part of my body crossed, hoping he'll see promise under the rust. He's not exactly talkative, as his flashlight skitters over the bridge and down the companionway to the engine room. Charles Hutchison is trying desperately to get the generators to work. No luck. But when Nick turns to me, he pronounces the boat 'very suitable'.

The *Rainbow Warrior* has her first captain.

Now we just have to find the ship, under the rust.

London's West India docks are generally pretty dead at the end of the 1970s. Nick says shipping companies have taken their business to Rotterdam and Antwerp, because of ongoing labour problems. So we really shake up the place. A swarm of hippies, buzzing round this old Fisheries boat, hammering and scraping and painting, and singing, 'you can't always get what you want, but if you try some-times, you get what you need.' Could have been our theme song.

Complete strangers are showing up to help with the back-breaking work of making a rainbow warrior out of this tarnished trawler. A taxi-driver offers to drive us around for free. A vegetarian (sigh!) restaurant gives us free food.

Most of the work is done by a core of regulars who work from dawn until last light. It's the change-the-world spirit of those times made real, made practical. Some of these people will never lose the spirit, the belief that we can each make a difference. One of the best of them is Chris Robinson, a long-haired, bearded Australian who comes aboard because he's Susi's boyfriend, and stays because it's where he belongs. Chris greets us each morning with a cheery 'g'day' and then works his butt off.

We still haven't figured out the engine room. Rather critical. The *Sir William Hardy* is a combined diesel-electric ship – in fact the first-ever built in the UK – and those of us who know a bit about engines know nothing about this. Finally Denise calls up the previous engineer, and he actually comes down from Aberdeen, Scotland, to help! It takes him about two minutes, and he has her purring. Whew.

Our 'design committee' is an art student who shows up with a brilliant idea, and the time to execute it. He paints rainbow stripes on the side of the ship, doves of peace on the bow, and animals on the side of the bright green funnel.

Everything's fantastic. Except for one huge bureaucratic pain. We're having a continuing battle over whether or not we can register the *Rainbow Warrior* as a yacht. We should be able to, since she's under 500 tons. And it's important. There's no way we've got the money to upgrade to Class Seven standard. Day after day, Nick heads up to the Board of Trade offices. They politely arm-wrestle, and we get no definitive answer.

I feel like I'm in Auckland in 1972, trying to get *Vega* underway. These guys just don't like the cut of our jib, and they're going to make it as difficult as possible for us to get out of port.

Sometime during the final days of our preparations, the bureaucracy smiles. We're a yacht. Officially. Whew. (Nick's always thought I bribed somebody. I would have, if I'd found someone susceptible, but I didn't. Honest, Nick.)

The inspector comes on board to clear our 'yacht'. Final inspection. And wouldn't you know it, we don't pass. It seems we have to have the ship's name hammered into the hull *and* into the main beam, too. Something in Denise's passion, or in her honest eyes, gets to the inspector, though. He says he'll sign the clearance, if she gives her word that the words 'Rainbow Warrior' will be driven into the beam before we cast off in the morning. She promises. The inspector's made a safe bet; Denise is a woman of her word. They work all night.

On 28 April 1978, we are ready to sail. A large handful of beautiful young people, prepared – no, eager – to take on the world. And one middle-aged man.

It's late afternoon when we go through the main lock into the Thames. Night is falling as we head out of the estuary into the sea. There's a mild swell, and many of the green crew rapidly get greener. I can't tell yet how much that's inexperience and how much is celebration. We've left on a wave of cheap champagne, and optimism.

The *Warrior*'s hull cuts confidently through the water. She's ready. We're ready – I hope.

Chapter Twelve

BUT THERE'S A difference between hope and blind optimism. Nick and I know that this crew, as willing as they are, badly need some experience before we come up against the tough Icelandic whalers. Partly to shake down the crew, and the *Warrior*, we first head up the east coast of Britain, destination Torness. A nuclear plant is to be built there and people don't want it.

It's an amazing scene. Thousands of people, maybe as many as 5,000, have marched miles along the Scottish coast and pitched tents among the sand dunes on the seashore. We anchor the *Rainbow Warrior*, and I stay on board as a Greenpeace party zooms ashore in inflatables. Our guys look a little James Bond in their bright wet suits, landing amongst the tweeds and walking sticks.

But the crowd is overjoyed with our support and soon starts insisting that they want to hear from McTaggart. I don't want to do it, *really* don't want to do it, hate public speaking. But the crowd won't take no for an answer. My people finally coax me ashore and up onto the platform in front of that huge crowd. I'm following good speakers, like Brice Lalonde, who understand a lot of the technical detail about nuclear power. I'm uncomfortable about my lack of knowledge, and the size of the audience. It's such an awkward situation that I don't even really remember what I said, but have it on good authority that it was short, if not particularly sweet. Something like, 'Has anybody got a joint?' and 'Let's go get the ****ers'.

The assembled throng lets out a huge cheer. A very generous bunch.

The next day, we get serious. Start having our first zodiac drills.

Including skipper Nick Hill, only half a dozen of the crew of 24 on the *Rainbow Warrior*'s maiden voyage have any real sailing experience. The rest of the crew have a pretty romantic notion about bouncing off over the bounding main in little inflatables to put themselves between the whales and the whalers. Good for them, without that spirit there wouldn't be a Greenpeace.

But Nick Hill and I are worried about the practical end of things, such as how we'll find them again. We don't yet have a reliable way of communicating between the *Rainbow Warrior* and the inflatables, and Nick and I worry that once they're out in the fog and swells of the North Atlantic, we may lose them. The radar won't pick them up unless the water is like glass, and that's unlikely. We decide there's nothing for it, except to keep vigilant watch from the bridge. Every time there's a zodiac in the water, it'll be like a 'man overboard' drill. One of us on the bridge will keep our eyes on the inflatable *at all times*.

And there's the matter of getting the inflatables into the water and away from the *Warrior* quickly enough to catch the whalers. As we head off on a public relations tour of northern Europe, we spend part of every day doing zodiac drills. We practise over and over and over, until these enthusiastic young men beg for mercy. And then I make them go again. They think the old man is off his rocker, but this is important.

By now the ship is developing a lot of character. One of its unique qualities is democracy – everybody takes a turn at everything, from steering to washing up.

Actually it isn't entirely democratic. We aren't that crazy.

The bridge is totally serious, with Nick in charge. One of the things I'll always remember fondly is the approach this serious-minded seaman took to his amateur crew. It's a big part of what makes him the ideal man to captain the first voyage of the *Rainbow Warrior*. Nick treats everyone with respect and patience. He doesn't seem to be afraid of his crew's inexperience, just compensates for it whenever he needs to. Example: calmly making sure professional seamen are always on deck when we're coming into port.

Nick has a quiet, deep understanding of why we're here, and of who these people are, underneath their hippie garb. He even puts ashore one of his few professional seamen because the man isn't treating the hippies with enough respect.

Below decks, things are not so serious. Charles Hutchison has been nicknamed Charles Duck, because he keeps hitting his head when he goes through a hatchway. Charles and Denise are sharing the old laboratory under the bridge and have made it very homey, even put curtains up around the portholes. This becomes a popular meeting spot, which is a good thing because Remi Parmentier is in the habit of falling asleep in the saloon where we take our meals. This is driving everyone else a little crazy, but that doesn't seem to stop him. When he's awake, Remi provides a real continental flare, marching around the ship in a short black cape. It's quite a scene, especially when our cook, Hilary, is out on the bow playing her violin. The saloon itself is a bit of a statement. Potted plants hanging everywhere – that should be interesting in a gale.

It's in this setting that we hold our big meetings, and right from the start, it gets pretty hot over one issue: are we there to save whales, individual whales, or are we there to bring the world's attention to whaling so that we can totally stop it in the future? You can probably guess how it went. Denise passionately leads a large group that can't see why we should waste time on a tour of European ports – Calais, Rotterdam, Amsterdam, Hamburg, Aarhus, Bergen. They just want to get out to the whaling grounds and save a whale. I feel we have an obligation to thank the Dutch branch of the World Wildlife Fund, and the Dutch people, for the contributions that made it possible for us to buy the *Warrior* in the first place. It also seems obvious that the more people who join our cause, the more clout we'll have. Politics isn't complicated. It's power. And in democratic nations, that's public opinion. Let's go get it. In truth, I don't care so much about the individual whales but am focused on the political war.

It gets pretty hot. Denise is not pleased with me, but we do the tour. And it's fantastic! Lots of press at every stop. In Hamburg a popular pianist holds a concert on the deck of the *Rainbow Warrior*, and everywhere big groups of schoolchildren turn out to see 'the ship that will save the whales'. You can almost feel our power grow.

But it's never easy.

It's our intention to present a paper to the Norwegian government, asking them to stop killing the minke whale off the coast of Norway. Sailing between Denmark and Norway, Nick takes the shortest route. Of course. But what the charts don't show us is that this is through an unmarked Norwegian military zone. When we get to Bergen, I head off to have a drink with our Icelandic interpreter and when I get back to the *Warrior*, Nick's gone. Arrested. Quite an honour, now that I think of it, to be the first *Rainbow Warrior* skipper arrested. He won't be the last, by a long shot. He's released with a small fine, and a clear message: the Norwegians don't want us here. They're still whaling, and they don't want to stop.

Well, we knew that.

In fact, we've decided to go after Iceland because we don't want to go after Norway.

They're both members of the International Whaling Commission, a body set up in 1946 to regulate the whaling industry. Membership is open to any country that adheres to its rules, and pays a hefty fee.

The IWC has the clout to protect species and to designate certain areas as whale sanctuaries. They do it all in the name of managing 'whale stocks' so that countries can keep 'harvesting' them. But since its power is generally accepted among the whaling nations, the Commission is also the place to be if you're against whaling. If it has the power to regulate whaling, it has the power to stop it.

Iceland, Norway and Denmark are the Scandinavian bloc at the International Whaling Commission, and they're each democracies, with a vigorous press. We want to sway all three votes at the IWC, and the best way to do that is to get public opinion on our side. Norwegian whaling is mostly families, operating their own small boats. Icelandic whaling is one big company, operating a fleet of ships. If we want to be on the right side of the David and Goliath equation, it's pretty clear we don't want to be interfering with a family's livelihood. We want to go after the big guys.

And there's a curious irony at play. At the United Nations Conference on the Environment in Stockholm in 1972, Iceland and Norway both voted to ask the IWC to consider a ten-year ban on commercial whaling. It was a bit of a charade – they look good in the world's eyes at Stockholm but then kill the moratorium idea at the next IWC meeting. There's obviously a conflict here between international principles – or at least international image – and economic reality. Where there's conflict, there just might be energy for change.

So we turn away from the familiar waters of the continent and head north towards Iceland. Have you ever realized how much closer it is to Greenland than to the UK? God, it's a long way. And cold. And damp. And grey.

We put in to the Shetland Islands, off the north coast of Scotland, to refuel and – unbeknownst until now to the rest of the crew – to officially change the name of the ship's master. Nick's understandably concerned about losing his licence, should he be brought up in front of a professional tribunal for endangering the ship, or crew. And, of course, we plan to deliberately put ourselves in danger. I don't have a licence to lose, so it makes sense. And it's only paperwork. Nick's still in charge of the day-to-day running of the *Warrior*.

It's now early June 1978. The fin whale season opens 5 June, and the International Whaling Commission meets in London on 26 June. So we have three weeks to find the Icelandic whalers, interfere with the hunt, and get pictures dramatic enough to enrage and engage the public. I want to be in the IWC meetings, lobbying member nations, and I want the delegations to walk into the sessions through a noisy public protest. The delegates need to know that the ordinary people who elect their governments are questioning the business of whaling.

Now if we can just survive the seasickness and the boredom, and find the whalers.

As we cruise further and further north, into the world of perpetual daylight, the ocean gets rougher. The *Rainbow Warrior* rolls and creaks with every wave breaking on her foredeck. People are starting to get a little crazy. Not much can be done about the seasickness, but we combat the fear and boredom with attempts at humour. We pick actors to play each of us, as if this were a Hollywood movie. Here's a partial list – anybody who's under 40 can skip ahead:

Nick Hill – Gregory Peck

Chris Robinson – Kris Kristofferson

Athel von Koettlitz (soon-to-be legendary inflatable driver) – Jack Nicholson

Tony Marriner (photographer, and inflatables expert) – Terence Stamp

Charles Hutchison – Woody Allen

Denise Bell – Vanessa Redgrave

Remi Parmentier – Dustin Hoffman

Allan Thornton – Omar Sharif

Susi Newborn – Katharine Ross

David McTaggart – Marlon Brando.

A week away from the Scottish coast, Iceland looms out of the sea. What a landscape! Geysers boiling up out of plains of ice, towering mountains, and flat, dry valleys, bare of vegetation. We've obviously come to a tough place.

Each summer, as the fin whales pass through Icelandic waters on their migration north, the Hvalur whaling company kills something like two hundred and fifty of them. The second largest of all great whales, the fin whale is on the endangered species list. But it's complicated. Fishing and whaling are part of Iceland's marine heritage, to say nothing of its Gross National Product.

And, remember, these guys had just fought Britain to a stalemate in the Cod War, by filling the bows of their boats with concrete and playing chicken with the Royal Navy's warships. Somehow I don't think they're going to be intimidated by a bunch of hippies in a brightly painted boat. We're going to look to them like the kindergarten-of-the-sea.

But our immediate problem is just finding the whalers. Hvalur's four ships work about two hundred thousand square miles of ocean. They start in the south at the beginning of the season and slowly move northwards as autumn approaches. We have no idea what the pattern is, or even if they repeat the same pattern each time they come out. We do know that every two hours the ships communicate by radio with their shore station. We hope to locate them through those radio signals. It's a painful waiting game, and even when we establish a whaler's position, it's just too far away.

The crew is feeling extremely frustrated to have come all this way, prepared to engage in the battle of their lives, and then be unable to find the enemy. We spend endless hours in the saloon, discussing the best strategy, and finally decide we'll simply start in the south and plot a zig-zag course north. Not too technical a plan, but hopefully it'll work.

On 5 June, we get a radio communiqué from Kristian Loftsson, Hvalur's director and himself a delegate to the IWC: 'We wish to draw your attention to the fact that the intended operation of the Greenpeace group in attempting to prevent the fishing for whales inside the Icelandic Fisheries limit constitutes illegal interference.' These guys plan to play tough.

But we haven't come this far to back down.

On 9 June, we're cruising off Reykjavik when we see it, *Hvalur 7* carrying three dead whales back to the station. For most of the crew, this is their first look at a whale, and it's a terrible picture – these magnificent creatures lashed by the tail to the side of the catcher, being most unnaturally dragged backwards through the water. Silently, the *Rainbow Warrior*'s crew lines the deck and stares across the water. Even for a hard case like me, it's difficult to look at.

It'll be another week before the crew gets to put all that emotion to work.

It's almost midnight when, through the perpetual dusk of these northern latitudes, the bridge crew sights a school of dolphins bearing down on the *Warrior*. I know this sounds just too perfect, but it's true. And just a few minutes later a mast appears on the horizon. It's *Hvalur 9*, towing one dead fin whale.

As sad as it is, this is our perfect scenario. You see, we'd earlier made the awkward discovery that our inflatables weren't fast enough to catch one of these whalers. But once they're loaded down with the weight of one dead fin whale, we have a chance to stop the second kill.

Now the hours of endless drilling pay off. We hop right from bed into our wet suits, and jump into the zodiacs bobbing up and down beside the *Warrior*. Three teams mobilize, so that two can take up positions on the whaler's bow, and the third act as a rescue craft and a gasoline jockey. I'm with the crazy cowboy, Athel. He drives the inflatable so hard that we take off from the tops of waves, and then crash down low, losing sight of both the *Warrior* and the whaler.

I keep thinking of our inflatables as a bunch of bulldogs on leashes, when the leashes have been cut.

Hvalur 9 is about a mile and a half away when we start out, so it takes us ten minutes to catch up and pull in front of its bow. *Hvalur*'s chasing a pod of fin whales, and we just ram ourselves between the whales and the crashing steel hull. Every time that ugly hull rises up, I can see the dripping bottom of the ship with its lead paint. We all know if our engines cut out, we'll be smashed before the whaler can react. Hell, the guys on the bridge can't even see us, since we're below their angle of vision.

Then there's the whale. Right in front of us, tired and terrified. One swipe of that tail, and we'll be flipped in the air and under *Hvalur 9*'s bow. It takes constant concentration to stay in position.

Occasionally we see the harpooner run down the catwalk, flip the safety catch off, and try to line up a shot. Most of the time the harpoon gun is pointing right down at us. From our vantage point it looks like a small missile launcher, silhouetted against the grey sky.

It's a tough, tough night. By morning, we're exhausted, but not finished. We can sense a change in attitude from *Hvalur 9*'s crew. When we'd first pulled up to the ship, they'd hurled tomatoes and lit cigarettes at us, and given us the finger. But as we hung in there hour after hour, one inflatable replacing the other, their contempt turned to respect.

Finally, at about 5 p.m., the whale-spotter climbs down from *Hvalur*'s crow's nest, and the ship turns back towards Reykjavik. If they don't get their catch home within thirty hours, the meat will spoil.

Back on the deck of the *Rainbow Warrior*, we open a bottle of champagne and pass it from hand to hand. Dog-tired, soaking-wet and very battered, this little band of hippies has won against the tough Icelanders.

But it's clear to me that winning a battle at sea won't be worth much if we can't also turn it into a public-relations victory. We head into Reykjavik and call a press conference. Allan Thornton has the brilliant idea of inviting Kristian Loftsson, owner of the whaling company, and challenging him to a debate. Almost unbelievably, he accepts. We have a ready-made media event.

Loftsson is a thin, nervous-looking guy, who opens by saying he doesn't really understand the fuss, that Iceland's whaling quota is officially set by the IWC.

Thornton – you'll recall he somewhat resembles the darkly handsome actor Omar Sharif – responds by saying the IWC has no idea how many whales there are in the ocean, so the quotas it sets are irrelevant.

Then an *Icelandic* psychologist stands and speaks against the morality of killing intelligent mammals and says, 'We have a moral responsibility to protect these fin whales for future generations.' He sits down to loud applause. Wow. It doesn't get much better than this for public pressure. Applause for the protesters' point of view right in the heart of whaling country.

After the meeting, Loftsson and I meet in the bar for a drink. (You've got to admire the man's balls for agreeing to the debate in the first place.) He presumes we've got what we came for and will be heading back to London. I have to tell him, no, the *Warrior* will be leaving in the morning alright, but back to the whaling grounds.

I don't tell him that he and I will meet again, very soon, at the IWC in London. And that I'm planning a little surprise.

Chapter Thirteen

A YEAR OR so earlier, as we were setting up the London office, I spent time looking for tough, tough people to run campaigns. I kept hearing about this guy who'd been a driving force behind Friends of the Earth in the UK, and then quit in a bit of a huff. I was told he'd wanted more responsibility, to be put in charge of a campaign, and felt FoE was holding him back because he didn't have the right accent or any academic credentials. I was also told he was the most ornery sonofabitch they'd ever had working for them. I liked the sound of that.

I tracked Pete Wilkinson down at the Halstead Post Office, where he'd taken a job in a misbegotten attempt to settle down into regular society with his new bride. I called up Pete out of the blue, told him we should talk about his joining Greenpeace.

We went to a football game that Saturday, each wanting a little time to get a sense of the other, but I knew the second I laid eyes on Pete. He was only about five foot seven, but looked as if he could handle himself physically in any situation. And he had the face of a sensitive boxer, if that makes any sense. Rugged, but not mean. And smart. You could see the intelligence, and the soul, in his eyes. Pete'd be a great friend, and a tough opponent. And I'd come to know him both ways.

We watched a terrible game, Millwall, I think, and then retired to the Deptford Arms pub to talk. Pete was fantastic company, still is, and we just got on. He asked why I'd looked him up, and I told him. We need ornery people. I offered him twenty-five pounds a week – a fraction of what he was making – and all the trouble he could get into. He took the job.

It's Pete who first suggests an orderly invasion of the International Whaling Commission.

I fly from Reykjavik to London to prepare our little surprise for the 1978 IWC meeting. In a complicated round of international politics, there'd been a proposal put before the Commission for a ten-year moratorium on commercial whaling, and then withdrawn. Japanese pressure on the proposing country, I think.

We want the public to know about it.

I arrive in a pretty strange frame of mind, a kind of heightened sense of being, my senses just about humming. Two days before I'd been crashing around in the North Atlantic, staring up at a harpoon, and over at an exhausted fin whale swimming for its life. It's very strange to go from that seascape to this – schools of blue and grey suits bobbing along through the Mount Royal Hotel. These guys talk about 'harvesting' whales as if they're turnips.

I manage to get a phoney German press pass to the meetings. And a graphic designer makes official-looking passes for Pete and a dozen others, all bearing the names of different fictitious magazines and newspapers. Works like a charm. Dressed in our Sunday best, we have no trouble getting through security and into a room I've rented. We'll keep out of sight until it's time for our carefully rehearsed invasion.

As the one with the 'real' press pass, I head into the meeting to gauge the most effective moment for us to strike.

About thirty minutes later, I run up two flights of stairs to signal Pete. When I barge into our room, I can barely see him there's so much smoke – guess they're a little nervous. I bark, 'Go!' And then head back into the convention to watch the fireworks.

Pete leads the company quickly and quietly down the fire escape, through the main doors, and into the international private men's club that is the International Whaling Commission.

He struts up to the podium and announces that Greenpeace is taking over the meeting. The IWC chairman takes what is probably the wisest course: 'The floor is yours.'

Pete shines. He makes a fantastic speech about the IWC presiding over the extinction of whales. While he talks, our people present big bouquets of flowers to countries with good conservation records, like France. Those with lousy records, like Japan, get huge signs, saying 'For crimes against nature you stand condemned.'

Then Pete declares an indefinite moratorium on whaling, as decreed by international public opinion, and ends a very successful, *very* photogenic protest with two minutes silence for the whales.

As our guys start to leave, the room actually bursts into spontaneous applause. It would have looked so good on the evening news.

Would have.

Unfortunately, all the world will see was what happened next. As they file out past the Japanese delegation, somebody in the protest group, *not* a Greenpeace member, pulls out a bottle of red ink. It's supposed to symbolize whale's blood. He tips it over the head of the Japanese delegate, and all hell breaks loose. I'm seeing red myself. This guy has just single-handedly spoiled a very effective protest. When two heavy Japanese guys grab him, I'm tempted for a moment to let them have a go. But that'll just make a bad scene worse. In .001 of a second, I see that if he goes to jail, we'll be in a hell of a political spot.

I don't want to be forced to defend a stupid action like this.

Somehow I get into the crowd, manage to extricate him from these sumo-types and slip away with the little bastard in tow.

Sure enough, that night on the news there's no mention of our peaceful protest. Only shots of that fool grabbing his thirty seconds in the limelight. Even though this guy would turn out to be one of the good ones, dedicating years of his life to the environment, thinking of that day still makes me mad.

That summer we decide to broaden our attack and take on pirate whaling. Example: Spain isn't a member of the Whaling Commission. It *is* the base for a whaling company that's killing endangered species and shipping the meat to Japan. We call it pirate whaling, because it isn't regulated *at all*, not even by the IWC. Furthermore, Japan is in violation of IWC regulations by buying whale products from a non-member nation.

We want proof that it's happening, and we want to confront the whalers at sea. We just have to find them. They aren't exactly advertising their filthy business.

I fly to Paris, borrow back my old VW bus and drive down along the west coast of Spain. On the way to Iceland to – hopefully – launch the protest against Spanish whaling, the *Warrior* will put in at the big port of La Coruna. So near there, I pull off the highway on a steep hill from which I can see the shoreline for miles. Take out my binoculars. Nada. Then I look down. There's a little paved road that stops behind a 'Do Not Enter' sign. I bump down the road to the sign hanging on a chain-link fence. Behind the fence are three big steel buildings, and behind them, invisible from the highway, a tiny bay. And I can't believe my eyes! A whale is being winched out of the water by the tail, up a long concrete ramp.

During the next two days, I walk around quietly, collecting as much information and as many photographs as possible. When it turns foggy, I figure I've got enough photos anyway, I might as well go say hello. I walk into the station itself and walk around. I knock off a few shots, before I'm stopped and booted off.

It's one of those times when you really have to think somebody up there is on our side, and it just keeps happening to us.

When the *Rainbow Warrior* and her crew put in at La Coruna, they tie up not two hundred yards from a Spanish whaler. When it leaves in the morning for the killing fields, it has a shadow. The

Warrior slips out of harbour to spend three days harassing the whalers. It's a very different scene than Iceland. The Spanish sailors are quite friendly, even passing a bottle of wine down to our guys in the inflatables. The weather's glorious, and some of our guys even strip down and go swimming with the dolphins.

But the pleasant mood doesn't last. When the *Warrior* heads into La Coruna to refuel, the Spanish navy requests that they stay put. Our guys agree, but at nightfall think better of it and make a run for Portuguese waters. Thank God they made it. If we'd lost the *Rainbow Warrior* at that point, I don't know what we'd have done. It's our only real asset, and the campaigns are running us into the red.

But the *Warrior*'s crew, including Allan Thornton and Charles Hutchison, just want to keep going, forget about money, forget about strategy. They want to head the ship down into the Mediterranean to campaign against chemical dumping off Italy. I think the tension of the past few months is getting to them. They're exhausted, starting to run on empty, and beginning to believe that they are the only true warriors in the organization. Understandable, since they've been the ones constantly in the field. But we just can't afford it.

I believe in picking good people and letting them make their own decisions, but sometimes you just have to step in.

On the flight down to Portugal, I realize I've been driving myself pretty hard, too. Looking down at the Spanish coastline, the blue, blue sea rolling up a long white beach, for a moment I think we're flying over the Atlantic on the way from North America to the UK. If you've ever had the disorientating sensation of waking up in a hotel room that's familiar, but for a moment not having any idea where you are, that's what it's like, only I'm wide awake. I quickly get it straight, but the feeling lingers, the feeling of having lost a place of identity.

Marching onto the *Rainbow Warrior* a couple of hours later, I'm not in a very good mood. We meet in the saloon, and although nobody's downright hostile, it isn't very pleasant. I have to order the boat back to the UK.

And that's really the beginning of the end for Allan Thornton and me. I take him aside and essentially tell him it's my way, or the highway. If he wants to be part of this organization, he has to get behind me.

I decide to take Thornton off the ship for now. He's too much of a wild card.

As we wait for a plane at the airport in Santiago de Compostella, Spain, Allan keeps his distance. Across the waiting room I can see him chatting up a good-looking redhead, helping her place a phone call. She's wearing jeans and a T-shirt – a girl-next-door type with longish curly hair, and a very nice figure. Good for him, I think.

But when we board the plane, she's directly in front of me and I can see that she has a *very* nice figure. I think, what the hell, follow her past my assigned seat on the plane and ask her something inane, like 'Is this the smoking section?' She says, 'Not if you're still standing.' So I sit down beside her.

And suddenly this irritating trip to discipline the troops is getting interesting.

Annette has a sparkle about her, one of those impossibly wide smiles and a real twinkle in her hazel eyes. She's young, maybe mid-twenties, a special education teacher on her way home to Amsterdam after a holiday spent crewing on a boat. I'm going to Paris, and she has to change planes there. I don't have a lot of time.

We drink rum and cokes, and smoke all her Silken cigarettes. And talk and talk and talk. By the time the plane touches down in Paris, I've convinced Annette that she'll never make her Amsterdam connection. It's too tight. She'll have to stay in Paris that night.

And, really, that's how Greenpeace Europe – a few years later – came to be based in Amsterdam. It was a sound choice politically, too. By 1980, the Dutch office was a rising star in Greenpeace, bringing in a lot of money and getting a little arrogant. Several of my colleagues thought that moving the head office to Amsterdam would make it easier to control the Dutch, and the dollars. But I have to admit that my following Annette up the stairs to that plane in Santiago de Compostella, back in 1978, helped swing my vote.

The third weekend in August 1978, we hold the Greenpeace annual meeting in Amsterdam. And then I grab a train from Centraal Station to Hoorn, forty minutes north, over countryside cross-hatched with canals. This is where Annette lives and teaches, and it'll turn out to be the first of many times I make this trip during the next four or five years.

Hoorn is on a big bay that sweeps in off the Markerwaard, the waterway that defines the east side of the north Holland peninsula. Named for the shape of its harbour, the city was one of the principal ports of The Netherlands, before the Zuiderzee silted up in the eighteenth century. I love the feeling of history all around me, and I love the water. This place would be good, even without Annette.

And what a welcome! I step off the train into a fantastic party. Seriously. As it turns out, the third Monday in August is Lappendag, a festival to celebrate the end of the summer, the beginning of autumn. The tradition is that the women get up at 7 a.m. to go to market and buy cloth for winter garments, and the men go to the pub. By the afternoon, when I arrive, everybody's pretty happy! Annette and I wander through the crowds to her flat, upstairs in a little house just a few minutes walk from the station.

I start feeling more like I belong in Europe. On the train to Hoorn one day, I write to my parents: 'I could easily settle down, and everywhere I go I look in windows, visualizing people inside, content, warm, secure, eating regularly and I have very large twinges wishing for the moment I could just stop. But the feeling passes. I am giving direction to the younger people I work with, maybe sometimes I'm too hard, but the object is to win or there really is no reason to start.'

I don't mention to the folks that I have a home when I want one, with Annette. I actually get pretty settled, for me. We even buy bicycles and spend some deliciously ordinary days cycling around the harbour, with me always keeping one eye on the boats moored there. Through the wild expansion of Greenpeace during these next few years, Hoorn and this warm and gentle woman will be home base, a safe anchorage when I have to get out of the eye of the storm.

Of course, most of the squalls I need to escape are of my own making, with a little help from my friends.

I've been in Hoorn for about two minutes – story of my life – when Pete calls me back to the UK for another one of these warm and fuzzy campaigns, seals this time. It's the autumn of 1978, and UK Fisheries wants to cull half the grey seal herd resident in the waters around the Orkney Islands, off the north coast of Scotland. The local fishermen are blaming the seals for reduced whitefish and salmon catches, somehow ignoring the Russian ships that come into the area and just hoover up the fish. Anyway, the grey seal is a protected species, has been since 1914. This should be a conservation success story. But the British government has caved to political pressure and called in Norwegian seal hunters to cull mother seals and their pups.

Well, I learned my lesson from our Newfoundland experience. Cute animals make good press. And there's even a sound scientific argument here. These seals were teetering on the edge of extinction. It's perfect for us – warm pictures, cold science.

Instinctively, I know this is it. An issue which could get us talked about at every breakfast table in Europe.

I decide to go to the Orkneys personally. I'll be on the *Rainbow Warrior*. Pete Wilkinson will be onshore, managing the press.

Our plan is simple, another non-violent direct action. We'll put ourselves between the seals and the sealers. Only one little problem, the seals aren't exactly organized. They're spread out over several outlying islands. So we drop volunteers with camping gear on each one of them, people brave and loony enough to put themselves in front of a pissed-off Norwegian marksman.

The northern coast of Scotland hasn't seen as much action before or since. There are boatloads of journalists following the *Warrior*, which is shadowing the Norwegian ship, *Kvitungen*. Even a Japanese film crew has turned up. People are hiring helicopters to get aerial shots. And Pete Wilkinson is holding a press conference every night at the local hotel. We're on the front page day after day. Kids are hitchhiking up from London to join the protest.

What a zoo! All kinds of craziness. One of our inflatables, buzzing the *Kvitungen*, has a steering failure and rams right into the Norwegian ship at high speed. The three people on board the inflatable are thrown overboard, and the *Kvitungen*'s crew pulls them out of the water. I think that's pretty classy, especially when just that morning we'd delivered a message to them, asking that the hunt be stopped.

I wait until very late that night, when everybody's asleep, and then slip over to the *Kvitungen* in an inflatable. I spend a couple of hours with the captain, drinking rum. Not raising the issue that keeps us apart, just talking about what we have in common – the sea. It was his instinctive belief in that deeper seaman's code that compelled him to pull my crew from the water. I respect that and want him to know it.

I've never discussed that middle-of-the-night visit with anyone. Maybe I should have. It's the things we have in common that will save this world, not our differences.

Aboard the *Rainbow Warrior* during these days, I'm about as content as I get. The campaign is wildly successful, and I've even got Annette tucked into my bunk for part of the voyage. Can't for the life of me remember why she was off school, but it was good to have the moral support.

About day eight, the *Kvitungen* anchors, so the *Warrior*'s crew goes ashore. I was just about to enjoy my first decent meal in a few days when one of the press guys comes running in to say the Norwegian ship has weighed anchor. I run down to the quayside. Not pleased. It seems like I can't turn my back for five minutes. In the ensuing panic, a woman reporting for ITN falls in the water. We get back to the *Warrior*, and you know what? Nothing happens. We just chase around after the *Kvitungen* for a couple more days.

But that's okay, we're still on the front page.

Day ten, actually evening ten, about six o'clock, the Department of Fisheries has a press conference, and bans Pete from it. So, sensible man that he is, he goes to the bar. Which is where he sits, nursing a pint, when the full pack of press comes running at him. Fisheries has announced that they're calling the whole thing off. Seems the Prime Minister's Office has received almost 17,000 letters of protest.

On the *Warrior*, we'd have been celebrating, if only we knew. In the flurry of interviews, that's the one thing that's been neglected. Nobody's told us that it's over. So when we see the *Kvitungen* steam away, full speed ahead, we pursue, figuring maybe this is the start of the hunt. About ten o'clock that night, and thirty miles away, we get a call from Pete. Come home. We've won.

It takes us almost two hours to get back to Kirkwall Harbour. We cruise into a halo of light, artificially created by the press, but still very nice. There are champagne corks popping and cheering, so much cheering. I'll never forget our captain, Pete Bouquet, when he can't get his orders heard over the crowd. He barks out, 'Excuse me, I'm trying to park this ****in' boat.'

It's okay, we've landed.

Only the Pope's death keeps us off the front pages that day, and it doesn't really matter. We're on the map. This kind of publicity is high-octane fuel to an organization that draws its power from the people.

Things start to move really fast, even for me. By now Greenpeace has something like forty 'branches' around the world. Really more like 'buds' just starting to bloom – points on the globe where people with a concern for the environment do good work in our name, although they don't necessarily have any legal standing. But by the end of 1978, we do have *official* Greenpeace offices in Canada, USA, New Zealand, Australia, France and the UK. We also have groups ready to open offices under the Greenpeace banner in Germany, The Netherlands and Denmark. Whew. Not bad for basically three years work.

The organization is really an alliance of three spheres which have grown up around the campaigns in each area – North America, the South Pacific and Europe. But Europe is where the action is, where the power base is growing fastest, and solidifying.

I've more or less got the European groups operating under one banner, but sometimes that's as tough as taking on the Icelandic whalers. Everybody's so bloody concerned about their national issues. I want them to think *internationally*. Screw the borders. They don't exist, except in people's minds. They sure don't exist for the whales, or for nuclear fall-out, or for chemical pollution.

That autumn, while I'm struggling with the politics of this international organization – at least I *want* it to be international – I get a letter that makes me think we just might be getting somewhere.

It's from Sadruddin Aga Khan, *the* Aga Khan's brother. He's heard about our campaigns and he wants to know if he can help!

Oh, yes, he can help. We arrange to meet in Geneva, in a few weeks' time.

Chapter Fourteen

HE'S STANDING BESIDE a carved antique desk, alone. My first impression is that I'm looking into a mirror, only the image staring back is considerably more handsome. Prince Sadruddin Aga Kahn is about my height, about my build, about my age, and he's wearing a tweed jacket, which is my uniform of choice when it's necessary to wear something other than jeans. He even likes his coffee the same way, short and strong.

We're at Château Bellerive on the shores of Lake Geneva, the Prince's main residence. And in spite of his fabulous wealth and Harvard-educated English, I feel immediately at home in this man's presence. He's a sailor and a skier. He appreciates a beautiful woman – as a young man, his name was linked in the gossip columns with a number of lovely ladies. Born in Paris, educated in the States, a citizen of Iran, and a resident of Switzerland, he's also as inter-national as I'm beginning to feel, and as I'd like my organization to be.

He's quite relaxed and friendly, yet there's a sense of distance from him, of privacy, as if he protects his personal self from public view. I know the feeling.

Sadri, as I'll come to know him, had been the United Nations Commissioner for Refugees until a year earlier. In 1977, he left the UN and started his own independent commission – called the Bellerive Foundation – studying world problems. That's why he's written to us. He sees Greenpeace making waves on the nuclear issue, and on whaling, and he thinks we might be natural allies. He's right.

I'd thought earlier about asking the Prince outright for a big financial contribution, but as we talk it occurs to me that Sadri's connections are probably worth as much as his bank account. And, anyway, I don't want to ask him for money; I want to work *with* him. Don't yet know when or how this new alliance will be needed, but by the end of the meeting I do know he'll be there when I call.

Fantastic! When you consider that not ten years before, I was a California real estate developer who didn't see much beyond his own nose.

And while I had just been following my nose – my instincts – at the beginning of this adventure in environmentalism, now I have glimpses of how far it can go. With the numbers who are joining Greenpeace, and with friends like Sadri, we can do anything, we can change the world. We just have to stay focused and all keep moving in the same direction. Like that'll be easy!

The bigger the organization gets, the harder it is to control. Example: Iceland, 1979. The *Rainbow Warrior* makes two voyages to the whaling grounds. The first is very successful.

By June of 1979, we're much better equipped to have a go at Iceland than we were the previous year. We've got a hydrophone that will pick up whale sounds. We've got experience. And most of all, we've got a much, much faster inflatable. The RI28 (stands for Rigid Inflatable – 28-feet long) can be quickly launched from the bow with a derrick, and can travel at speeds of up to 35 knots. We won't have any trouble catching the whalers.

We head directly for the mouth of the fjord, and quite quickly into a confrontation with the whaler *Hvalur 8*. Nick Hill and Chris Robinson leap into the RI28 and they're off! Way off, zooming over the horizon. They have no trouble catching the whaler but the

Rainbow Warrior doesn't have a hope of keeping up, and the direction finder isn't working.

We can hear Nick and Chris, driving back and forth in front of the *Hvalur 8*. We hear Nick saying, 'He missed that shot, he missed that shot!' Then, 'Jesus, he's released the safety catch. He's pointing right at us.' Then silence.

We are utterly helpless. The only thing we know is what direction they were going when they went over the horizon, now three, now five, now twelve hours ago. They're halfway between Greenland and Iceland, in a big rough sea. All alone, except for a whaling ship, which as you can guess probably doesn't have their best interests in mind.

We use the only thing we've got: the sky. A message comes from RI28: 'Can you see that shaft of light? It's to the south of us. Repeat. To the south of us.' Great, except there are shafts of light all over the horizon. We just keep going in the general direction, nothing else we can do. The *Warrior*'s bridge is tense and silent, each of us praying to the spirits, hoping for a miracle.

Around midnight, still light at this latitude, we spot a whaler on the horizon. Maybe. Just maybe.

As we draw closer, we see the inflatable, buzzing back and forth in front of the *Hvalur 8*, like a fly bothering a charging bull. Out in front of them both is a pod of fin whales.

We launch the old inflatables and join the action. And let me tell you, it's not as easy as it looks on film. At water level, you feel so small, so fragile, cutting in front of that gigantic steel hull, looking way up at a hunter behind his harpoon-launcher. You're pretty sure he won't fire directly at you. And you're pretty sure the ship won't run you down on purpose. But this is a war of nerves, and nerves can give out. One mistake, and we pay with our lives.

This goes on for hours, until at about 7 a.m. the *Hvalur 8* just stops dead. Maybe they're getting tired, too. I know I'm about ready to pass out.

We refuel the inflatables, and sure enough, three and a half hours later, black smoke comes belching out of the ship's funnel, and they start hunting again. We pursue.

Late that afternoon, I'm on the bridge of the *Rainbow Warrior* when it happens. The whaler's captain gets a shot off, and an injured fin whale leaps out of the water in agony. For the next several minutes it looks as if the whale is pulling the whaler. I radio Nick and tell him to get the hell out of there. Don't want to risk the harpoon cable slicing through one of our guys.

Hvalur 8's captain fires a second harpoon. From the *Warrior*, we watch for an awful hour as the sea turns red. Then the whaler fires again, a *coup de grâce*, and we are close enough to hear the harpoon's explosive tip detonate inside the whale, with a sound like muffled thunder. Then silence.

I'm not one of those people who's seriously soft on animals. I don't think they are, individually, as important as human beings. But this is disgusting.

When we pull into Reykjavik the next day for repairs to the RI28, we're arrested and charged with harassing Icelandic fishing vessels within their 200-mile economic zone. We sit it out for three days, and then late one afternoon decide to make a run for the 12-mile limit. We're about halfway and I'm actually starting to think we might make it, so I go below for a nap. I am just dozing off when I get called back to the bridge. There's a coastguard gunboat tailing us. Oh, hell. They'd like us to return to Reykjavik. Pronto. I stall, by radio, as long as I can. Sloooowly read them the legal opinion we've pulled together. But, remember, these guys won the Cod War against the Royal Navy. I'm not planning to get into anything more serious than a war of words.

I insist that they record in their logbook that we are returning *under protest*. We ask for sea room and turn around.

Walking back and forth between the Reykjavik docks and the lawyer's office, I start to notice something. People sure are friendly.

I don't know if it's because of the graphic film footage of the kill or the courage of people like Chris and Nick and many others. Whatever it is, we're starting to sway public opinion. I can feel it. So when the authorities agreed to release us if we agree to head directly back to the UK, it's okay with me.

They may have won the battle, but I think we're winning the war.

You may have noticed by now that we always time these voyages to the whaling grounds to coincide with the opening of the International Whaling Commission's annual conference. At the 1979 conference, in London again, Iceland refuses to support a ban on sperm whaling, but does end up supporting some conservationist measures, such as an Indian Ocean whale sanctuary and a partial ban on deep-sea whaling.

It looks to me as if public opinion is getting to the Icelandic government, so it's time for us to ease up and let the people do the work. This is not the time to push Iceland up against the wall!

Unfortunately, the crew of the *Rainbow Warrior* doesn't agree. They essentially mutiny.

At our last press conference in Reykjavik, we said we'd be back if Iceland voted against the moratorium on sperm whaling. I want to give it a little time before we honour that promise. With an injunction hanging over our heads, we could lose the ship. Even more important, Iceland's position on whaling is softening. The last thing I want to do right now is get them mad. It'll backfire on us. They need room to back down a little gracefully.

But the *Warrior*'s crew is living in their own world – very black and white, good guys and bad buys, no room for compromise. I understand the kind of revolutionary psychology at work. These guys feel like warriors. Hell, they *are* warriors. They want to have a go at 'the enemy'.

As much as I admire their courage, I can't write enough expletives to tell you how mad I am when Pete Wilkinson calls to say Denise and Chris and the others are heading back to Iceland, and Pete's going with them.

I get another call from Pete a couple of weeks later. They're in Reykjavik, under arrest and flat broke. Pete's proud that he refused to return to Reykjavik under power, and the coastguard had to spend gas money towing the *Warrior*. (To this day, he thinks the Icelanders respect Greenpeace more for going back again in the big seas and almost constant darkness of November. I don't agree.)

I fly in with a hundred quid, which the crew promptly spends on a little rice, and a lot of booze. I feel like the father who said 'I told you so.' With the help of the lawyers, I'll get them out of this mess, but it's a bloody hassle and it's accomplished less than nothing. If we'd been Iceland's conscience the year before, now we're just the enemy. A proud nation has lost face. It'll be tough now for them to back away from whaling. My guys have effectively shot us in the foot.

Frustrating! It feels sometimes like I'm the only one who realizes what we've got here. We aren't a little band of outlaws, anymore. We've captured the public's imagination, and if we stay focused, we can win big time. But it's like in badminton; if you lose concentration, your game will fall apart.

While all this crap is going on with the third Icelandic voyage, or maybe I should call it the mutiny, I'm trying to stay focused on the real game, building an organization so big – and popular – that no democratic government can afford to ignore us. If we've got the public behind us, we can force their governments to stop whaling, ban nuclear testing, clean up the environment – all the things that need to get done in order for our children to make it safely into the twenty-first century. But we can't do any of that if we're seen as a fringe organization of eco-freaks. We need to be so big that we can rightfully say we speak for the people. Politicians need to respect us, maybe even fear us. When they're deciding public policy, they need to know that our popularity can sway elections. For them, or against.

And I know I'm about to repeat myself here, but it's important! Getting this next point across *inside* Greenpeace was one of my biggest challenges in building the organization. Since most environmental issues are absolutely international – whales don't stop at border crossings, and neither does pollution – we need to work together internationally. Partly it would just make us bigger, and our voice harder to ignore for any government. But it also would mean that we can focus our energy on the paramount issues, instead of dissipating it getting involved in little national campaigns. Essentially, I don't want to build small fires around the world that could go out in the first big storm. I want to build one big fire that *can't* be put out.

I'm succeeding in Europe. Occasional mutinies aside, we're getting big and strong, and, for the most part, we speak with one voice. But in 1979, in North America, a civil war has broken out within the organization that threatens to destroy them, and weaken us all.

Greenpeace Vancouver is in trouble. Floundering under a huge debt, they're threatening to take the good Greenpeace name under with them. Looks to me like Vancouver is jealous that San Francisco is doing so much better at fund-raising, so they've decided to sue the San Francisco group over use of the Greenpeace name. San Francisco has counter-sued. Talk about shooting yourself in the foot, again. It shouldn't happen, but it looks like it's going to. Here we are a couple of steps away from creating a powerful international organization, and they want to get into a schoolyard squabble about who can join the team.

I gather as much intelligence as possible, and then fly into Vancouver a couple of days before the case is scheduled to go to court.

We meet in a lawyer's office near the docks. It's all ferns and hardwood, very tasteful. A funny setting for a street fight. There are four or five Greenpeace Vancouver people in the room, including my old friend Bob Hunter. But mostly it's me toe-to-toe with the

July 1982. Victory! The International Whaling Commission passes the moratorium on commercial whaling. Sidney Holt on the left, and on the right Ian MacPhail of IFAW (International Fund for Animal Welfare).

After the victorious IWC meeting of 1982, protesters finally have a reason to rejoice – and later join in with the festivities on Brighton beach.

Bono uses his celebrity for a good cause. U2 joins us on the beach at Sellafield for an anti-nuclear protest.

Early 1984, off the New England coast. From left to right, colleague Patti Forkan, Sir Peter Scott, and American newsman Walter Cronkite.

In the final hours of our innocence. The *Rainbow Warrior* in Auckland Harbour, 10 July 1985, shortly before she was sunk by the French, and our much-loved photographer, Fernando Pereira, killed.

The following day. The *Rainbow Warrior* on her side in Auckland Harbour. The dove of peace struggles to keep her head above water.

The bombing ripped a huge hole in the *Warrior*, and the aftershock reverberated through our organization for years. I went after the French for damages, although there were those in Greenpeace who felt any settlement would be blood money. I thought it was the best way open to publicly establish France's culpability.

With my friend and ally, American media mogul Ted Turner, at his retreat on St Phillips Island, South Carolina in the mid-1980s.

1986. Being treated like royalty, *by* royalty. Prince Bernhard of the Netherlands presents me with the Order of the Golden Ark.

Greenpeace protests piles of rubbish at the US Antarctic base.

1989. The world watches through our dramatic photographs. Greenpeace protesters fly banners to protest Japanese whaling in the Southern Ocean around Antarctica.

I went to the Ukraine in 1990 with a group of doctors, including my brother Drew, to see what could be done for the children of Chernobyl. I took great pleasure in meeting the people – such survivors! But overall, the experience was profoundly saddening.

My friend Bryan Adams wears his heart on his sleeve. He was a major player in the campaign to save Antarctica.

Greenpeace made several trips to Antarctica to claim the continent for all citizens of the world, not just the oil companies! In 1995, we succeeded in getting it declared a World Park.

Greenpeace crew members raise a glass to World Park Antarctica. That's my old friend and occasional adversary, Pete Wilkinson, in the middle foreground.

28 August 1995. They never give up! A French patrol frigate looms over the shoulder of the *MV Greenpeace* during an anti-nuclear protest.

Back again, 23 years after my first voyage to Mururoa. Preparing to get lost on the atoll and delay French nuclear testing, underground this time.

With Henk Haazen (left) and Chris Robinson, back on board *Vega* after our 'holiday' on the atoll. Didn't realize until I got home to Italy that this little protest made some serious headlines.

Home is where the heart is, my organic
olive farm near Paciano, Umbria.
November 1999, harvest time.

After David's death, four of his five grandchildren gathered
at Paciano to remember him. In this picture from the left,
Kerin, Julia and Lisa – David's eldest who spoke at the
memorial service of tolerance and forgiveness.

current Vancouver chairman, and one of the earliest members of Greenpeace in Vancouver, a fuzzy-haired academic type called Pat Moore. Normally, I'd say he's a smart guy, but this isn't a smart move. He's afraid the Americans will grab too much power. It's such a small-minded typically Canadian point of view – always worrying about the big bad Americans – that it's all I can do to stop myself from being really insulting. I do say something about not wanting to step on anybody's little knackers. Really, why worry about the Americans? Or the Canadians? Think beyond your little North American boundaries. Think international. That's where the power is.

We're there for hours, no food, no booze. Just coffee and endless discussion. Finally, Moore agrees to bring Vancouver, as Canada's head office, into an international Greenpeace – one nation, one vote. In exchange, I agree that Greenpeace Europe will pay off Vancouver's $160,000 debt.

Moore doesn't know I'm bluffing. I haven't yet told our European offices about their major contribution to the cause of internationalism! But I'll worry about that later. If my plan works, I know I'll be able to sell it.

Next stop, San Francisco.

They're relieved the court case has gone away, and it's an easy day's work to pull the twenty or so American offices together into Greenpeace USA. Somebody produces a map, and I draw nine different regions onto it. That's about it. Deceptively simple.

I don't like patting myself on the back, but this day I'm delighted with what I've accomplished. More than delighted, ecstatic! And it's an oddly private ecstasy. I don't think anybody else has really taken in what's happened. The North Americans are just happy the fight's over, and of course I still have to deal with Greenpeace Europe over the little matter of their $160,000 contribution. But I've won big, we've won big, all of us. I've just brought my strong European organization together with the world's democratic superpower.

Overnight, we've increased our power monumentally.

We climb out onto the fire escape afterwards, to toast our success. There's a stunning sunset, and I can see across to Angel Island, Alcatraz and the Golden Gate Bridge. And something else. Another of those moments that nobody outside Greenpeace can ever believe. A rainbow.

Greenpeace International is stirring to life. And the heavens approve. A month later, in November 1979, in Amsterdam, we make it official. The first meeting of the international board is held in our Dutch office at 99 Damrakstrasse, right off Dam Square. With a bit of grumbling, it's agreed that we'll pay off Canada's debt.

Oh, and I'm elected chairman.

Greenpeace is well on its way to becoming *the* environmental organization, the name that springs to mind when you say the word 'environmental', the organization that governments sometimes despise, but must always respect.

I know I haven't always been very nice to my fellows, maybe trampled on a few toes, and sometimes ignored the finer points of leading a democratic organization – like voting first on all the big decisions. But I'm proud of the part I played. If anybody outside the organization remembers me, it's likely to be as 'that crazy guy who sailed to Mururoa'. But I know that to insiders, when the history of Greenpeace is written, pulling the thing together into Greenpeace International will be seen as my biggest victory. That's what gave us our power.

As the new decade opens, 1980, we do have some clout. And we're going to need it.

The 1980s are only a few months old when Pete Wilkinson, Allan Thornton and I head to court in London, looking at jail time. We're charged with defying a court order, in our ongoing campaign against the dumping of nuclear waste at sea.

It started somewhat by chance two years earlier, as the *Warrior* headed southwest towards Spain, from Iceland. We'd noticed 'dumping grounds' marked on our marine charts. Seems we were headed right for the UK's nuclear garbage dump.

Pete Wilkinson and cameraman Tony Marriner went to where the stuff was loaded, at the port of Sharpness, in the Bristol Channel, due west of London. They managed to walk onto the ship that the Atomic Energy Authority had commissioned to do its dirty work. And they got the goods – confirmation that the ship was being loaded with spent nuclear fuel, including nuclear rods, and *that* was clearly illegal.

At the dumping grounds, we shot incredible footage of the *Gem*'s crew dropping barrels right on top of our guys. One campaigner suffered a concussion when a barrel hit the front of his zodiac and flipped him ass-over-bow into the waves of the North Sea. Only fast action from the now-mandatory safety zodiac saved him from drowning. We made sure that footage hit every television screen in Europe, calling renewed attention to the dumping of radioactive waste at sea. Bringing this covert operation into public view didn't endear us to the British authorities. Remember, Margaret Thatcher had just been elected Prime Minister for the first time. With our growing popularity, we're a thorn in the side of the Iron Lady.

We started to make a regular event out of parking at the entrance to Barrow-in-Furness, the nearest port to a nuclear plant at Sellafield, northwestern England. The waste from this plant was going out into the Irish Sea, and we thought people should know about it. We obstructed ships trying to dock. Once we nearly lost a crew, including Pete, when an inflatable was caught between the stern and the rudder of the ship, and crushed. Great footage, though.

We were served with an injunction restraining us from 'causing or assisting in causing or encouraging, any physical obstruction which may impede or interfere with the free navigation of vessels in and out of Barrow Docks, Barrow-in-Furness.'

That was in January 1980.

In March, when a ship called the *Pacific Fisher* arrived at Barrow to unload spent nuclear fuel from Japan, three inflatables launched from the *Rainbow Warrior* began cutting across the *Fisher*'s bow from port to starboard. The next day, we tried to delay the ship's unloading.

The British Transport Docks Board was not pleased. They wanted a pound of flesh – our flesh – and in this political climate I'm a little nervous they just might get it. The Board asked the court to jail Pete, Allan and myself for contempt, and to seize the assets of Greenpeace in Britain. Only Pete was aboard the *Warrior* for the action, but all three of us, as directors of Greenpeace, accepted responsibility.

But we argued that it was never our intention to endanger the ship's navigation, only to prevent it from unloading its deadly cargo.

We have to pay a five-hundred-pound fine from Greenpeace, a hundred quid each from the three of us.

We don't get off so lightly after another nuclear protest in 1983. We tried to disable the discharge pipe at Sellafield. End up with a fifty-thousand-pound fine.

The judge called our activities indefensible, but said 'that they are honourable people, I accept. I do not think prison is the place for people like them.'

It's almost worth it to hear a British judge call us honourable! We've come a long way.

But in 1980, it's out of the frying pan, into the fire. Just a month after our court appearance on the *Pacific Fisher* case, the *Warrior* is arrested in Spain.

By now Spain has joined the International Whaling Commission, but we've been hearing reports that Spanish whalers are going way over their quota and quietly shipping whale meat to Japan. The *Warrior*'s crew wants to have another go at the whalers, another chance to rally Spanish public opinion.

If I hadn't been quite so preoccupied with the setting up of

Greenpeace International, and with our nuclear campaign, I might have thought this through a little more carefully.

Spain really, really doesn't like us. They've just come out of a long period of Fascist rule, so they're without a history of peaceful protest. And we'd made this macho nation look a little silly with our escape from La Coruna a couple of years earlier.

Just before our arrival, terrorists planted underwater bombs in the harbour and sank two whalers. Wasn't us. Definitely not our style. But Spanish authorities are in no mood to hear philosophical arguments about terrorism versus non-violent direct action.

The second day out, Spanish warships appear and force the *Warrior* into the military port of El Ferrol near the northwest tip of Spain. To ensure there's no midnight dash this time, they take a vital piece of the propeller shaft.

Now what? The ship is tied up to a military pier and put under round-the-clock guard. Our crew can go ashore to the local bars for a drink but that's about it.

A Spanish court rules that the *Rainbow Warrior* will only be freed when we pay fines equivalent to the value of the whales we've saved, and they put that at a half a million dollars.

The world press is on our side. The Spanish could not care less.

The weeks roll by in stalemate. There's no way we'll pay any fine, but we desperately need the ship back. The *Warrior*'s absolutely become our symbol. The ship and Greenpeace are almost synonymous.

There's nothing for it but a jailbreak.

To pull that off, we'll first have to replace the thrust block, the part of the propeller that the Spanish authorities have removed. We get a copy made in the UK, and then Tony Marriner and a colleague smuggle it across the French border in my old Volkswagen van. Now we just have to get it into a Spanish military port, swarming with guards, and onto a ship that's under 24-hour watch.

Tony devises a plan that makes good use of the crew's bad habits.

He pulls the van up right beside a police Land Rover, gets out, meanders up to the *Warrior* where he meets his mates and joins their nightly bar patrol.

A couple of nights later, they're joined in the bar by another mate, an older fellow. Me.

Around midnight, we stumble back towards the ship, pretending to be a little worse for wear. The biggest of our guys, Athel von Koettlitz, stops at the van and pretends to fumble around for something inside, while the rest of us create a diversion of drunken revelry. We do quite a good job. Athel manages to stumble up to the *Warrior* without raising suspicion. He's staggering under the weight of the thrust block, but the military police just think he's had a few too many. Unfortunately, we hadn't calculated on the low tide! Athel has to jump twenty feet down onto the ship. Rips his arm from wrist to elbow. But he makes it!

Over the next few days, we talk our escape plan through, over and over. We know there'll be one crack at this. If we fail, we'll probably lose the *Rainbow Warrior* for good. I leave it up to Captain John Castle to say when we go. I'm here to make sure he has all the information. Example: I notice that when they change our guard there are often two or three minutes when nobody's watching the ship very closely. The late afternoon shift-change looks particularly opportune, since it's already dark at this time of year, November.

Quietly, quietly, we install the thrust block. Then intrepid Tony – he's a photographer, an inflatable expert, *and* a diver – slips below the water to scrape the seaweed off the *Warrior*'s propeller.

We're ready.

And on 8 November when I walk into the saloon and see the crew all sitting quietly, dressed in dark clothing, I know John Castle has made his decision. It's tonight.

At about 6.45 p.m., the changing of the guard begins. From the darkened bridge, John and I can see the two guards standing in a pool of light, deep in conversation. One guard draws the other away, into the street beyond the gate.

It's a dream come true.

The engines come on. Thank God. That was a question mark, after five idle months. We'd turned them on a couple of times on the pretext of wanting the lights, but we didn't want to be too conspicuous, so we haven't exactly tested them out.

Tony and Chris Robinson hurl the lines on board, and we ease out into the harbour.

The weeds that have accumulated on the boat's bottom during its time in harbour slow us down. We're only making about seven knots, and we're anxious as hell. When bright lights suddenly illuminate the *Warrior*, we dive for the decks, half-expecting bullets to rip through the hull. But it's only a car's headlights. We're travelling a narrow channel to the sea.

Through the night and into the morning, the Spanish navy *is* looking for us. But in the wrong place. First off, they aren't expecting us to be moving so slowly. Many thanks to the Angel of Seaweed. We can actually see the helicopter lights ahead of us. Also, we don't immediately set a course for the UK, as the Spanish expect. Instead, we hug the coast, creeping across the French border.

When we come into port at Jersey around midnight, journalists are waiting for us. We step off the *Warrior* into a pool of light from atop some guy's television camera. By now the press so loves us that somebody's even brought a bottle of champagne.

And that's how we look on the next day's news, unshaven seadogs quaffing back bubbly. Home. Free. And bloody famous.

Chapter Fifteen

THE SUITS AT the Whaling Commission may be a little shaken by our growing popularity, but they're sure not letting that get in the way of business-as-usual. The 1980 IWC meeting is a bloody disaster.

Peru, Chile, South Korea and Spain have joined the Commission since the last meeting, and they're all pro-whaling countries, all of them whaling for the Japanese market. When the vote on a sperm whale moratorium comes up, it's defeated. And the part that really gets to me is that Canada votes with the whalers. Not because my home country has a whaling industry, no, the logic is much loopier than that. The Canadian commissioner thinks Japan and the Soviet Union might leave the IWC if the moratorium's voted in. It's such Canadian logic – do nothing in case you piss somebody off. Infuriating. I feel like we're rowing backwards, and my country's got one of the oars. I'm embarrassed to be a Canadian.

The nation's biggest newspaper, the *Toronto Star*, runs an editorial calling Canada's vote a shame and a disgrace.

In Brighton, on the beach in front of the Metropole Hotel where the meetings are being held, protesters burn a Canadian flag. Can't say I blame them.

I retire to the bar of the Metropole, depressed as hell, and order a rum and coke. I'd really like to chuck it all. I'm 48 years old, broke, exhausted, homeless, pretty much estranged from my children.

And for what? All this bashing around in boats is great for the young guys, but I don't really need another grand adventure, had enough for ten lifetimes. If this isn't going anywhere, maybe it's time to think about getting out. Leave it to the kids, and start making some money for my old age. Which feels like it started yesterday. God, I'm tired.

I've just ordered another rum when a slender, grey-haired gentleman asks to join me. I know him to see him. As the founder of the World Wildlife Fund, Sir Peter Scott is probably *the* most famous champion of the natural world. He's a fixture at IWC meetings, a member of the British delegation, but we've never really talked. Frankly, I consider him several rungs up the evolutionary ladder from me, especially right now. Feeling like a pariah, after Canada's unbelievable performance, I'm especially pleased that Sir Peter would even acknowledge me.

His intelligent blue eyes peer intently at me over a pair of half-moon glasses, and I suddenly know that this isn't a social call.

My depression starts to clear in that instant, and it takes only about two more seconds for us to agree on a strategy. The whalers are working from a different rulebook than the rest of us. They don't care about world opinion – for years everybody from the UN Environment Conference on down has been saying there should be a moratorium on whaling. The whaling nations don't seem to care about wiping out the whole species. They're stuck in some strange parallel universe, where the rules of the Commission are all that counts. Like God himself wrote them.

Okay, then, we'll have to get *inside* the IWC, and beat them by their rules.

We move to a table in the corner of the Metropole bar, and Sir Peter takes out a little notebook. We quietly write down the names of every country either of us thinks might be persuaded to join the IWC on the side of the whales, and once inside, vote to end whaling. For all we care they can be land-locked countries; the IWC is open to everybody. They just have to understand that all of us have a stake in the fate of the whales.

We'll take the shortest route possible, using every contact we have, at the highest level of government. If we don't have a contact, we'll find somebody who does.

It's an age-old strategy: if you can't beat them, join them … and then beat them.

We also talk about ways to put more pressure on the marginal whaling nations, countries like South Africa, Denmark and Canada, which sometimes vote with the whalers and sometimes abstain.

Again, we'll use contacts if we can. Otherwise, it'll be the strong arm of democracy. Together our two organizations represent a lot of people. And if we can build an alliance of all the conservationist groups, it'll appear a formidable force to any democratic government, a significant voting bloc.

The tough year I just went through suddenly makes sense. Ramming all our various national offices together into Greenpeace International was more an instinct than a plan. But now that there's a project that needs a truly international organization, well, we've got one.

As I step outside into the moist sea air of Brighton beach, I'm feeling pretty good. I love a good fight, and there's no win more enjoyable than one from behind.

But I don't want to leave the impression that we were starting totally from scratch, and that it was all just Sir Peter and me. This was the beginning of a beautiful friendship, and a powerful alliance. But we had help, lots of it. And some serious groundwork had already been laid.

The small island nation of Seychelles, in the Indian Ocean, was already an important player, along with a couple of British friends of theirs, and of mine. The best-selling nature writer Lyall Watson lived in the Seychelles for a couple of years and became friends with the President, France-Albert René. Watson and the President got talking about how you never saw whales anymore in the Indian Ocean. René was particularly concerned because the Japanese were just finishing three years of so-called scientific whaling in the area, with a view to opening a new commercial whaling stream. At the end of 1978, Seychelles decides to join the IWC.

That simple, really. The right people in the right place at the right time. In the early days of the environmental movement, we got a lot done that way.

As an interested observer at the IWC, Lyall Watson met British biologist Sidney Holt, a mad scientist type with flowing beard and flying hair. Sidney had represented a UN agency at the Whaling Commission for many years. Watson put Holt together with President René, and the two of them worked out the idea of proposing a moratorium on sperm whaling, and an Indian Ocean sanctuary for all whales.

Together, and with the World Wildlife Fund's help, they convinced a number of Indian Ocean countries to join the IWC and support the sanctuary. And that's what got the Indian Ocean sanctuary passed at the IWC in 1979, the year before Sir Peter and I have that drink together in the bar of the Metropole.

So it's pretty obvious what we have to do now. If we can quietly, quietly encourage enough pro-conservation nations to join the IWC, we can get the long-awaited moratorium passed before there's time for the opposition to react.

But it's got to be fast, and it's got to be quiet, or Japan will counter-attack.

I get that surge of energy you feel when, in a flash, you see your opponent's game, and how to beat him. I feel incredibly focused. This next year will be crucial.

Since secrecy's important, I give the project code names. The work with other non-governmental organizations, trying to keep all the NGOs heading in the same direction, I call Project Mary, after my mother. The work we'll do with national governments, trying to persuade them to join the IWC, I call Project George, after my dad.

It might sound foolishly cloak-and-dagger, but it's important! If we have a leak, if the Japanese find out what we're up to, you can say goodbye to the whales.

On Project George, one of my first moves is to meet with Sadri. Prince Sadruddin Aga Khan will be our key to persuading Middle Eastern countries to join the IWC. None of the rest of us has connections outside the West. It'd be tough for even Sir Peter to walk through some of the doors that are open to Sadri. He agrees to set up several meetings, including one with King Hussein in Jordan and one with Anwar Sadat in Egypt.

In the autumn of 1980 I make the tough decision to move the Greenpeace International office from Amsterdam to Washington, DC. We're recruiting new members in The Netherlands at the rate of about a thousand a month. If we're ever going to see that kind of action in America, ever going to tap the huge potential of Greenpeace USA, it'll take some hands-on attention.

And we need to convince the American government to use their influence with the marginal pro-whaling nations. Not even Washington can sway Japan, I know, and obviously not the Soviet Union, but they might get to countries like Peru, Chile, South Korea and Spain. And that could get us the moratorium.

You'd think that, given how little time I spend in any one place, this move to Washington wouldn't be a big deal, personally. But I really feel it. I write in my diary for the week of 3 October 1980: 'Sad to leave Hoorn, Annette. Tough to leave Holland. Have no home.' Annette and I don't officially break it off, but I know in my heart that I'm lousy at turning back.

The guy sitting ahead of me on the plane stands up and asks me why everybody's lining up to buy Scotch. I tell him, 'Because some folks are going home ... to their own homes.' Feeling a little sorry for myself, I guess.

But, in fact, I do see quite a bit of my old home with Annette during the next year, even welcoming 1981 in from Hoorn. I leave a colleague in Washington, a tough young Brit named Cornelia Durrant who had been working with Lyall Watson and Sidney Holt on the Seychelles delegation to the IWC. I'm back and forth to Europe constantly, meeting with Sir Peter, meeting with Sadri, travelling between our various offices, and the other NGOs. Trying to keep everybody focused on persuading enough pro-conservation countries into the Whaling Commission to end the bloody butchery.

It feels like we're gaining momentum. At the CITES meeting – Convention on International Trade in Endangered Species – there's overwhelming support for a resolution putting an end to the international trade in most whale products. That's seriously important! If Japan can't buy whale meat from other nations, then for many countries there won't be any reason for whaling, since their kill goes to Japan.

On a grey, wet English summer day, we're back in Brighton for the 1981 Whaling Commission meeting. Behind police barricades, hundreds of demonstrators stand in the drizzle outside the Metropole Hotel, singing to the tune of 'Give Peace A Chance'. 'All we are saying, is peace for the whales.' Above them floats a 28-foot blue-and-white inflatable whale called Flo. Sir Peter and I cross the street to thank them for their support, and for providing such a cheerful, human send-off for those of us about to do battle with the suits inside.

We're all incredibly tense. The plan to encourage conservationist nations to join the Whaling Commission has worked. China and India and Oman and Kenya have joined the IWC, as well as St Vincent, St Lucia, Dominica, Jamaica, Costa Rica and Uruguay. That should be enough to get the 75 per cent margin needed to pass a moratorium. But we know Japan's been heavily lobbying China for a pan-Oriental policy, and we're not sure if we have other soft spots.

As the meeting opens, I'm elated when the American commissioner, a big bear of a man, stands up to read a message from President Ronald Reagan: 'Our cooperative efforts so far to regulate whaling have been tragically unsuccessful and species after species have been successfully overexploited and reduced to protective status. We have no basis to believe that commercial whaling will not continue to reduce whale stocks.'

Wow! To come from a conservative, business-oriented President, this is good. I can see that it makes an impression on the South American delegations and on South Africa.

The first important vote is on a proposal to end all whaling.

As each commissioner barks out his vote – a simple yes or no – I'm scratching them down on a piece of paper, and I get that sinking feeling. Please don't let this be a repeat of last year.

The vote goes: Yes – 14; No – 8; Abstain – 4.

We've won a moral victory, but because of the IWC's 75 per cent majority rule to change a regulation, that's all. I hear someone from Friends of the Earth sum it up for reporters: 'The nations of the IWC voted two to one to stop whaling, but the slaughter of these magnificent creatures will continue.'

When we step outside at the break, I see a very disheartened group of protesters standing on the seawall across from the hotel. Even their mascot, Flo, looks a little less buoyant, floating against the grey sky.

'Don't worry,' I tell them, 'we're stronger than we look right now.'

God, I hope I'm right.

That afternoon, Japan's control of the whaling bloc begins to crack.

The IWC's technical committee must approve resolutions before they're put to the plenary session. It reports that two conservationist resolutions will be voted on by the convention as a whole before this session ends. One is the ban, for most whales, of a particularly cruel type of harpoon. The other is the moratorium on sperm whaling!

As the week rolls on, the buzz in the room is constant, and so is the action in the hallways and the bar. Lobbyists from both sides work on the fence-sitters. I don't go to bed as long as there's a conversation to be had, a vote to be swayed. It's really intense.

On Saturday the delegations reassemble in the Winter Room for the final voting.

The harpoon ban passes.

The chairman begins to read the motion to set a zero quota for sperm whales. As the votes are called out, finally it all seems worth it.

Country after country, YES! Only Japan casts a dissenting vote. It is 25–1, for the whales. At least one species is protected.

It's a beginning.

We have 12 months to build support for a total moratorium on commercial whaling, 12 months during which we know the Japanese will be working like hell against us.

That autumn we hold a strategy meeting aboard Sidney Holt's houseboat in London. We painstakingly review each vote from the IWC meeting. Who can we move to our side? Who might we lose? Who else can we convince to join?

And there's a great omen for me, personally, about this time. My old boat *Vega* turns up in California, a bit the worse for wear, but still my *Vega*, the boat on which a private Canadian citizen challenged the French state, and won. It's got to be a good sign.

Greenpeace buys *Vega*, and I put together a crew to go again to Mururoa. I'm maybe just a little stir-crazy from the endless meetings of the last year, but there's also a good political reason. France has stopped atmospheric nuclear testing at Mururoa, but they're still testing underground. And now a report has been leaked to the French press that reveals that the atoll has sunk about five feet and that there's a big crack – a good chance it's leaking radiation. So if the fall-out didn't get the islanders, maybe the polluted fish will. Jesus, it's terrible.

I persuade a couple of the old *Rainbow Warrior* crew to come with me. Tony Marriner's a hell of a navigator, as well as a radio operator and a diver, and by now Chris Robinson is one of the ablest seamen I know, plus a great cook and even better company. I join the boat in Manzanillo, Mexico, and bring with me Brice Lalonde, my old Paris colleague. Six months earlier Brice ran for the French presidency, under the Ecology Party banner, so he's got some stature in France. You may recall I lived at Brice's house for a while in Paris and – foolishly – got involved with his lady. Don't know that I'll be able to bring myself to raise that topic, or that he'd want me to, but I welcome the chance to be in Brice's company and somehow put the past behind us.

Off Mururoa, we encounter *Vega*'s old enemy, *Hippotame*, and get a warning that we'll be arrested if we cross the French territorial 12-mile limit around Mururoa. Brice relays a letter back to Mitterand via the commander at Mururoa. It asks that France suspend their atomic testing programme and take the initiative in proposing a Comprehensive Test Ban Treaty.

France decides to ignore us. For forty days.

We're getting a little bored, and more irritable.

Tony and I have a disagreement about his navigation, and he goes on strike for a day and a half, until I apologize for doubting him.

We have some tequila on board, one of those bottles with a worm in the bottom. Inevitably, we crack it open in an attempt to beat back the ennui. I end up with the last shot and just can't face the worm. When I refuse, Chris – who's our cook, remember – takes the thing and tells me I'll have eaten it by the time I get off the boat. Chris being a man of his word, I imagine I did.

Finally, on the fortieth day, we're running out of food and water, and about to give up when we receive a message, relayed from the

Greenpeace office in Paris. The French won't agree to stop under-ground testing. They will agree to an independent scientific survey of Mururoa's flora and fauna.

We decide to call that a victory and head home.

The next six months are a blur, mostly travelling fast towards the 1982 IWC meetings, and getting those crucial votes to end whaling.

My diary from 5 March, four months before the IWC meeting, gives you an idea of the level we were working at:

Argentina – diplomatic pouch; USA to Argentina

USA – coastal whaling as long as eaten locally

Chile – Lyall says Chilean rep was advised to vote with Japan

India – Cassandra keep an eye on this

Norway – David to go

China – wait for Sidney's report

South Africa – telephone rumours, withdraw

Russia – Sadruddin with me.

We are so close, pushing hard. I ricochet between exhaustion and euphoria. Maybe that's why my diary's getting so much use. Flying from Washington to Vancouver to visit my folks that spring, I even get a little poetic:

Sailing – the love is its unpredictability.

The front moves below us
man above the clouds.

Three years in the Pacific
first full use of the hair shirt.

Blasting back to Vancouver.

South Dakota: nine kids and an old log cabin.
Montana – it was a start.

Scratching through the grey area.
Survival is the problem.

Past the plain,
the cabin
to the high mountains.

Returning home
the plains, the high peaks
the sun crashing over the lagoon
the four reasons – the blue blue sky – the passing fronts
the fragrance the flower
this delicate world.
And man.

The third week in July 1982, we're back at the Metropole Hotel in Brighton for a rematch. I'm tense as hell, and just as excited.

We just might have the numbers. I'm still fairly embarrassed by my own country's showing. Canada stayed in her favourite position – firmly planted on the fence – couldn't decide whether to support the whalers or the conservationists. But at least we were able to convince Canada to drop out of the International Whaling Commission. Not as good as a vote for the moratorium. But, with the 75 per cent majority rule, it was three times better than a vote against us.

By Friday we are all in a serious state of sleep-deprivation from the endless hushed and hurried meetings to shore up our vote. But as the delegations file into the Winter Room for the big vote, the place fairly hums with energy. You can almost see the buzz. This is it.

The delegates sit in a U-shape, with the non-governmental organizations all sitting behind the delegations at the bottom of the 'U'. It's not a bad vantage point for me. I can't see everybody's face, but I can see body language, and who glances at whom as delegates pass in and out of the room throughout the day. That's important. Seriously. If you really look, you can see which way a vote is moving, long before anything actually happens. Then you've got a chance to get in there and maybe make it go your way.

Seychelles has a proposal on the floor that would effectively end whaling. They're suggesting three years to phase out whaling – give the people reliant on the industry a chance to find something else – and then in 1985/86, the Whaling Commission catch limits on commercial whaling would be zero until further notice.

Japan's been just as busy behind the scenes as we've been all week. I know they have a little notebook like mine. Well, probably something a little fancier, but the same idea – lists of countries, how they're voting, whether or not their vote is firm. And if it isn't, how to get in there and make sure it goes your way.

By now, I know we're strong. And Japan knows.

They're fighting from behind, and it's going to get ugly.

The Japanese delegate takes the floor to say that the moratorium proposal is in violation of the International Whaling Convention. He says it's political, not based on scientific criteria, and science is the only criterion the Commission is supposed to consider. Japan says: 'You cannot change the duties or the obligations provided under this Convention. We therefore maintain that should a proposal for a total moratorium as proposed by the Seychelles delegation lead to the eventual collapse of the IWC the responsibility for such an outcome should not be attributed to my delegation.'

It's a threat. A very effective one. Vote for this moratorium, and just see what happens to your precious whales. Japan will walk out, the IWC will collapse, and the whales will be left with no protection whatever.

I may disagree totally with their point of view on whaling, but I've got to admit, these guys are good. Their threat really spooks some of the conservationists. One really important NGO delegate on our side totally freaks out. Just before the vote she scurries from delegation to delegation, begging conservationist nations to vote *against* the moratorium.

As the vote is being called, the Japanese delegation stands up. Single file, they walk along the side of the room to the back and out the door. Very dramatic. Except I notice that they've left one man behind to vote. Japan's not withdrawing from the IWC.

The electric buzz of energy is still in the room. Only now it's silent, like a vibration underneath the sound of the nations' delegates shouting out their votes.

Netherlands – yes!

New Zealand – yes!

Norway – no.

As the vote rolls through all 37 countries, I scrawl in my little notebook, continually, repeatedly, doing the math. Will we get the three-quarters we need?

It's impossibly close to the very end.

Korea – no.

Mexico – yes!

Monaco – yes!

And that humming vibration erupts into unrestrained cheering!

From the rows of NGOs, and from some of the delegations themselves, comes the sound of absolute joy, a release of hours and days and years of tension. We've won. We've bloody won! We've brought the outside world into this archaic institution, forced the whalers to face world opinion.

We've got the three-quarters majority we need.

The whales are saved!

As the chairman repeatedly thumps his gavel in a hopeless attempt at restoring decorum, the NGOs spill out of the Winter Room into the Brighton summer. Somebody produces the required bottle of champagne. We drink it, and then much, much more. The party goes on all night, on Brighton beach. Some people even go swimming in the chilly English sea. I just stand and watch and smoke and listen to the contented rumble of the rocks tumbling in the surf. A good day's work.

Chapter Sixteen

MY PERSONAL LIFE and Greenpeace are both in a state of flux at the end of 1982.

With the moratorium vote behind us, we don't need to stay based in Washington for lobbying purposes. And it's too far away from our powerbase in Europe. By now we have offices in ten countries, six of those European. We talk about a move to Geneva, which appeals to me because of Sadri, and because – well – it's Geneva. But everything's expensive there, accommodation's hard to find, and the bureaucracy is stifling.

We decide on Lewes, near Brighton in the south of England. It's the perfect location – an hour from London, a half-hour from Gatwick Airport, ten minutes to the Channel ferries. And not expensive.

To tell you the truth, I'm not sure which comes first – sudden clarity that the south of England is the ideal place, or Rose Cottage.

During the long weeks stuck in Brighton for Whaling Commission meetings, to keep from going crazy I'd sometimes take off in the car to explore the countryside. Nine miles out of Brighton, and three miles from Lewes, I come across this fantastic little house with a thatched roof, beautiful big gardens, and a fascinating history; it's just round the corner from a cottage where the British writer Virginia Woolf once lived, and the river where she took her life. But mostly Rose Cottage appeals because it's quite secluded and absolutely peaceful.

Rose Cottage feels like home.

In August 1982, I buy it with the little bit of money I've put aside from the sale of my Canadian property.

And I have an idea about who I want to come home to.

By now, Annette and I have parted for good. There are no hard feelings, only great sadness on both sides. She's a fantastic lady and will always be a good friend. It's difficult to say goodbye, but I just can't get this other woman off my mind – Christina, my old friend Ingemar's daughter.

We've been dancing round each other since we first met in 1976 when she was just 19. Back then, Ingemar was very clear. He wrote me a tough, tough letter, saying that as close as he and I are as friends, he considers me a lousy match for his daughter. Too old, and too many times divorced.

I wrote him back that he didn't need to worry. As much as I wanted Tina, and believed she was the one woman who might be able to make me happy, Tina didn't think she loved *me*. (In fact, Annette thought that's why I couldn't get Tina off my mind, because I couldn't have her.)

Don't know about that kind of psychological crap, but I sure didn't give up. When there were occasional moments of quiet in my crazy schedule, my mind would wander back to Christina. Sometimes I'd send her little poems, written over one too many rum and cokes on long plane flights:

Tina
the old earth
has been good to me
if you could just say
just say
just whisper
like an offshore breeze
yes
we could try.

By the autumn of 1982, I've convinced her to have a go. Tina joins me at Rose Cottage, and her parents even come over for a week at the end of the year. Ingemar and Karin must figure Tina knows her own mind by now – she's 26. But I'm 50, so it's still a little complicated.

Tina's just finding herself, fighting to be her own person. And I'm too old and too selfish to have much patience for her quest.

With decisions to be made on all our campaigns, the move of the office, and the rate at which Greenpeace is growing – almost half a million members by the beginning of 1983 – I'm stretched to my limit.

I'm not sure what would have happened to our relationship, if fate hadn't dealt the next couple of cards.

It's a Thursday morning, 13 January, a clear crisp day. We made love that morning, and so I'm quite late for the office. Just before 9 a.m., we're barrelling along the road towards Lewes. Christina's in the car with me. We power up over the brow of a hill and – wham – into a garbage truck sitting broadside right in the middle of the road.

I'm out cold.

When I come to, I can barely breathe. Broken ribs. But I'm more worried about Christina. Through the shattered windshield, I see her lying on the road, paramedics working on her.

We're both rushed to Sussex Hospital by ambulance. Neither of us seems to have any really serious injuries. But as they're about to X-ray Christina, I have an out-of-the-blue flash that is *totally* serious. I tell them to stop. No X-rays. She's pregnant from our morning's love-making. Somehow, I just know it.

During the next few weeks while we wait for the doctor to confirm my intuition, Christina and I prowl the house like a pair of caged animals. We're both in some pain – physical and mental. I'm crazy about her but, to put it bluntly, we don't make each other very happy day-to-day.

One night a couple of weeks after the accident, I stay up late watching a movie, *A Man Called Horse*, starring the Irish legend Richard Harris. It's just my kind of movie – a man loses everything, and starts over in a simple, primitive life. And he's a lot happier. In the bathroom to take another pain-killer for my ribs, I catch a glimpse in the mirror, stop and stare at this man who appears to have everything – beautiful woman, house, serious work. But the truth is, I don't feel free, or happy. I have failed to take responsibility for my children, and now there might be another on the way. I even have the passing thought that my work for the environment might come out of some kind of guilt. Get a grip, McTaggart. Too many pain-killers.

I'm back in the living room of Rose Cottage, cheering up by listening to Willie Nelson sing 'Blue Skies', when Tina wakes and comes downstairs.

All the days are hurryin' by
When you're in love, my how they fly
Blue days, all of them gone
Nothin' but blue skies from now on.

I want her to come and listen to the music with me, want to connect. But she's too chilly and goes back up to bed. Now that we're finally together in this perfect setting, it feels like we're further apart than ever.

By the beginning of February, we decide it's better if Tina goes back to Sweden for a while. We're not saying goodbye, just struggling to find a way to make it work. Tina's a strong and very private person; I don't think she even tells Ingemar and Karin that we're having problems. She just gets on with it.

I try to get on with it, too, but fate's not finished proving to me that even McTaggarts are just human beings.

I'm in and out of Lewes, dealing with setting up new offices in Sweden and maybe Austria – Greenpeace countries numbers nine and ten. Luckily, I get a top executive director about this time. John Frizell is another of those eccentric professor types, kind of a younger version of Sidney Holt. Frizell keeps the office together. He and Sidney and Sidney's brainy young paramour, Leslie Busby, keep working on our anti-whaling strategy.

I need them all badly, as I seem to be getting worse since the accident, not better. Nobody can figure it out. By mid-March, I'm back in Sussex Hospital, so sick that I think I'm going to die. And unfortunately the doctors agree.

I've got heavy, heavy headaches – unbearable pain at the back of my skull – and I'm drowning in sweat at night. My temperature randomly shoots up and then drops down, leaving me shivering. Things are starting to close in. Sussex Hospital does dozens of blood tests and X-rays and scans and biopsies. Nothing. At one point through a semi-conscious haze, I hear two doctors arguing about what I've got. One thinks it's cancer. The other bets on some kind of blood disorder. It's terrifying.

Three or four people die on the ward during March and April, and I come to know the hospital routine well enough to recognize that the little flag they put on the chart at the end of my bed is not a good sign. It means they think I'm next.

My brother Drew is carefully following my progress – or lack of it – from Vancouver. He begins to think that what I've got sounds an awful lot like an extremely acute version of something from which our father has been suffering for years. Drew goes on his own medical research mission and zeroes in on another possible diagnosis – giant cell arteritis.

I've dropped 35 pounds and my doctors in the UK are pretty much at the end of their very long list of possibilities, so they decide to take a piece of artery out of the back of my skull and test it for this obscure disease that causes inflammation of the arteries in the head. Giant cell arteritis comes with headaches, fever, weight loss, depression – sounds right – and can lead to stroke, heart attack and blindness. Great. I don't know whether to hope they've finally found the answer or not, but the biopsy comes back negative anyway.

I'm wheeled to the phone to hear my brother say he's talked to my doctors and – positive diagnosis or not – I'm going to take the heavy doses of steroids they use to treat the disease. No arguments. As sick as I am, I'm paranoid about taking drugs, especially when we don't even know if they're treating the right thing. But it's Drew, so I do it.

Just eight hours later I feel like eating for the first time in weeks. Within ten days, I've gained a little weight, and the headaches are easing up. I'm ready to go home, feeling bloody lucky, and certain that I've used up at least one more of my nine lives.

I'll spend a full year on steroids, but within just a few weeks I'm back in the land of the living, starting to worry again about how to steer this giant ship called Greenpeace. With no one at the helm, there's been an escalation in the squabbling between – and sometimes within – national offices. (John Frizell had actually visited me in the hospital to say he was quitting as executive director if I didn't get out and make peace.)

Bloody maddening. There's so much to be done, and people waste time fighting among themselves.

The birth and growth of our German office is a prime example. By the time they're after official Greenpeace status in 1981, Germany's already a going concern. But our North American offices, and even our other European offices, argue that we don't need another office in Europe. Crazy! And near-sighted. Obviously, the North Americans are afraid it'll tip the balance so that Europe has even more power in the organization. And the Europeans know how powerful Germany will become. They already have more members than France even before officially opening, in Hamburg in February 1981.

By the autumn of 1982, Greenpeace Germany is big – and noisy.

People aren't sure they're happy anymore with the woman who's largely responsible for getting them this far. A couple of years earlier, I'd personally asked Monika Griefahn to help organize Germany. We'd met at some kind of international youth conference in Hamburg; she was there because she worked for the YMCA. Monika stands out physically; she's tall and strong, with a big head of dark curly hair. And then she opens her mouth. A very smart lady. And she speaks excellent English, too.

Anyway, Monika and her team do an absolutely great job getting Greenpeace Germany launched, and now there's this move afoot to kick her off the board. Some people feel the organization isn't grassroots enough; it's becoming too professional. I don't agree, but I've got to listen.

We have a six-hour meeting in Hamburg. The grassroots people insist that it be in German, so everything comes to me through a translator. I stare out of the window of one of those long, sterile meeting rooms and think that the River Elbe flowing by outside is going a hell of a lot faster. Finally, we reach a compromise. Monika stays, but she'll no longer be the sole director. She'll be joined on the board by a couple of others.

It's pretty much what I'd planned, but if I'd announced it when I walked in the door, they never would have been happy about it.

On 3 October, I'm back in Lewes with Christina when the best event of the year – no, of the decade – happens.

In Royal Sussex County Hospital, where I'd almost died six months earlier, Christina gives birth to a gorgeous baby girl – Julia Christina Gustafsson-McTaggart. It looks as if she's going to have the McTaggart colouring – dark hair and blue eyes.

There's something special about her, and about this second chance. Almost immediately, Julia steals my heart. I know this is one love that will last my lifetime.

By now, my three older daughters are talking to me again. They've each even spent a little time with me in Europe. But I know I'll never really be their dad. Too much time apart, too much hurt and anger. Baby Julia and my second-oldest daughter, Kerin, share the same birthday. Kerin's now 23 and, in personality, I think she's the most like me. Kerin can be quite tough. She writes to tell me that her mom says my new daughter strongly resembles Kerin's baby pictures, but she doesn't stop there: 'I suppose you know that this baby has three guardian angels on the west coast who feel very protective and would like to see this baby lead a *normal* life. You can do it, David. Don't blow it this time. I'm sorry to be so abrupt, but I'm worried about this child. I know what it's like to be fatherless – so do Tamra and Lisa.'

Ouch.

But she's right. I haven't been much of a dad, and I want to do better for my Julia.

My health is still a major worry, so I choose Julia's godfather very carefully. I want someone who'll be able to look after her no matter what happens to me. I ask Sadri, and he graciously consents. Ingemar and Karin come over for the baby's christening, at the Swedish church in London. When we're signing the documents, and I tell the minister that the baby's godfather is Sadruddin Aga Khan, he looks at me like I've got a screw loose. At first we assume it's just because it's such an illustrious name, but – no – it's that he's not sure anyone with a Muslim surname can be a godparent in the Swedish Church. What a joke! And what a statement about the kind of stupid barriers that exist in this world. I tell them there's no negotiating; he is Julia's godfather and she's just been christened in their Church. We get the papers in the mail a couple of weeks later.

Don't know if I ever told Sadri the story – too embarrassed – but coincidentally he and I spend quite a bit of time together during the next couple of years, on a project that goes right to the heart of those kind of ignorant divisions. It's also absolutely fundamental to humankind's survival – disarmament.

These are pretty freaky times in the early 1980s. Iron Lady

Thatcher's in power in the UK. And in the USA, President Ronald Reagan seems to think he's still an actor in some old Wild West movie, playing the part of the sheriff eager for a showdown with the bad guy. But as far as I can see, there is no bad guy and any showdown could be the end of humanity.

In 1983, Reagan announces the Strategic Defence Initiative – Star Wars – an anti-ballistic missile umbrella over the United States. If this goes ahead, it's a clear escalation of the arms race. The Doomsday Clock that indicates how close we are to a nuclear holocaust moves to three minutes to midnight. Three minutes to the end of the world.

Our disarmament campaign doesn't have the warm, fuzzy appeal of the whales, but when I hold my new little daughter in my arms, nothing seems more important. We've got to get our children into the twenty-first century.

To be worth taking on, Greenpeace campaigns must be winnable, and winnable in a clear and short time-frame. It doesn't work to chase 'world peace'. The goal has to be specific. The Nuclear Non-Proliferation Treaty is opened for discussion every five years, the next time in September of 1985.

So we've got a date.

Our target is also clearly visible. 124 countries are signatories to the Nuclear Non-Proliferation Treaty, and only three of them actually have nuclear weapons – the UK, USA, and the Soviet Union. The other countries have all agreed not to arm themselves because the big three promise to actively pursue disarmament.

Only they don't.

So there's our goal. Basic. Just force the big three to make good on what they've already contracted to do.

It's simple, but we know it won't be easy.

I circulate an article published around the time of Julia's birth, in the *Bulletin of Atomic Scientists*. The author is Aaron Tovish, an American working for a Swedish peace group.

Tovish proposes an elegantly simple idea. Come in the back door. Get the non-aligned countries to push the disarmament agenda, to force the superpowers to talk to each other.

This becomes the backbone of our strategy. And it's a little – no, a lot – like our whaling moratorium strategy. Work quietly, quietly behind the scenes to get members of the club to force the big guys to play by the rules. In this case, to get the superpowers to live up to their treaty obligations and disarm.

Cornelia Durrant and I get on a plane for Geneva. Cornelia earned Sadri's respect during the campaign for a whaling moratorium. She's charming and witty, and possessed of an absolutely cold and precise intelligence. Her nickname inside Greenpeace is The Ice Queen. Just the right person to lead this top-level campaign.

Sadri is eager to see us. He's just come back from ten days in Moscow and brings another layer of insight to our strategy. The Soviets want to get the Third World involved in disarmament. They think the discussion has been too East–West, and should open up to become a North–South dialogue, too. The Soviets say the Southern Hemisphere nations don't understand that there will be no bystanders if the superpowers blow themselves up in a nuclear war. Nobody will be left to pick up the pieces.

Sadri will again use his considerable influence to lobby various governments to stand up to the superpowers on disarmament. And he wants to go further. He suggests that his organization, Groupe de Bellerive, host a conference on the nuclear issue *before* the treaty meetings – a conference of mostly Third World countries.

At the end of January 1985, the Group of Six (Argentina, Greece, India, Mexico, Sweden, Tanzania) convenes in Athens. It's a symbolic meeting that's difficult for the three nuclear weapons states to ignore. This isn't another meeting of a group of hippies-for-peace; these are people of the stature of Andreas Papandreou for Greece, Julius Nyerere for Tanzania, and Olof Palme for Sweden.

Disarmament is no longer a discussion among superpowers. The world has invited itself in.

The Athens meeting is significant to me for another reason – Yevgeny Velikhov. It's my first meeting with this distinguished member of the Soviet Academy of Sciences. Velikhov's a round, jolly-looking guy. Strikes one more like a farmer than a physicist. But he's sharp as a tack and absolutely committed to the peace movement. In response to Reagan's Star Wars announcement, Velikhov made a brilliant counter-move. He founded a group called the Soviet Scientists for Peace, and invited American scientists to Moscow to meet with their Soviet counterparts. Obviously a man willing to stick his neck out, and I want to get to know him.

After Athens, I court Velikhov by mail, encouraging him to press the Soviet Union to declare a unilateral moratorium on nuclear testing and force America's hand. We send him newspaper clippings that might be of interest – like the huge positive response to the Soviet rescue of beluga whales trapped in the Arctic. I want to demonstrate how the Soviets can get the power of the international press behind them.

I'm playing poker at two tables here, also gently nudging Velikhov towards using his considerable influence to get the Soviet Union to withdraw their objection at the International Whaling Commission to the moratorium on commercial whaling. Japan, Norway and the Soviet Union are the only hold-outs. World opinion is going to love the Soviets if they join the moratorium to save the whales. And it'll be a stronger moratorium – more resistant to whatever the Japanese throw at us next.

In July, I'm back in the south of England, Bournemouth, for the IWC. The scientists – Sidney Holt, along with Australia's Bill de la Mare and the UK's Justin Cooke – have done a great job preparing arguments to get both Norwegian minke and North Pacific sperm whales on the Commission's Protection Stock list. If you wonder why we'd even bother, given that there's a whaling moratorium about to take effect, it's because the Japanese are still whaling under an objection that they've filed to the moratorium. After the moratorium goes into effect, they'll find another rationalization – that they must still do 'scientific' whaling. Whale meat on the table in the name of research.

During our usual preparation week before the IWC convenes, I decide to hold a quick meeting on Greenpeace International board business. We've got the usual crises unfolding – mostly gripes that my small executive board has too much power, and the council of trustees from all the national offices doesn't think it has enough. Well, excuse me, but sometimes we need to move quickly. I'm happy to go with democracy most of the time, but when we need a quick decision between board meetings, we can't afford to get into a six-month telex war.

I call a meeting in my hotel room. Monika Griefahn's there, and Pete Wilkinson. He's raving on about what a beautiful ride it was along the coast on his motorbike, a perfect midsummer's day. We're just getting down to business when the phone rings. Pete grabs it off the wobbly little bedside table, and I remember feeling quite irritated at the interruption.

But it's a collect call from New Zealand where the *Rainbow Warrior* is preparing to head out on another protest aimed at stopping the insanity of French nuclear testing at Mururoa.

So I take the call, prepared to tell them to call back unless it's really urgent.

Something in the tone of voice tells me that it is.

The room goes dead quiet around me.

It's 13 years since I first sailed to Mururoa. Not a lucky number. I am being told that the *Rainbow Warrior* has sunk. Explosions, two of them. And at least one of our people is missing, maybe more.

Our guys in New Zealand are a couple of steps away from hysteria, but for me this is one of those times when the world goes into slow motion, every second has at least ten seconds worth of information in it. A surreal calm.

The first investigators on the scene consider the most likely cause of the explosion to be some kind of problem with the *Warrior*'s fuel system. I don't think so.

My instincts tell me this was deliberate.

Chapter Seventeen

THE FIRST EXPLOSION happened at 11.38 p.m. New Zealand time, in the *Rainbow Warrior*'s engine room. It tore a hole in the ship's side big enough to drive a car through. The crew scrambled to get off the boat as the water rushed in, forcing the *Warrior* over on her side, and then down towards the bottom of Auckland Harbour.

The second blast came just minutes after the first, and disabled the propulsion system with what looks like brutal precision – shearing off the thick bolts that held the propeller to the shaft and bending the shaft itself. It was obviously aimed at making sure this ship went nowhere.

That second explosion took more than the guts of the *Warrior*; it took a piece of her heart, too.

Fernando Pereira, the ship's photographer, was a handsome fun-loving Dutch-Portuguese guy who'd just celebrated his thirty-fifth birthday. He was also very dedicated to his craft. After the first explosion Fernando went below to grab his cameras. He was hurriedly stuffing a camera bag when the second bomb went off.

He's found in the cabin next to his own, face down and drowned, his legs entangled in his camera bag.

Two little children have lost their dad, and our organization has lost its innocence. It's our first casualty in this war to save the planet, and it looks like cold-blooded murder.

I sit in Bournemouth, glued to the BBC. It reports that the

explosions were caused by two limpet mines, attached to the *Warrior*'s hull and on timing devices. At first, I think this must be the work of some renegade military-type, a right-wing nut of who-knows-what nationality. Doesn't really matter, just a nut. Just a murderer.

No way my mind wants to accept the obvious, that this could be the work of my old nemesis, France.

I know Greenpeace is a thorn in the French government's side. They're frustrated at not being able to keep their nuclear testing programme out of the harsh light of our continuing Mururoa protests. Like anybody with something to hide, they'd far prefer to do their dirty work in the dark. But it's a big, big jump from knowing France hates our presence in the South Pacific to believing that a democratic nation would commit a terrorist act against a legitimate non-governmental organization. And do it in the sovereign territory of an ally – New Zealand.

It's unthinkable.

New Zealand is as enraged as we are, and their police force reacts fast. They interview anybody who'd been around Auckland Harbour on the night of 10 July. Passers-by had seen an inflatable launched. A fisherman heard it cross the water. And then the police hit pay-dirt: a boat club night-watchman saw a man in a wetsuit load gear from an inflatable into a van. And he's noted the van's licence number.

The police trace the van to a rental company near Auckland Airport. It was rented by a married couple carrying Swiss passports.

When the couple returns the vehicle, New Zealand police are there to grab them, and bring them in for questioning.

The pair's Swiss identification is false. They turn out to be French secret service agents Captain Dominique Prieur and Major Alain Mafart, members of the DGSE – Direction Générale de la Sécurité Extérieure. You have to think Mafart and Prieur are not the smartest secret service agents, to commit a terrorist act on foreign soil and then return their rent-a-car. I might have just grabbed the first plane out of there. Hilariously, we'll later find out that the French secret service agents spent a fantastic amount of time worrying about getting reimbursed for expenses while on their mission – as well as fiddling their expense reports! Returning the van had something to do not only with maintaining cover but also with ensuring that Mafart and Prieur got their money back from the petits bureaucrats in Paris.

But that's why, three weeks after the bombing, I am in Paris working underground to nail it, to prove the unthinkable.

The New Zealand police and Greenpeace have been swapping information. They have Mafart and Prieur in jail in Auckland, but we all know there are more members of the DGSE terrorist team still on the loose, and one of them is a doctor specializing in treating victims of diving accidents.

Dr Xavier Maniguet is the one member of the team who is not a professional agent. I figure he just might be scared for his life, and talkative. We locate Maniguet in Paris, and – through intermediaries – arrange a meeting.

Six o'clock on a hot summer evening, 12 August 1985. Nine years since I wandered the streets of Paris with Lison. Same time of year, same sand-coloured buildings glowing in the evening light, but the city somehow doesn't look so golden.

Maniguet will meet me beside a lamp-post outside this famous brasserie, La Coupole, in Montparnasse. I get there early, in case this is a set-up. The French government actually offers me protection while I'm in Paris, which I refuse, but it serves to underline how dangerous and desperate the DGSE must be. If they're immoral enough to blow up the *Rainbow Warrior* with people on board, it's a short step to sending a sniper to silence the two of us.

At five minutes to six, from the bar where I sit, I see a nervous-looking man pass by La Coupole and cross the street to a news-stand. I slip in behind him, confirm it's Maniguet, and we start to walk. He keeps saying, 'I'm an ecologist. I've always been an ecologist.'

We go into a bar, and Maniguet proceeds to tell me about the whole operation – even drawing little maps for me. I don't know if he's repentant or scared shitless. Probably both. Maniguet says his lawyer thinks he should get out of France, but this is the only country where he's certain he won't get prosecuted – executed maybe, but not prosecuted. The French police know where Maniguet's living, and he's now afraid they'll come for him and hand him over to the secret service. So he didn't go home last night, and he won't tonight. He's got the shifty, anxious look of a man who believes he's become prey for a hunter much stronger than himself. A haunted man.

There's no doubt now that the DGSE is behind the bombings. The question is how high up does the guilt go. The Defence Minister? How about the President?

I underline in my diary: 'I should be very careful in Paris.'

The Greenpeace team helping me in Paris includes Brian Fitzgerald, a great American kid who'll become my right hand throughout most of the next decade. I get Brian to keep moving my little red Fiesta around town. I don't want it parked in the same spot long enough for the DGSE to plant a bomb.

The French government under François Mitterand scrambles to contain the political damage. A high-ranking civil servant, Bernard Tricot, is charged with conducting an independent investigation. The Tricot report is published at the end of August, after 17 days – not exactly an exhaustive investigation – and at first glance it looks like a complete whitewash.

From his review of documents and interviews with – among others – the head of the DGSE and Defence Minister Charles Hernu, Tricot concludes that the secret service operation in Auckland was ordered to spy on the *Rainbow Warrior*, not to blow her up.

But it's important because Tricot's report is the first official confirmation that there *was* a DGSE operation focused on the *Warrior*. Also, he can't point to any other perpetrators. And – quite subtle, I thought – Tricot says he can't exclude the possibility that he's been deceived: 'I do not exclude that there may have been a kind of general agreement … not to tell me the truth.'

Wow. That would mean a conspiracy that went as high as the Defence Minister.

The world press grabs the story and hangs on like a starving dog. I do what I can to feed the frenzy, giving interview after interview.

On 17 September, the respected French newspaper *Le Monde* declares that there's no doubt that Defence Minister Hernu and the head of the DGSE had been aware of the operation to sink the *Rainbow Warrior*, and had very likely ordered it.

The head of the secret service is dismissed, and Hernu resigns.

Two days later, France admits it: the *Rainbow Warrior* was sunk by French agents, acting under orders. Then the walls of silence go back up. Admissions stop. And we all prepare for the court case coming up in six weeks' time, against the two DGSE agents in New Zealand.

The New Zealand police have the pair under very careful watch in their Auckland jail cells. If the French are capable of killing a civilian, no reason to think they'd have scruples about silencing witnesses. I personally think it's not a bad thing for agents Mafart and Prieur to be frightened for their lives. Seriously. It might make them a little more co-operative in court.

Greenpeace happens to have a helicopter available in Auckland. It's there for a totally different campaign, but I get thinking that it's perfect for sticking the needle in. On the morning of the trial, I ask the pilot to take me up and just circle around Waitemata Harbour until he sees the escorted van carrying Mafart and Prieur leave Mount Eden prison. We spot it, and swoop in until we're right over the van. The VHF radio's going crazy: 'Get that ****ing thing out of here.'

I tell the pilot to turn off the radio if it's bothering him. We concentrate on staying low enough that the sound inside the little tin box beneath us must be deafening. I want to rattle their brains. Make them wonder if the next sound they hear will be the last – a blast that will end their roles in this French farce. I want them to arrive at court feeling like they need to make some friends.

At 10.30 a.m., as Prieur and Mafart take their places in the courtroom, they do look a little shaken. Don't know if that's because of their escort or because they've had a peek at the size of the press corps hungry for a piece of their story – 147 press, from around the world.

But the day's pretty disappointing for the reporters, and for me. Instead of a six-week murder trial, it's all over in a matter of minutes. In English, in very low voices, the two agents plead guilty to reduced charges of manslaughter and arson.

It's just not enough. Not enough for the murder of an innocent man. Not enough for the *state-sanctioned* murder of an innocent man.

Not a chance we'll leave it here.

And that's where Lloyd Cutler comes in.

Lloyd is the kind of personality you'd cast in a courtroom drama as the crusty older lawyer, the deceptively slow-talking guy with a rapier-sharp mind who is almost unbeatable in court. Just who we need to represent Greenpeace against France. Lloyd had served as White House counsel to US President Jimmy Carter, so he's got stature; and, maybe because he's been inside government, he's particularly outraged that a democratic state could authorize terrorism. That's got to be a good thing – righteous indignation in a lawyer as skilled as Cutler.

Some elements in Greenpeace think he's wrong for us, a 'bad guy' because he once opposed consumer activist Ralph Nader in court. Hell, I couldn't care less. I think Lloyd's the best. If the devil could win for us against France, I'd hire him. And Lloyd, about to retire, agrees to represent us without pay. It doesn't get much better than that – a prince's lawyer on a pauper's pay-cheque.

Now we know who all the main players are, we just have to figure out what theatre we'll take our case to. French courts? No, that's a joke. New Zealand? France might just refuse to show up. The Hague? France has a reputation for ignoring the International Court.

Lloyd has another idea. We'll just make the case a simple claim for damages. Since this is a unique situation – a sovereign state attacking a non-governmental organization inside the territory of another sovereign state – we'll effectively create our own international court of justice, an arbitration hearing between France and Greenpeace.

There's just one small complication. How do we get France to agree to come to our court?

Suddenly, I feel like I'm in very familiar territory. We're talking about good old arm-twisting, negotiating. I know this stuff. And Lloyd seems to enjoy the game just as much as I do. We go looking for another legal option that will be more unappetizing to the French than sitting down with us to negotiate damages. Lloyd finds it: France does not want to go to civil court in New Zealand, where anybody and everybody involved in the bombing could be called as witnesses, and the whole sorry affair made very public.

A week after the Mafart-Prieur trial in Auckland, Lloyd does a little press conference. Says we plan to file a civil suit in New Zealand. He does mention that we have another strategy – going for damages – but tells the cameras that maybe a civil trial would be better. 'We may even be able to satisfy our own – and the public – curiosity as to what did happen.'

Jeez, he's good.

Ten days later, the two agents are sentenced to ten years apiece for manslaughter and wilful damage, and France has decided to sit down with Greenpeace to negotiate the terms of an arbitration on damages ... much more appealing than a civil suit that would air dirty French laundry in public.

It takes another month to get agreement on the terms of the arbitration. The last item is location: where will it take place? We want a neutral location. France says Paris – no negotiation. I've finally had enough, and pass the message back to the French, fine, no negotiation – sign now, and I mean *right* now, or we're going to court in Auckland.

They sign.

On 27 April 1987 – 21 months after the *Warrior* was bombed and Fernando Pereira murdered – the Republic of France sits down with Greenpeace International at the Hotel de la Paix in Geneva.

I won't bore you with all the details, but you have to appreciate the setting. Hilarious. France chose the hotel and is paying for it. It's so luxurious that it's laughable ... at least to those of us who only get out of our blue-jeans when forced. And because it's the Hotel de la *Paix*, its symbol is the dove of peace. They're bloody everywhere, even on the door handles of the big conference room where the arbitration is held. They inadvertently chain the birds down each night when they lock up the room. Seriously.

Lloyd Cutler orders two models of the *Rainbow Warrior* made showing the ship before and after the bombings. He has the 'after' model sent back once – doesn't think it looks quite grim enough. Those reminders of a dirty night's work in Auckland Harbour sit in front of the Tribunal. Don't know that they influence the esteemed judge overseeing the arbitration, but I like looking at them.

Lloyd and I do have a couple of disagreements. He suggests Greenpeace ought to leave France alone for a while, stop our protests at Mururoa until the case is settled. I tell him that's just not possible, ever. In fact, Chris Robinson and *Vega* head for Mururoa only days after the bombing of the *Warrior*.

The other disagreement I have with Lloyd is also a reasonably big one. Early on in the arbitration, France offers quite a large settlement, but no apology. Lloyd thinks maybe we should take it. After all, we might get nothing. It's a long tough discussion, but we end up passing on the offer, and going for it.

One morning, when Lloyd comes down to breakfast, he says he has an announcement. Now you have to remember what a quiet, unhurried man he is. 'I had … a very hopeful indication … on the case … this morning … gentlemen,' he says. 'Over the lake … I saw … a beautiful rainbow.'

Lloyd's closing statement before the Arbitration Tribunal ends like this: 'Remember, you can't sink a rainbow – without paying actual, aggravated and exemplary damages.'

After nearly two years of arbitration, a panel of judges orders France to pay Greenpeace a total of $8.16 million, including aggravated damages.

Not everyone inside the organization is popping bottles of champagne. Some people feel this is blood money and we've taken a wrong turn. Greenpeace is a big sprawling organization by the mid-1980s – more than a million members, in 15 countries. There are bound to be some differences of opinion. And to get the arbitration off the ground, I had to push a little.

One of the conditions before France would agree to sit down with us, with Greenpeace International, was that we have authorization from all our national offices. Well, it took a little arm-wrestling, and with one office – Hawaii – I was forced to get a bit blunt. I asked Brian Fitzgerald to send quite a simple telex warning them that, if they didn't sign, they could 'expect immediate proceedings to terminate your right to use the Greenpeace trademark and seizure of your assets and office'. The agreement got signed on time, but not everybody appreciates a game of hard-ball.

And there's lots of it being played in the mid-1980s in Greenpeace. It's tough to keep everybody heading in the same direction. I do the best I can. But it's not always pretty.

In 1986, I come nose-to-nose with the UK board, and that includes my friend Pete Wilkinson. There are a couple of things going on with Greenpeace UK that I'm not happy about.

Number one: Greenpeace absolutely can't be partisan to any political party. If we're labelled, we lose our power. I'm serious. But Pete and the UK office don't agree. Pete keeps trying to build an alliance with the unions around closing down the Sellafield nuclear reprocessing plant. It's not a stupid idea in the short view. If the unions refuse to deliver spent nuclear fuel to Sellafield, it'll force the government to find alternatives and the Irish Sea will be a much cleaner place. So we maybe would accomplish that, and in the process get labelled as just another left-wing organization, in bed with the unions. No way. But Pete's almost as stubborn as me, and he just won't let it go. He's even brought a friend of his who's a former Labour candidate onto the UK board. I am not comfortable with this situation.

Number two problem: UK just can't seem to think internationally. They want to spend the money they raise on national issues – like the Orkney seal campaign. Nice, but not enough. I keep telling them they've got to expand their horizons, get real; none of the other European offices is so bloody introverted. Pete and I go several rounds on this one. Jeez, the man's hard-headed.

The UK decides to do this anti-fur campaign. In isolation, it's alright. In fact, it's so good that if you're over forty, you might even remember their main campaign image – a beautiful model on a fashion runway, dragging a fur coat behind her. And the coat is leaving behind a trail of blood. The caption reads, 'It takes forty dumb animals to make a fur coat. But only one to wear it.' Well, the UK board's insistence that they ought to be able to run a regional fur campaign gets a bit of a wake-up call when the ad wins an international award and gets airplay worldwide!

In the UK animal rights issues are practically mainstream. But our offices in Sweden, Denmark, and particularly in the USA and

Canada, go ballistic. They see it as placing us on the fringe, detracting from our focus, and all for an issue that other groups already have well in hand. It's also complicated in some of those countries because they've got indigenous people who still trap fur for a living. Furthermore, even in the UK there are people who see the ad as anti-women. For me, it just isn't worth it. It's a very small issue compared to the problems the world is facing. And Greenpeace *International* can be a powerful force on the side of Mother Earth if – and only if – our opponents know that when the organization speaks, it speaks for people from 15 different nations. 15 nations: one voice. More than a million people all saying the same thing. That's powerful, and it's simple.

So the anti-fur campaign has to go. And I want some kind of assurance from Pete and the UK board that there'll be no more rogue campaigns, no more of this kind of nationalistic bullshit.

After a certain amount of bitching and belly-aching, Pete calls me up at home in Lewes the day before a UK board meeting. He reads me a letter of apology. I tell him that isn't enough; he's got to offer his resignation. Same for the rest of his friends on the board.

Pete has the impression this is just for show, that they'll be invited right back, so he convinces his four colleagues to resign, too. Well, maybe, if it had just been the fur campaign, but there's the problem of their political leanings, too. I'm sick of constantly arguing with these guys, constantly trying to get them to see past their own navels.

The meeting is held at 10 a.m. on a Monday morning, in the scruffy little boardroom of our office on Graham Street, London N1. The chairman – whale expert Sidney Holt – calls the meeting to order and immediately moves Item Number 14, the resignations, up to Item Number 2.

He accepts the five resignations. And closes the meeting.

All hell breaks loose, but there isn't much they can do except retire to the Earl of Essex across the street and drink the place dry. It's a pub where Pete and I have held many strategy meetings, over a beer or two.

This time, I don't join him.

Chapter Eighteen

MAYBE IT SOUNDS cold-blooded, but I don't regret sacking Pete. At least not right away. He's a casualty of the biggest battle I'll ever have inside the organization – over nationalism. I have to win or we'll just be another nice little organization with good intentions and no clout.

The second biggest battle I have is underway about the same time, and it's related. It's over the West understanding the East. By the mid-1980s the Cold War has been going on so long that ordinary people have been brainwashed into fearing each other. My brother's a child psychiatrist, and he explained it to me. If you take small children, from age one to age seven, and put fear into them, they'll be afraid for the rest of their lives.

That's what the military industry in the USA did; made Western children so fearful of the Russians that even after they grew up and the Wall began to crumble, they still couldn't get over the fear. And that's what I'm facing inside Greenpeace when I try to move us into the Soviet Union. West versus East, as if pollution respected boundaries or ideologies. It's tough.

Most Greenpeace members aren't more than thirty years old, and they've been told since a child that Russians and communism are evil. You can't change that. So I decide if the organization can't move towards Russia, I'll just have to go to the Soviet Union and build from within.

The whole thing really starts playing on my mind after meeting Yevgeny Velikhov at that disarmament conference in Athens just after New Year's 1985. He's the Deputy Director of the Soviet Academy of Sciences, a very educated man, but there's something very basic about him. We can talk to each other.

Then in March, Mikhail Gorbachev becomes General Secretary of the Politburo.

The Soviet Union takes the initiative on disarmament, calling for a re-opening of negotiations towards a Comprehensive Test Ban Treaty. Alright! I write to congratulate Gorbachev, and to encourage him, even going so far as to suggest he declare a moratorium on nuclear weapons testing and challenge the USA to do the same.

I start flying into Moscow frequently – there'll be more than forty trips before I'm done. I want to establish Greenpeace in the Soviet Union, but know that'll be a long-term project, inside a communist country that doesn't have any non-governmental organizations. My more immediate goals are trying to get the Soviet objection to the moratorium on commercial whaling removed, and constantly pushing the disarmament agenda.

During the next several months, Gorbachev does declare a three-month unilateral moratorium on nuclear testing; and when the Americans drag their feet, he renews it, even calls for the dismantling of all nuclear weapons by the year 2000. Hard to paint these guys as the enemy.

Until 28 April 1986, Good Friday.

Computer screens at a nuclear plant north of Stockholm start going crazy – signalling extremely high levels of radiation. Something is terribly wrong, but a frantic search of the facility reveals no leak. Where can it be coming from? Prevailing wind patterns point to the Soviet Union.

Silence from Moscow over the Easter weekend.

Then on Monday morning, a stony-faced Soviet newscaster reads a statement: 'An accident has taken place at the Chernobyl power station, and one of the reactors was damaged. Measures are being taken to eliminate the consequences of the accident. Those affected are being given assistance. A government commission has been set up.' That's it. The worst man-made disaster in history, and that's it.

I am in the USA for meetings with Lloyd Cutler, and with Greenpeace USA. We sit staring at CNN in horror as the story unfolds. Sketchy details coming from the Soviet Union, but satellite photos tell the story – a nuclear reactor burning out of control. The accident happened two days earlier, and the wind is carrying the radiation north and west. Wherever the spring rain falls across Ukraine and Scandinavia, it brings down this invisible poison. My precious Julia – now two and a half – is in Stockholm with her mother, in the path of the radioactivity. This is much more terrible, and more personal, than having French commandos beat my eye in. Almost 15 years of having no life, of fighting to do a little bit for this planet, and here's where I am – halfway across the world from my daughter, and unable to protect her anyway. I call Christina and tell her to keep Julia inside, but I know it's late, and little.

The Western press really has a go at the Soviet Union, for not immediately telling the public about the accident, thereby giving northwestern Europeans a chance to protect themselves. I have to agree, but Chernobyl is all the more reason not to demonize the Soviets, but to build bridges into the Soviet Union and get working on their pollution problems.

Flying over the Atlantic back to Lewes, I start composing a letter to Yevgeny Velikhov: 'Please accept my condolences for the great national tragedy which struck the Soviet Union with the Chernobyl fire. I would be remiss if I did not say in the strongest terms that I think it irresponsible that people downwind from the fire were not warned by Soviet officials, but this will not save the lives that were lost, nor prevent the appearance of the cancers that will result.' I push for full disclosure, for shutting down all reactors that don't have secondary containment, and for the establishment of international protocol: 'Such accidents and radiation respect no national boundaries and should therefore be treated as problems requiring immediate and concerted international cooperation.'

I'm trying to say, let us help, let us in.

I write to Gorbachev, too. Don't mention Chernobyl in this one, just congratulate him on his persistent efforts to get a ban on nuclear weapons testing, and say Greenpeace would like to help push his agenda. At a Whaling Commission meeting in Sweden six weeks later, the Soviet commissioner asks me for clarification on a couple of points in my letter. Good. They're listening.

That summer, 1986, I go to Moscow at Velikhov's invitation to attend the International Forum of Scientists for a Nuclear Test Ban. When I arrive, Velikhov's in the hospital – probably the after-effects of too much time spent at Chernobyl during the crisis. But he's out in time for the meeting of dozens of top scientists from around the world. In such over-educated company, my only role is to remind them of the impact they can have if they all go public. I remind them, too, that it's science that brought us the bomb, maybe it's scientists who have the moral obligation to bury it.

On Sunday night, Christina and I have dinner with Yevgeny and his wife at their private home in the woodlands surrounding Moscow. By now it looks like the Soviets will extend the weapons testing moratorium again, so I go after my other priorities. After a sauna and some vodka, Velikhov and I talk about some kind of East–West musical event – on either side of the Iron Curtain – to break down the psychological barriers inside young people who grew up during the Cold War. Velikhov also agrees to push for an immediate end to Soviet whaling, and we decide to set up some kind of joint East–West project. I know that sounds boring. But it's huge, seriously. There's never been any kind of organized venture between the Soviet Union and the West. This would be a first.

I don't want to make it sound as if I'm the only Westerner fighting to bring the Wall down. Far from it. During the summer of 1986, my good friend Ted Turner opens his first Goodwill Games in Moscow, an athletic competition that brings together East and West. It's Ted who got me my first visa into the Soviet Union – not his first, or by any means his largest, contribution to environmental causes.

Turner's an amazing story. You probably know him from founding CNN, or marrying Jane Fonda. When I think about it, both those things are pretty indicative of his character. Ted doesn't see walls much, of any kind. If he wants something, he goes and gets it. I remember him telling me – before they knew each other – that Fonda's a woman who could hold his interest. Next thing I know, they're in love.

There are some similarities between Turner and me. He moves fast, makes quick decisions. He's an athlete – won the America's Cup. He appreciates women – got kicked out of university after being caught with a lady in his room. Ted doesn't have a lot of formal education and doesn't let that stop him. Also like me, I know he gets pretty down sometimes, but that doesn't stop him, either. There's just too much to be done.

We met a year or so earlier, when I was looking for big money for an important campaign that Greenpeace couldn't finance without help. I took pride in the fact that the organization's fund-raising was based on tiny donations from millions of people. We didn't accept money from governments or corporations, and normally I'd shy away from large donors as well. We needed the freedom to have a go at what we thought needed doing, not what some fat-cat donor wanted done. With Turner, though, my instincts told me there'd be no interference; he'd just let us get on with it. And also, since his business was news, it couldn't hurt to have his attention.

I'd spent time with Turner on his little island retreat, near Atlanta, and we'd done something very foolish, at least from my point of view. I've mentioned how I like my smokes. No. Correction. I hate smoking, but I can't quit. I'm one of the small percentage of people who are totally addicted. Some people can smoke for a while, and then quit, no problem. I'm not one of those people. When I try to quit – and I have many times during the years – I get so depressed that life doesn't seem worth living. But I know the bloody things are killing me, so ... I make a bet with one of the wealthiest men in America.

After getting back from Turner's island, we're sitting having dinner at some restaurant in Atlanta and I give Ted a rough time for chewing tobacco, tell him it's disgusting. And he challenges me – he'll give up cigars and chew, if I quit smoking. The bet will be a hundred thousand US dollars. I say yes. What the hell am I thinking?

The bet is to start at midnight, 31 July 1985. That evening I send a little telex from Lewes to Ted in Atlanta: 'Tonight – midnight – bet begins – would wish you luck, but under the circumstances will just say best regards.'

In two years, I'll be collecting a hundred thousand dollars.

I don't last two weeks.

And that brings us back around to Moscow a year later.

For months I've been watching out for CNN crews whenever I light a cigarette in public. I'm pretty sure Ted's alerted them to the bet; maybe even offered a little bonus if they bring home videotape of McTaggart smoking. And now, I'm in a limousine with Ted on the way to the stadium in Moscow for the opening ceremonies of the Goodwill Games and I'm already dying for a cigarette. Even if I make it to the stadium, the place will be full of CNN crews and I stand a good chance of getting caught sneaking a smoke. A little humiliating. If I had the money, I'd give it to him right now and end the agony. But I hardly have a thousand bucks to spare, let alone a hundred thousand.

The nicotine starvation must be affecting my brain. I decide to bet him double or nothing, starting – or rather stopping again – in a few weeks.

Several months later, when I lose again, Ted lets me negotiate the bet down to something I can pay – barely – but he doesn't let me off the hook entirely. Turner says I'm too valuable to die young. I'm flattered, if not exactly grateful.

For me these years – the late 1980s – are exhausting but absolutely exhilarating. It's amazing to help negotiate the end of the Cold War, amazing to play even a small part in building a new world order.

It consumes me.

There isn't much left over for my family, for any of my families. Christina and I are married by now, a very small ceremony, mostly to 'make it legal' for my old friend Ingemar who's very ill with a brain tumour. As much as I love Julia, and her mother, it's complicated from the start. Apparently love doesn't conquer all, since Tina and I just can't get along. I won't live in Stockholm – it depresses me – and we can't seem to agree on another location for home base.

We spend some time at the Gustafsson family summer home, trying to work things out and not getting very far. It seems to me that the only thing that will please Tina is if I quit Greenpeace. And I can't – partly because the work seems important, maybe mostly because it's too bloody interesting, this close-up view of the twenty-first century being born.

Still, in October 1986, Tina's with me in Amsterdam when Prince Bernhard makes me a Knight of the Golden Ark. There are some lovely pictures of her from that time, with her thick blonde hair braided to the side, and wearing a blue dress that deepens her eyes.

It's good she has those memories to take home to her father in Stockholm, my last gift to my old friend. Ingemar dies just before Christmas.

They say bad news comes in threes. Wish you could count on it to stop there. Fortunately, I couldn't see into the future, to know just how heavy the next few years would be.

But at least our push into the Soviet Union is going well, although it's a bit of a wild ride. For months and months I work at setting up a music concert – names like U2, Bryan Adams, Peter Gabriel, Eurythmics, Chrissie Hynde, David Byrne … we even talked to Paul McCartney about a reunion of the surviving Beatles. If it's held in Moscow and broadcast simultaneously around the world, a concert like this would break down some of those psychological barriers in the young people – music being their language, to say nothing of mine. But while French commandos could never stop me, I have to admit defeat at the hands of the Soviet bureaucracy. Even with Velikhov and other powerful friends behind me, we never quite pull it together.

It frustrates the hell out of me, but it's not a totally futile exercise. After all the main point here is to get an East–West dialogue going. We've succeeded in doing that – way too much dialogue, too little action, for me.

But the many, many meetings about the concert turn out to be the seeds of the International Foundation for the Survival and Development of Humanity. Remember, the Berlin Wall is still up. It's a big deal just to get a visa into the Soviet Union. Yet Velikhov and I sit making lists of top Soviet and Western people we'll put together in one room, basically to build a new international political system – and solve a few pollution problems while they're at it. I'm sure I can get Sir Peter Scott and American physicist Frank von Hippel on the board. Velikhov will invite Roald Sagdeev, head of the Soviet space programme and Andrei Sakharov, the dissident who's finally being allowed to participate again in Soviet life.

And we pull it off.

Gorbachev comes to one of our first meetings, held in this

typically ornate Russian meeting room – lots of red and gold with big chandeliers. Very formal. I even wear a jacket and tie for the occasion, so I don't feel too out of place in this august company. Five people away, around the corner of the table, sits Gorbachev, and he's sure impressive. You can feel the energy radiating from him.

Velikhov chairs the meeting, and he keeps signalling me to speak up. I hate giving any kind of speech, and this is very intimidating company, but finally I raise my hand and Velikhov cuts across the list of waiting speakers to call on me next.

I'm nervous as hell, but manage a little speech about pollution respecting no boundaries, and Greenpeace having the honour of being arrested in *both* the West and the East during our struggle for disarmament and for the environment. I hope this group will have the guts to take on the difficult questions that will embarrass the Soviet Union, the USA, and many other countries. I end by thanking the group for including me, an activist: 'I don't have a "sir" or a title. I'm from the streets, and I started fighting from the streets, and I appreciate being here.'

Well Gorbachev brings down the house when he says something like, 'It's good to see that there are at least two of us here from the streets.'

One of the sweetest public moments of my life, to have Mikhail Gorbachev draw even that kind of flippant comparison between us.

A few months later, Greenpeace makes a musical breakthrough – literally. In 1989, we release an album called *Breakthrough* which is the first major offering of new Western rock music in the Soviet Union. We actually manage to get promoted on Soviet television, and we bring Bono, Peter Gabriel, Annie Lennox, Chrissie Hynde and David Byrne to Moscow to sign albums for their fans. It's quite a scene. We plan to sell three million records and a million cassette tapes, each including a booklet with an overview of the global environmental crisis, and an introduction to Greenpeace.

At the end of 1989, the Berlin Wall comes tumbling down, and six months later Greenpeace becomes legal in the Soviet Union. We're in place, ready to help clean up the pollution problems that have been hiding behind the Iron Curtain.

The 1980s end for me personally on a miserable note. Sir Peter Scott dies, at just 79, and it's hard to take. I can't believe he's no longer with us, this humble, sensitive, quietly powerful man. His memorial service is held at St Paul's Cathedral in London, where his father – the Antarctic explorer Robert Scott – had been similarly celebrated 75 years earlier. After the service, Peter's wife Philippa – Phil, he always called her – hugs me tightly for a few seconds, and the sea of black suits behind her blurs. I know it's a cliché, but the world won't see another like him, seriously.

I haven't climbed out of that sadness when my father dies. George McTaggart made it to 90, a good run, and there's comfort in knowing that his life was happy – other than the heartache I caused him.

Our father dies in January of 1990, and in March my brother Drew and I set off on the first professional joint venture of our lives, to see what can be done for the children who were born and raised in the shadow of the Chernobyl disaster.

It's Velikhov who first raises the situation with me. He's concerned that all sorts of illnesses are showing up that wouldn't necessarily be associated with radiation. It's very sensitive. People are on the verge of panic and don't trust Soviet doctors. Velikhov wonders if Greenpeace can arrange some kind of programme to take children out of the area on lengthy vacations.

I immediately call my brother. His reaction is typically quick and certain – a month away won't fix anything. We need to find out quickly what the medical situation really is for these children, and then we might be able to help. So in March 1990 I fly into Kiev with a team of Canadian doctors, including my brother who'll look into the children's psychiatric problems.

I've seen a lot in my life by 1990, but nothing could possibly have prepared me for the power and the pain of this trip.

It's a beautiful spring in Ukraine, sunny and warm, but early enough that the land is still dormant when we arrive, still wearing a coat of autumn gold.

We go from village to village, all of us crammed in a rickety old bus. When we stop at a clinic, knowledge of our presence spreads like wildfire. Within minutes the clinic is swarmed with mothers anxious to know if their children are being irreparably harmed by this invisible poison. We see hundreds of children. Some whose teeth are blackened stumps from drinking irradiated milk. The doctors take blood samples and promise that any results will be sent back to the village. Occasionally we see a very enlarged thyroid, which the doctors identify as potentially cancerous. I'll never forget one two-year-old girl in her grandmother's arms – a beautiful child with fair skin, very large blue eyes and that serious demeanour that small children occasionally have, an old soul. Her Baba is so proud of her, showing her off to all of us. It comes as a shock when the team's paediatrician checks the little girl's thyroid and says quietly to me, 'I don't like the look of this.'

It's difficult to look round the packed waiting room at families waiting patiently for something we can't give them – reassurance that their children will be okay. I feel helpless, and can't stop thinking about my own little girl. Julia's just six. This could be her.

But the worst of the epidemic so far is really psychological, and my brother spots it right away. Whether their children are sick or not, many of these mothers are panicking and passing on this fear of the world to their children. It's post-traumatic stress syndrome, deep and widespread ... and so very understandable.

As we walk, villagers stop and beg us to test their kitchen gardens with our Geiger counter. People are preparing to plant their vegetables – they really need the food – and they want to know if the ground is poison. Imagine!

One Sunday morning we stop at the sound of singing, coming from a tiny little church almost hidden in the long dry grass alongside the main street, a dirt road, in a little village called Nosdriche. Inside, the youngest person there is the priest, a man about 30. Everyone else is very old, and as he raises the Bible, these ancient figures all dressed in black swarm forward to kiss it, and then fall back. This is what remains of a once vibrant village – the old people who would not leave when the younger folks were evacuated. It is so bloody sad.

After church, the old women sit along the road in front of the bright turquoise fences that are everywhere in Ukraine. It's quite eerie; a sunny Sunday morning with no children on the street. And maybe a hundred yards away, there's a heavy metal gate across the road that divides one side of the village from the other. The radiation on the far side of the gate is so high that the place is uninhabitable. And the old women can see it from their bench, see the abandoned homes of their friends ... maybe even their own homes.

It seems strange the radiation would be so different in such a small area, but it's because of the rainfall. It scattered its way across Ukraine right after the accident, bringing down heavy radiation where it fell.

A few of us go behind the gate, and the Geiger counter chatters violently. I've never seen any place so empty. The only sound is the wind, picking up a gate and letting it go with a squeak. We quietly walk through the abandoned homes, and you can feel the panic with which they were evacuated – even beautiful handmade tools left behind. These people don't have much, so to leave such things behind, they must have really been terrified. The thing that gets to me the most is a little doll – a bride – left standing behind the sheer lace curtains of one living room.

Before we leave Ukraine on this trip, we go into the Chernobyl power station, into the heart of darkness. (Velikhov got us in.) As we're standing in one of the control rooms, I notice a pop-bottle cap wired over one of the switches. One of the workers tells me it's the power-down switch for the reactor – not the only one, but still ... not a very reassuring sight.

Leaving Chernobyl, we travel through the town next door to the station – Pripyat – where most of the workers lived. It's mostly high-rises, empty now, windows staring blankly out over blossoming trees. There's a big Ferris wheel standing idle, and beside it, a weathered painting of Lenin on the side of one of the buildings. But it's the sound of that place that will never leave me. Standing in the deserted town square, you hear a radio blasting out from huge speakers on top of one of the abandoned buildings. Apparently, the workers bulldozing up the poisoned earth have been going crazy. This is supposed to help, but it's like the world ended and nobody turned off the radio.

God, it's depressing. Back home, I try to show a friend some of the videotape we shot on this trip, and I can't do it without this jaded old man dissolving into floods of tears.

But taking the children out of there clearly isn't the solution. We can't take all fifty thousand or so, and we can't take them for ever. So we do what we can during the next months, setting up a clinic just outside Kiev to upgrade the quality of medical care for all the children of Chernobyl.

That's what I'm trying to protect when I fly into Kiev in August of 1991, during the hardline-communist coup against Gorbachev. By this time, I'm good friends with Konstantin Masyk, Deputy Prime Minister of Ukraine, so it's natural that I'd go to his office to find out what's going on. Natural, too, that we'd whack a few shots of vodka. Gorbachev's edict against booze notwithstanding, this is the way things are done in the Soviet Union.

Even for me, it's fairly exciting to watch Masyk handle the phone calls asking him to shoot down the plane carrying Gorbachev's enemies over Ukrainian territory. He won't do it; doesn't want

Ukraine in the middle of a Russian civil war. You know the rest: Yeltsin leads a huge demonstration on the streets of Moscow, and the coup collapses. Our building is safe, and I have a very interesting afternoon.

If it all seems a little reckless, maybe it's because I don't feel there's a lot to lose.

In 1991 I've got my own health problems and go to see a doctor in Vancouver. I'm expecting that what's dragging me down is related to spending time in highly irradiated zones around Chernobyl. But, nope. The news is lousy; it's my own personal demon that's got me – emphysema from smoking. I've got maybe seven years if I quit, three if I keep smoking. Even with a death sentence hanging over my head, it's bloody hard. Can't quit, so I start smoking just the first half of a cigarette, figuring it's better than nothing.

Knowing you're going to die sure focuses the mind.

When I coldly assess my leadership of Greenpeace, it feels like I've been dragging the organization behind me for the last several years, certainly since the push into the Soviet Union. I'm tired of it. At one point we even had a chance to buy our own satellite from the Soviets. Imagine that, Greenpeace with our own objective way of assessing environmental degradation. But it's just too big and wild a project for the organization. Maybe it's natural that when an outfit gets big, it gets slow, and safe. But I don't like it.

If I've only got a few years left, I sure as hell don't want to spend them pushing boulders uphill.

On 2 September 1991, I quit as chairman of Greenpeace International, issuing one of those nice, bland letters of resignation that says very little. You know, 'the time is right' – for sure – 'my contribution to the basic foundations of this organization is complete'. I guess that's true, too.

All I know for sure is that I'm bloody tired, and I want out.

I fly to Vancouver for some peace and quiet, and so my brother and I can finally take our father's ashes out to Buccaneer Bay. George wants his final resting place to be the waters in front of the family cabin. It's a blustery winter day when Drew and I set out. We'll make a private little ceremony for Dad and stay the night in that place of our childhood – remembering George McTaggart, remembering the family he built. Being grateful. And, for me, mourning both my father and Greenpeace.

Well, we get into a little too much remembering before we deal with the ashes. Drew's brought along his favourite beverage – a good bottle of Scotch – and the short autumn day gets away on us. Night's falling and there's quite a wind blowing by the time we set out with dear Dad to make our way down to the rowboat and out into Buccaneer Bay.

We don't quite make it. George McTaggart's ashes topple and spill, not far from the deck of the cabin. A little sheepishly, we decide it's okay. He's got a helluva view.

The next spring, broom sprouts there, as it does now every year. You know, that tough yellow bush, very common in Scotland. My father would have liked that.

Chapter Nineteen

I FIND OUT fast that it's a lot easier to resign than to quit.

No longer chairman of Greenpeace International, I still keep the title Honorary Chair. Greenpeace will use me for my high-level contacts built up over twenty years, and I'll have the clout I need to clean up a couple of projects.

The closest to my heart is Antarctica. This is where Sir Peter Scott's father perished leading an expedition in the early 1900s. Robert Scott's tiny hut is still standing there, perfectly preserved by the incredible dryness. In the last letter he wrote home, the explorer advised his wife to 'make the boy interested in natural history'. 'The boy' Peter grew up to be probably the world's most famous – and effective – naturalist and environmentalist, as well as a glider pilot, diver and painter. And I had the honour of working with him before he died, on the preservation of the wild continent that claimed his father. It feels right to finish the job.

It had started for me in 1979, with a proposal from Michael M'Gonigle in Vancouver, a Greenpeacer who was involved with the Washington-based Antarctic and Southern Ocean Coalition. M'Gonigle proposes that Greenpeace mount an expedition to Antarctica and claim the continent as a 'common heritage of humankind'. It's a big idea, and it's dead simple; so it's got appeal.

But even for me, this is pretty ambitious. And extremely expensive. This isn't Tahiti we're talking about. We need an icebreaker and a crew that can cope with the cold and the isolation, and with the risk. Maybe more important, we also need an iron-clad argument. Just because we claim it, doesn't mean it's ours.

But it's got possibilities, because Antarctica doesn't belong to any one nation. A treaty among interested countries has been in place since 1959. It's got a couple of key points: the continent will be used only for peaceful purposes, mainly scientific research, and the contracting parties will sit down occasionally to negotiate what happens next i.e. figure out how to divide up the spoils. And that's what they're about to do in the late 1970s – open Antarctica to mineral exploration, even though nobody knows what an industrial accident would do to an ecosystem this delicate. Under another Antarctic agreement, they're also talking about a commercial krill fishery in Antarctic waters. Krill is the main food for whales, so over-fishing means disaster for the whales.

It's obvious that the commercial exploitation of the world's last remaining wilderness is not a good idea.

At every Greenpeace council meeting for the next few years, we bash around the idea of what to do to save Antarctica. Everybody agrees it should be done, but not necessarily by our going there. It's just too huge, and costly, and uncertain. It would cost close to a million dollars, and we're still operating on a shoe-string budget in the early 1980s. And what if we do somehow manage to get there and the incumbent treaty nations tell us to piss off? Even I can see the logic in hesitating. But the idea keeps simmering away on the back burner. We help the Antarctic Coalition lobby against commercial exploitation, but nobody's going boating just yet. We play it safe. Never my favourite approach.

By early 1985, we've put together a couple of impossibly rich budgets for an Antarctic expedition, but during this period I'm focused primarily on getting into the Soviet Union, and on disarmament. That's why I go to hear a debate about nuclear weapons between the American evangelist Jerry Falwell and New Zealand's Prime Minister David Lange. Lange looks to me like a natural ally on disarmament; he's just banned nuclear ships from his country's harbours. Very radical at the time.

Anyway, this event's one of the famous Oxford Union Debates – as close as I'll ever get to a higher education – and I quite enjoy the atmosphere. A very old chamber, all dark wood with tiered benches three or four deep around the sides. The debate promises fireworks, and the place is absolutely packed. But for me the real sparks fly before the main event. I sit at dinner beside a skinny, auburn-haired young Kiwi, about 25, who's studying international law at Cambridge. He seems pretty bright, so I tell him about our problem with Antarctica – how do we legally justify going there to claim the continent for all the people of the world.

We discuss it a bit, the fact that no nation has sovereignty. Duncan Currie tells me he doesn't really think we've got a problem. In simplicity, it's just like the Law of the Sea; international waters belong to nobody. Fantastic. Suddenly it's very clear. And we will be going boating, somehow.

I ask Duncan if he can write it up for me – a tight legal document that we can wave in the face of the Antarctic Treaty nations. In about six weeks, I get a forty-page legal paper that powerfully asserts our right to go to Antarctica, and does a damn good job of arguing that the Treaty parties have no right to divide the continent up between them like an apple pie. Here's the heart of it:

The legal invalidity of the various claims to sovereignty over the Antarctica, combined with the State practice since 1957 and the refusal of the United States and the Soviet Union to recognize or assert sovereignty claims leads to the inexorable conclusion that the Antarctica is 'terra nullius', under the exclusive sovereignty of no country. It is emphasized that a claim to sovereignty is not the same as a right to sovereignty, and at this junction no claim is strong enough to amount to such a right. <u>The way is thus clear in law for the development of the Antarctic as a common space, consistently with the new international order</u>. [My underlining.]

The legal road is clear for Greenpeace to claim the frozen continent for the world. But we still have a little budget shortfall. Even if we sell the world rights to a documentary film on voyage, we remain about four hundred thousand dollars short.

And that's how I first met Ted Turner. I've mentioned being totally against going to big donors for anything. It's just too easy to get compromised. But I'd been following Turner's spectacular rise through the media business in the USA, and it just felt right. A risk-taker with a conscience – and with money. So I wrote him. He had a senior assistant meet me in London in May of that year and offer two hundred thousand dollars. I said thanks, but no thanks. Two hundred wouldn't get the job done. It might seem funny to turn down that much money, but it worked. A month later, I'm meeting with Turner at his headquarters in Atlanta. He's trying to negotiate the purchase of CBS at the time, so we keep getting interrupted by urgent phone calls. But somehow, by the end of the afternoon, Turner agrees to fund our World Park Antarctica expedition to the tune of four hundred thousand dollars, and he'll throw in a small helicopter – another fifty thousand. I like to think it was my charm that did it, but not bloody likely. More due to the fact that Ted has the vision to see through to the simple beauty of the idea, and the fact that it just might work.

Of course, it appeals to both of us to stick the needle in at this level, a couple of entrepreneurs re-arranging the face of international politics. It's a high-stakes game, and all for a very good cause.

So we're ready to set the cat among the pigeons. Just have to figure out who's tough enough to lead an expedition through the icy waters of the Southern Ocean and set up our World Park Antarctica base. Well, really, it's obvious – Pete Wilkinson. Now this is a year or so before his 'resignation' from the UK board. Frankly, I wouldn't mind getting Wilks out of the way for a while, as it would give me a chance to suffocate the party politics growing inside the UK office. But it's not just that. I don't know a tougher bastard to go nose-to-nose with the superpowers on a frozen beach in absolutely the middle of nowhere.

The first attempt at the end of 1985 – Antarctic summers fall right around Christmas – doesn't make it through the ice, but Pete is actually game to go again. In 1986, the timing's perfect, politically. I've mentioned that Pete left the UK board meeting at which we finagled his resignation to go to the pub across the street. Well, the next day an extremely hungover Wilks gets on a plane back to Auckland for our second attempt at building a base on Antarctica and declaring a world park. He wants to murder me, but he doesn't want to kill the project.

This time they make it – just. One afternoon the *MV Greenpeace* comes close to being trapped in ice. The ship is tantalizingly close to open water and to a clear shot at making the Antarctic coast, but completely surrounded by ice floes. Non-essential crew is evacuated by helicopter. Pete hangs over the bow, shouting the distance to the next ice floe up to the skipper. A couple of men actually push the ice floes away from the ship with boat-hooks. They get back to clear water, and two days later the *Greenpeace* inches again into the ice-field ... and finally through to the open waters of McMurdo Sound, where the Americans have their base.

Our guys spend five weeks in the balmy Antarctic summer, minus 10 degrees, building the World Park Antarctica base. We leave a team of four there over the winter – brave souls who'll do research on this unique ecosystem and man's impact on it, with special attention to the US base.

But really the most important thing they're doing is staking our claim, *your* claim, making it crystal clear that we all have a right to be here, and to be included in the decisions about what happens to the world's last wilderness. In simplicity, if possession is nine-tenths of law, the ordinary people of this planet now have the same rights of possession as the superpowers.

As soon as Pete gets back to civilization, he heads straight for Lewes. Wants to take a piece out of me for excising him from Greenpeace UK. He barges into my office, bellowing at me that I'm a bastard. I don't deny it, but so what. He had a great time in Antarctica, and now he's a bloody hero. After Pete settles down a little, I mention we have plans for him to go again. I'll tell him about it over a few beers.

The early Antarctic expeditions are a logistical nightmare, fortunately we have an onshore co-ordinator with a much better head for details than me. Roger Wilson, a New Zealander, handles the first expeditions and then – after we've pretty much worked Roger into the ground – an American woman, Kelly Rigg, takes over.

Pete leads four Antarctic expeditions before he's done. And, by the way, he's one of my few professional regrets. Wish I'd figured out another way around our problems with the UK board and kept him on it. He's a good man.

By 1988 Greenpeace has almost two million members. And we've got the connections and lobbying expertise built during our run-up to the whaling moratorium. In June the Antarctic Treaty nations prepare to divide up the continent's natural resources, and we're ready for them. They sign the Convention on the Regulation of Antarctic Mineral Resources (CRAMRA). We strike back with an anti-ratification campaign.

We focus on key countries and their vulnerabilities. Example:

the USA needs a two-thirds Senate majority to ratify; the Democrats currently hold the Senate majority, *and* the US Antarctic base has very visible pollution problems. We'll approach Democrat Al Gore. Example: France is building an airstrip in a sensitive penguin habitat. We'll try Jacques Cousteau. Example: the UK has a special relationship with Antarctica because of Robert Scott's expeditions there, so Sir Peter has enormous authority there.

Alongside the Antarctic and Southern Oceans Coalition, we build alliances with influential institutions that are tough for anybody to ignore. We do it at the highest level, with Peter Scott and Sadruddin Aga Khan writing letters to heads of state. And we do it through the side door. We'd tried unsuccessfully to get to Jacques Cousteau through official channels, and then one of our people has a love affair with one of his people. A genuine love affair, but bloody well-timed. You'd be surprised, or maybe you wouldn't, at how much gets done internationally that way. Don't think Cousteau ever knew, not that he'd care.

After the *Exxon Valdez* ran aground off the coast of Alaska in early 1989, the campaign snowballed. This disaster was more powerful than any action we could have dreamed up – making it easy to imagine what gas and oil exploration could do to the ends of the earth.

Shortly after that the French Prime Minister said he supported Cousteau, and the Mineral Resources convention should be renegotiated. Then the Australians broke, the Prime Minister announcing that they wouldn't sign the convention. This is shortly before Sir Peter's death, and he mentions it to me in his last letter. In fact that's what his last words to me are about: 'P.S. Bob Hawke did a good job, didn't he?' Yes, he did.

All my trips to Moscow and all those shots of vodka pay off, too. The Americans have been saying they can't go for an Antarctic mining ban because they know the Soviets won't. Not exactly high moral ground, and I want to pull it out from under them. Through one of my high-placed Soviet sources, Artur Chilingarov, we get Antarctica mentioned in a major speech, delivered by Mikhail Gorbachev early in 1990. Chilingarov and Velikhov and I actually write part of the speech. It says the Soviet Union proposes 'the establishment of protected areas of unique ecosystems with special attention to the Antarctic. Our grandchildren will never forgive us if we do not preserve this unique environment. The Soviet Union supports the establishment of a Common Reserve.'

That pretty much nails it.

There's a special meeting of the Antarctic Treaty parties scheduled in Chile a little while later. They've set aside a week for talk about liability issues arising out of the new mining policy, i.e. what happens when there's an oil spill. The meeting takes less than half a day. There's no point. Nobody's going mining in Antarctica. The public won't let them. The rest of the meeting is spent discussing various environmental protection proposals!

On 4 October 1991 the Antarctic Treaty Protocol is signed, banning mining there for fifty years. It'll take another big push to get it ratified, but we're on our way.

The Treaty is signed a month after I step down as chairman of Greenpeace International. And it sure feels good. I've honoured my friendship with Sir Peter, and maybe earned a little rest before my next crusade.

I've also got some personal details to clean up. Shouldn't call it details. It's bigger than that, and much tougher.

Christina and I have really come to the end of the road, but we're just as bad at parting as we were at getting together. One of us steps back and the other steps forward. One of us is finally ready to quit, and the other wants to give it another try. It's an excruciatingly painful dance.

I write a poem in 1987 that says it all, from my point of view:

Christina
evasive flower
petals touched ...
by a faint breeze.
Sunrise and a tender caress.
Sunset awaits,
my soul awaits,
the opening.

And there's Julia. It's not as if I've been a normal dad to my youngest daughter either, but I love her and she knows it, and loves me back in spite of my frequent – no, almost constant – absence. I have dreams about losing her. Once in my dreams I give her away to one of my Greenpeace colleagues and her new husband. When I call Christina in a small panic the next morning, she tells me Julia has been sick all night. It feels like we've got a bond beyond words, and I don't want to lose my little girl, so I dance. Which, when you think about it, is quite interesting. Even I can see that there's been a bit of a pattern of running away in my family life. This time, I don't let myself get far. Tina and I try all kinds of different scenarios. We know we won't be an ordinary family, but we struggle to find a shape our relationship can take to remain *some* kind of family. Maybe we both should have paid more attention early on to the fact that we can't seem to agree on where to live. By where, I don't mean which house; I mean which country. We send dozens of letters back and forth about finding a third place, a holiday place, where we can come together from time to time to be with each other, and with Julia.

In 1989, Tina agrees to come live in Rome, where Greenpeace is starting a major push into the Mediterranean. It's wonderful for me to spend more time with Julia, now six, but once again Tina and I just don't get along. My schedule's a big part of it. She wants to plan things, and I just can't. Or won't.

She leaves after a few months, and early in 1991 I decide to put us both out of our misery, and write Christina that I'm filing for divorce.

So at the end of the year, after leaving Greenpeace, I'm as at sea as I've been in decades. A free man, painfully aware of that old song that says 'freedom's just another word for nothing left to lose'.

Only there's more, lots more.

Chapter Twenty

ALTHOUGH I'M AT sea emotionally at the end of 1991, I'm not exactly alone.

It's complicated.

Greenpeace Italy opens its doors in 1986, and a year or so later I decide to move the chairman's office down to Rome, to put some power behind our push into the Mediterranean. Also – to be blunt – our new executive director, Steve Sawyer, thinks the International office in Lewes will run a little more smoothly if he has some room to do his job. He might have a point.

So I move down to Rome and take Brian Fitzgerald along. He's the young American who was with me in Paris after the bombing of the *Warrior*. Among other things, Fitzgerald's a computer whiz and has begun setting up what was then a brand-new communications system among our offices. E-mail allows us quick communication even into the Soviet Union, where it still takes days to book a phone call. I have no idea about how any of this stuff works, but I know it's going to be important to a global organization based in northern Europe.

It's love at first sight – me and Italy, me and Rome.

I find this fantastic apartment in the heart of the city, Colle Oppio, about half a mile up the hill from the Colosseum. In the morning, about 7 a.m., I drive what must be *the* world's best commute to work – down through narrow streets to the broad road that winds around the ancient walls of the Colosseum, past the arena where the Romans used to stage their chariot races, and then I'm at the office. I park my little white CinqueCento and walk across the little park in front of the office to grab an espresso at the gelato stand. Whack back one of those – the Italians do not sip their coffee – and go to work.

Even though our office is just two rooms down the hall from Greenpeace Italy, the Italians are a little shy around 'the International', meaning Fitzgerald and me, and they generally stay out of our space. Except for Domitilla Senni. I don't think Domi's ever been afraid of anything. She's small and slight, dark-haired and olive-skinned, and she moves like a cat – a very confident cat. Domitilla speaks excellent English, since her paternal grandmother was American. Her mother comes from a very old Roman family. Put it all together, and this is one very self-assured young woman. She becomes a bit of a secret weapon for Greenpeace, a fearless campaigner who'll walk up to anybody at a political meeting and lobby them. Because she's a beautiful Italian woman, they listen.

Domi becomes a good friend, and through her I get to know Italy. For a North American, it's quite a trip to drive over the Seven Hills of Rome or to sit quietly on my balcony watching dusk settle over the Colosseum, with a woman who can rightly claim this as her family heritage. Sometimes when I fly into the international airport at Rome, coming back from some meeting or another, Domi picks me up and we have a meal in the nearby little town of Fiumicino. Off and on, *Vega*'s moored there, so we can have a look at my old girl and then drink *vino rosso* sitting in a vine-covered outdoor restaurant overlooking the canal. Domitilla seems to care about these old bones without expecting more than I can give, so it's quite a peaceful relationship.

By now I've sold Rose Cottage and turned our place in Sweden over to Christina, so I'm feeling homeless – which maybe sounds strange coming from someone who lives on a plane. But even if I don't get home much, I need to know it's there. I'm also approaching 60 and feeling every second of it. I'm sometimes nostalgic for Buccaneer Bay, yet can't imagine ever going back to Canada to live. Rose Cottage and the UK seem like ancient and sometimes sad history.

I start exploring north of Rome, into Umbria, near the Tuscany border. Driving through this area on either shoulder of a summer's day can take your breath away. Soft golden light spreads over fields of sunflowers and olive groves. Every house seems to have abundant vines growing up the walls, and a little garden with the biggest, reddest tomatoes you'll ever see. Coming round a curve, you may suddenly pass an arm's-length away from a stone wall that looks like it was built by the ancient Romans, and probably was.

My friend Sidney Holt, the whale scientist, and Leslie Busby, his partner in work and life, have an old farmhouse just outside Citta della Pieve. Their property sprawls over acres of vines and olive trees, and has a fantastic view out over the towns of eastern Tuscany. I'm more than a little envious. Only one way to fix that.

By the autumn of 1989, I've bought my own little piece of paradise. Actually, what I've bought is a couple of derelict farmhouses, although the land developer in me sees that my fifty acres have incredible potential. But mostly I'm simply drawn here, drawn to the peace and the light, and the history. My new home sits above Paciano, a little village of fewer than a thousand souls that dates back to the thirteenth century and is still largely confined by the old walls. It's off the beaten track, so no tourists, and the locals are friendly to a strange Scots-Canadian who doesn't speak a word of their language. Actually, I've picked up a little – *vino rosso* and *due capuccini* just about covering it. From the top of my property I can see miles along the valley and watch the sun set beside Lago Trasimeno. I've lived in some beautiful places, but this beats them all.

My house is surrounded by an over-grown olive grove, the trees hundreds of years old. And the best thing about it is that the groves haven't been farmed for fifty years, since before the chemical age. If these trees could be brought back into production, the olives would certainly be organic. Hmmmm. Maybe there's a worthwhile occupation here for an old man who can't sit still but has had almost enough of going out every day to do battle with the bad guys.

This will be one of the happiest accidents in my life.

A young man comes over with the small crew of friends from the UK who will clear the land in exchange for free room and board. When I come down on weekends to see how they're doing, we get talking, this tall string-bean of a lad and me. Rowan Holloway is partly here to escape the UK. He had a helluva time with the education system, to which I can relate. Rowan's got dyslexia – a learning disability that means nothing about how smart you are. But they didn't discover what was holding him back for a long time, so he struggled at school and maybe hated it even more than I did. Rowan's gentle and smart and hard-working, and very interested in this quirky idea I have to farm the olives. He came to Paciano for what was supposed to be six months and ends up staying years, living in a little house we build for him next to mine. He'll look after the trees, and sometimes he'll look after me. But I'm getting ahead of myself.

By the middle of 1990, the house is habitable, and I start spending weekends there. I plant vines in big red clay pots beside my house and nurse them along so they'll eventually cover the walls. I frequently marvel at the stone stairs that take me up to my living quarters. They're hundreds of years old and very uneven, and it gives me pleasure to know that they're worn from the footsteps of many generations. People were climbing these stairs centuries before my father left the Isle of Mull. In the morning I wake to the sound of the cuckoo-birds, and at night the last thing I hear is the chatter of insects. So peaceful after Rome. So peaceful period.

Domi comes up with me for the weekend sometimes and it's in Umbria, as we're walking along the shores of Lago Trasimeno, that she tells me she's pregnant. I tell her I've been a lousy husband and father in the past, and don't see that changing. I'm too old to go through the baby stuff again, and I've just been told I've only got a few years left so I'm not going to see this baby grow up. The best I can offer is that we look for a third place to share together once in a while as a family. Domi's tough. She says it's better the baby knows the truth from the beginning, and she doesn't care for a piece of paper, anyway. I'll be a father again, but she's too clear-headed to want me as a husband.

Six months later I resign from Greenpeace. As I've said, my health is a big part of the reason. I don't know in 1991 that I'm going to beat the doctor's predictions. He told me I had three to seven years, depending on whether or not I quit smoking. Well I didn't quit, and I'm still here, almost ten years later – taking medication for my heart and my breathing, but still here. When you think you're facing a death sentence, it's natural to want a little more from life than work – no matter how important your work is.

There are other reasons I step away from the active chairmanship into an honorary position. Or maybe it's just one other reason. In the early 1990s the organization is getting big and unwieldy. The professionals are taking over, and I'm not saying that's a bad thing. Just not my thing. I didn't build the organization to last for ever; I built it to take risks.

For example, I've mentioned the satellite we could have had for cheap when the Soviet Union was crumbling. I thought that was a risk we had to take, to be the first environmental organization with our own monitoring satellite. The board thought it was too risky, that we didn't know enough about the vendors, or the cost of upkeep. Okay, but we didn't know if it would work either, in 1977, when we bought a rust-bucket called the *Sir William Hardy* and turned her into the *Rainbow Warrior*.

My friend Pete Wilkinson says there's a certain kind of organization that needs a rogue to run it. That was Greenpeace in the early days. Not in 1991.

After my resignation, with another child on the way and that lousy medical prognosis hanging over my head, I move full-time to the farm at Paciano. I hang a picture of Rose Cottage on a white-washed wall in the living room. Above the fireplace go pictures of my parents, George and Mary McTaggart, in their youth. And on a cabinet at the end of the thick, rough dining-room table, I place my prize – those two models of the *Rainbow Warrior*, commissioned by Lloyd Cutler to help us win damages against the French.

At long last, I'm home.

I quickly fall into a routine. Up before 6 a.m. for a shot of espresso and a morning's work by fax and phone. Brian Fitzgerald has joined me in Paciano, so our projects continue fairly seamlessly. Then about 11.30, I head for Castiglione del Lago to buy some smokes, and the *Herald Tribune*. I contemplate what's shifted in international politics over a beer in the little town square, and then down for lunch by Lago Trasimeno at a little place I call Anna's. That's not the name of the restaurant, but the name of the woman who runs it, and she takes good care of me. Occasionally, friends join me, and that's a mixed blessing. I really enjoy a quiet meal alone, and I'm not very patient with the social niceties: how long it takes people to order, the fact that nobody ever wants french fries – tooooo unhealthy – but they always want to steal mine. Guess I'm getting a bit set in my ways. After a long slow lunch, I find it easy to fall into the Italian tradition of having a wee nap. By evening I'm up, restless, and tuning into CNN, reading between the lines to decipher what's happening in the world.

You understand, as much as I'd like to, I can't stop thinking about how it is possible to change the world, about where I could stick the needle in next.

Domitilla is expecting the baby around Christmas. It's not very nice, but as the event approaches, I really can't handle being around for it. It just gets more complicated when Domi has an ultrasound and says it looks like a boy. There hasn't been a McTaggart boy born in my generation. Drew and I each have four beautiful daughters, but nobody to carry on the family name. Yes, I know it sounds sexist, and it has nothing to do with loving my girls, but there's a part of me that wants a son.

I'm a bundle of inadequacies, of guilt ... of anxiety about what Christina's reaction will be. I don't want to lose her friendship and am terrified of losing Julia. By mid-December I just can't sit still any longer, and head back to Vancouver for Christmas with my brother.

On 13 January 1992 Domi calls me at Drew's. Actually, even a few hours after her labour, she's so tough and discreet that she has Brian Fitzgerald call me first to see if I can talk. She's just given birth to a healthy baby, a boy. And she's naming him George Godfrey, after my father.

When I tell my brother, I'm a little embarrassed to be caught in another messy situation. But, mostly, I'm bursting with pride that I have a son.

In Rome, a month later, when I first hold George in my arms and look into his deep brown eyes, I make a pact with myself, and with him. It's very clear between Domi and me that I won't be any kind of regular dad. But I want George to know his father, and to be proud of his name, the first McTaggart boy of his generation.

But I'm not around to change many of his nappies. George is born in the middle of the Antarctic sanctuary campaign, a campaign again named George after my son's grandfather. I hope my boy grows up to find some satisfaction in that.

It started over drinks at Sidney Holt's old farmhouse outside Citta della Pieve. Sir Peter's right-hand person, Cassandra Phillips, is there, along with John Frizell from Greenpeace, the scientists

Bill de la Mare and Sidney, as well as Leslie Busby and me. Very much the core anti-whaling group – no bureaucrats.

This is around the time when battery-operated coke cans are a fad, the ones that start dancing when you make a noise. We're in the middle of a heavy conversation when Bill de la Mare looks up and says, 'I don't know about you but I don't trust that coke can.' Very funny, but the issue's real. It's around this time that the local police catch a Japanese guy with a long-lens camera sneaking around up above my house. To the whaling nations we're the enemy, and it's no joke that security's important.

We're worried about a Japanese counter-attack on the 1982 commercial whaling moratorium. Just because we won it, doesn't mean it's unassailable. We start talking about a proposal for a whaling sanctuary in the waters around Antarctica that we've heard France may propose at the next IWC meeting. I'm fresh from the campaign to prevent the mining of Antarctica, so this sanctuary is especially appealing. Then Bill and Sidney start spouting off about how, if we get a Southern Ocean Sanctuary, we've got a crack at saving most of the world's remaining whales since the waters around Antarctica are the summer feeding grounds for most of the great whales, including the minke. It's the last whale species to survive in any numbers. So with a Southern Ocean Sanctuary, even if the commercial moratorium doesn't hold, the whales are safe. Bloody brilliant. By the spring of 1991, we know there's an Antarctic sanctuary proposal sitting with the French government in Paris, going nowhere. It needs a friendly push if it's going to be on the agenda at the next IWC meeting and it has to happen soon.

As the evening progresses, I become increasingly restless – and not just from the strain of pretending that Leslie's cats are not getting on my nerves. This is one of those moments of absolute clarity. This is *it*. The sanctuary idea is big, but it's simple, and winnable in a short time-frame. I want it on the agenda at the next IWC meeting. We've got to have a go.

I might even have left before the meeting broke up – not sure – just remember being absolutely focused on getting to Paris and to my old friend Brice Lalonde, who is now France's minister of the environment.

It is such a contrast from twenty years ago, from our meetings with Friends of the Earth at Brice's funky little apartment on Rue de l'Université. Now he has a huge office in a private hotel in Paris, rented by the government. It's all black leather designer furniture, with low glass tables and half-abstract paintings of mountains. So bloody big you could have a meeting of fifty people and not feel crowded. Brice understands the importance of the sanctuary completely, the beauty of the strategy – save the whales, no matter which way Japan turns. We sit happily plotting while the very serious people from the administration take notes. I am back with my old friend, and that feels good. And we are making trouble, and that feels even better.

Brice is about to resign over philosophical differences with the government but I convince him to put out a press release first, committing France to the Antarctic sanctuary.

France tables the motion at the IWC in Glasgow in 1992.

Now excuse me if this is boring, but it's important. Adopting a new regulation at the IWC happens in stages. After it's tabled, a motion must be seconded before it can go to a vote at the Commission's technical committee. Only if it passes a simple majority vote – fifty per cent – in technical committee will it be put to a vote the next year before the plenary of the IWC.

The 1993 International Whaling Commission meetings are held in Kyoto, Japan, and talk about walking into the lion's den! This is a very heavy scene. The Kyoto Conference Centre looks like something out of a science fiction movie. The Japanese have organized massive pro-whaling demonstrations outside, and there are black vans with dark windows parked near the entrance to the conference centre, loudspeakers on top going constantly in Japanese.

The young woman brave enough to be the face of Greenpeace in Japan, Naoko Funahashi, translates for me. As people arrive for the conference, the speakers blast out information on who's who, so the rent-a-crowd can applaud or jeer appropriately. It's wild.

Inside the meeting room, there are the usual rows of familiar NGOs. But this year, something new – this Japanese guy is constantly sitting right behind me, with the flaps on his briefcase pointing always the same way, in our direction. If you were suspicious, you might think he had a microphone. I *am* suspicious. I get into the habit of putting my shirt over the mirror in my room, in case it's a two-way mirror. None of us ever has an important conversation inside; we go outside into the garden for meetings.

The sanctuary proposal needs a seconder so that it can be put to a vote at the technical committee. After that it should be smooth sailing to the simple majority vote needed to pass technical, and move forward to a plenary vote at the 1994 meeting.

There are several conservationist countries that ought to be proud to second the motion, but one evening I see all our so-called like-minded commissioners coming out of a meeting room, looking grim. It's strange that they're meeting secretly. A little later in the bar I push one of my contacts who'd been inside the meeting. He says the Japanese foreign ministry has been applying such heavy pressure that they've all been ordered by their governments not to second the French motion.

This could kill it, for good.

But the Irish delegation hasn't arrived yet, and Ireland is one of those rare nations that doesn't always follow the pack. We have a strong campaigner there, John Bowler, and he goes to the environment minister and talks him into seconding.

When the Irish commissioner arrives at the IWC, we have the pleasure of handing him an Irish government press release – Ireland Will Back Whale Refuge. It's his first indication of new instructions from his minister – Ireland will be seconding France's Antarctic sanctuary proposal. The commissioner doesn't mind at all, hearing it first from us. Good thing the Irish have a sense of humour.

We're halfway there. Now we have one year to pull in the votes.

And all hell breaks loose. The Japanese begin a vote consolidation operation, pouring millions in fisheries 'aid' into poor Caribbean nations to get them to vote against the sanctuary. The Japanese are trying to create a voting block – remember they only need one-quarter of the IWC delegates to block a change in IWC regulations, to block the sanctuary or any other conservation measure. We don't have the money Japan has for 'aid' contributions, but we do have experience focusing public pressure where it can do the most good. We need to make it very unpopular for governments to vote against the sanctuary. In a democracy, that matters. If the people don't like you, you're out.

We organize a film to be made, *The Last Whale*, to show in IWC countries during the run-up to the vote.

I have another idea, a seed planted while organizing the release of the *Breakthrough* rock album in the Soviet Union. Bryan Adams is on a world tour; he's just done a benefit concert for the victims of the Sydney bush fires that summer. A big star with a conscience. Maybe he'd like to have a go at the sanctuary – hand out postcards at his concerts for people to send to politicians asking them bluntly to vote for the sanctuary. No mention of the green movement, just a direct message from person to politician.

Well, Bryan goes for it.

Bryan and I personally pay to get a simple one-page flyer printed. It's one half a plea from the rock star to his fans to write to their governments to support the Antarctic sanctuary at the IWC, or at least not to oppose it. (Remember, when you need a 75 per cent majority, every vote the opposition doesn't get is like three for you.) The other half is a postcard, addressed and ready to go to the head of state we're targeting.

Throughout New Zealand and Australia, we go after the Solomon

Islands. Every concert-goer gets a postcard saying, 'Dear Prime Minister, I am asking you not to vote against the IWC proposal to create a Whale sanctuary around the Antarctic Ocean, due to be voted at Mexico in 1994. Yours sincerely...'

I receive a private call from a senior official in New Zealand's foreign office. He's been talking to the Prime Minister of the Solomons, and they're drowning in postcards. Could we stop? Well, no, I say, until they agree to abstain on the sanctuary vote.

It takes a few thousand more postcards, but they agree.

I join Bryan for the European leg of his tour, making sure the flyers are printed and on the seats before each concert. And to tell you the truth, I have a helluva lot of fun. (Some of the boys in the band give me the nickname Axl after the wild man in the band Guns 'n' Roses. Okay with me; after twenty years of Greenpeace, I'm ready to let loose a little.) Halfway through each concert, Bryan shouts out at the audience, 'Do me a favour!!??' Of course, by that time they're eating out of his hands and, anyway, what young person wouldn't like to save the whales, if they knew how. Well, we're here to tell them how.

On this tour I have a small experience of what it's like to be a star and it's easy to see how people get hooked on the rush. At Wembley Stadium in northwest London, Bryan plays to a packed and very enthusiastic audience. As the show draws to a close, the band does a couple of encores and then leaves the stage. But Bryan's got a little surprise, and I'm invited to be part of it. As the audience shuffles into their coats to leave, we run around a little passageway at the outside of the arena, along a narrow walkway right through the audience, up onto a little makeshift stage in the centre of the auditorium.

The little stage is suddenly flooded with light, and the startled audience absolutely erupts with joy. You can barely hear the band begin to play one of their old favourites. It's fantastic.

But what's more fantastic is how the campaign's going.

By the time I arrive in Puerto Vallarta ten days before the 1994 IWC meetings, I'm feeling pretty good. Nervous as hell, but pretty good. We just might pull it off.

Our Mexican powerhouse, a quiet university professor named Martha Banuelos, has organized thousands of Mexican children for a torchlight parade through the hotel grounds in support of the whales. They also form a living work of art on the beach, the outline of a whale about a kilometre long. Beautiful.

But I'm worried about Chile, very worried about Chile. They'd been a whaling country and then started to come over to the conservationist side when they abstained on the 1982 moratorium vote. At Kyoto in 1993 I saw the Chilean and Japanese commissioners hang back at one of the breaks, to have a huddled meeting in the corner of the conference room. I put our team on the alert. Somebody's got to reel in Chile.

While everyone else is in closed meetings, Sidney Holt nabs the Chilean commissioner and takes him for a beer. Since Kyoto, Chile's had a change of government. Before his election the new President, Eduardo Frei, had actually signed a Greenpeace petition in support of the sanctuary, but Chile's still got problems with the boundaries of the sanctuary. So does Argentina, the other South American country that touches the sanctuary. Sidney and this guy work out a compromise that's still biologically sound, and we quickly get the 'Proposal for a Widely Accepted Sanctuary' over to the proposing nation, France. They'll go with it. And so, with a bit of arm-twisting, will the USA and the other countries with strong interests in the Antarctic, such as the UK and South Africa.

It's incredibly exciting, and excruciatingly nerve-wracking. If this proposal doesn't make it now, it's gone for good, and so probably are the world's whales. So much depends on the next 24 hours, and on what the Caribbean countries do. Japan's spent a lot of money there.

Then somebody overhears the commissioner from St Lucia at the travel agent's desk in the lobby of the hotel. He's going home early! Avoiding a confrontation with the Japanese.

On Thursday as the thing goes to a vote, it isn't just the Mexican weather that's making me sweat. We're still not entirely sure what the remaining Caribbean countries will do.

France puts the motion on the floor.

The Americans second it.

And the room quiets for the vote.

As it moves through the Caribbean countries, my spirits start to lift. One after another, they abstain.

My breath leaves me in a giant WHEW!

Only Japan votes against the Southern Ocean Sanctuary.

In a delicious repeat of the moratorium vote a dozen years earlier, we spill out of the conference room into the day. One nice difference, though, Puerto Vallarta is a helluva lot warmer than Brighton. And soon NGOs are tossing each other into the swimming pool, drunk on joy, and a little champagne.

We've won a big one. Won for the whales, and for Julia and George. Won for your children, and for their children.

I still have the piece of paper I carried with me throughout that convention, tracking the movement of votes. Funny kind of souvenir, since I'll never be able to unfold it. It got absolutely water-logged, and dried permanently stuck together. But just looking at it brings back the taste of that day – chlorine and champagne. And winning.

Chapter Twenty-one

THAT SHOULD BE enough. Time to retire properly to Paciano and the olive groves, to the long lunches and wee naps. Savour my remaining few years. And I try. I really do. For a few weeks I enjoy doing a little work around the farm, and sipping a beer beside the fountain in the square at Castiglione del Lago. Then I get restless again, something jumps out at me from the newspaper, something I'd maybe have a go at, if I were younger. And I get thinking, what the hell.

Which is more or less how I get myself lost on Mururoa Atoll in the summer of 1995, when France schedules another round of nuclear madness.

They had stopped their testing programme in 1992, responding to Gorbachev and Bush. But with Jacques Chirac's election to the French presidency in April 1995, they're at it again – planning to explode a series of eight nuclear bombs at Mururoa. These tests will be underground. We did manage to stop the insanity of tests in the atmosphere, raining radiation down on the people of Polynesia. But underground testing is causing the atoll to sink, at the rate of about half an inch a bomb blast. Imagine if Paris were sinking; people would be marching in the streets and banishing the officials responsible to political purgatory, for ever. But this is far away from 'civilization', these people aren't Westerners, and somehow it's easy to ignore. Or it would be, if we left France alone to get on with their dirty business out of the public eye.

There's an even bigger issue at stake than what's happening to the atoll. If France resumes nuclear testing that'll trigger other countries to go at it, killing the Comprehensive Test Ban Treaty. They have to be stopped.

I fly to Rarotonga to join the *Rainbow Warrior* – the new *Rainbow Warrior* – and on my sixty-third birthday am once again heading for Mururoa. Greenpeace has a strategy that, to be blunt, I don't agree with. On 10 July, the tenth anniversary of the bombing of the first *Warrior* in Auckland Harbour, they'll sail the new ship right into Mururoa, inside the 12-mile limit that marks international waters. They'll get arrested, grab a headline or two, and that'll be that.

My thinking is that we need a strategy that will go on and on, that will keep delaying the tests and irritating the hell out of the French. So if Greenpeace is heading in, and putting the *Warrior* out of action, I'm going off in another direction.

On the trip towards Mururoa, I spend a day painting an inflatable black and provisioning it with food and an extra motor. On the night of 8 July, near the atoll, Greenpeace launches several regular zodiacs beside the *Warrior* to create a diversion, while my old friend Chris Robinson, Greenpeace campaigner Henk Haazen and I slip into the black inflatable and shoot away towards Mururoa.

With three people 'lost' somewhere on these islands, I don't think France can risk setting off a nuclear bomb.

As dawn breaks, we are fifty nautical miles away from the *Warrior*, picking our way carefully through the coral reef surrounding a little island called Vanavana. We bury the zodiac in the sand, wipe our tracks off the beach and move into the temporary huts the islanders use when they come each year to pick coconuts on Vanavana. Our only company is a dog and her pup, left behind after the last coconut harvest. We name the little guy George.

Occasionally we risk turning on the radio, and so catch the fantastic news that a peace flotilla of sailboats is on its way from

New Zealand to Mururoa, apparently the result of a television interview with me that was broadcast the day we left the *Warrior*: 'I really hope that the Kiwis, who are the best sailors in the world, get together all the boats they can and just wander over to Mururoa … You don't have to go inside the 12-mile zone, but when you're outside the 12-mile limit they have to put a warship on you and it bothers them. The more that can get there the better. Please come.'

Of course the 'little wander' over to Mururoa is a month's tough sail on unpredictable seas, and yet 32 yachts risk everything to join the peace flotilla. It's one of those times when you have to believe there's hope for the human race.

We also hear over the radio that the French are looking for us. Several times helicopters fly over the island. Then after about ten days, they find out we're safe – apparently an information leak from our side – and I decide we've milked most of the impact out of our disappearing act. We motor back to the protest fleet, and I fly back to Italy, disappointed in an action that could have put a lot more pressure on the French, if our internal security had been better.

But when I get a look at the international press, we're doing better than I thought. Lots of stories about 'Scarlet Pimpernel' disappearing on the atoll. Opinion polls around the world condemn the French testing programme. Even in France itself, two-thirds of the people polled say the tests are a mistake. Several countries are boycotting French wine. Australia has frozen military co-operation with France, and French goods sit untouched in Australian ports. In all, a hundred and fifty countries register protests.

I decide we should keep the pressure on, have one more go.

By the middle of September, there are a half-dozen protest boats left in the zone off Mururoa. One of them is my old girl, *Vega*, skippered by Chris Robinson. The monsoon season is approaching and the protest fleet has to get home ahead of it, but we want to end the action on a powerful note.

Among the islanders now picking coconuts on Vanavana are 18 brave souls who agree to sail into Mururoa and claim it back from the French. That'll put one more needle into the French, and give a boost to the local protests.

On 26 September as *Vega* nears Mururoa, the Polynesians send a message to the French admiral there: 'We, the Maohi people, rightful owners of the atolls of Mururoa and Fangataufa greet you. It has been 30 years that you have been conducting nuclear tests on these islands. We are here of our own free will to ask you, President Chirac and Admiral, to terminate all nuclear testing.'

Some of the islanders plan to sleep on the shore of the atoll, a peaceful protest, but they don't get that chance.

As soon as we cross the 12-mile limit, the French warship that's been tailing us launches an inflatable. For me, it's a flashback to 1973. Commandos board *Vega*, in spite of my objections. At least this time they don't beat me senseless, just arrest us all. The French are very disrespectful of the islanders, quite abusive, but do eventually return them home. Chris and I spend a couple of days in a concrete cell, before being shipped, separately, out of Tahiti. He's sent to Sydney. I'm off to Paris for a few more hours of useless interrogation in a cell at Orly Airport. Then it's into a police car for a ninety miles an hour trip across Paris, complete with motorcycle escort, to Charles de Gaulle Airport. You'd think I was a terrorist, not a peaceful protester. They hand me an expulsion paper saying I'm banned from French territory for the rest of my life, and then put me on a plane for Rome.

As I walk onto the Alitalia flight, someone recognizes me and begins to clap. Other people look up, and the applause travels down the length of the aeroplane. Feels pretty good.

A year later France signs the Comprehensive Test Ban Treaty, saying they were planning to do it all along, after this last little round of tests. I like to think maybe Chris and I and *Vega* had a little bit to do with it.

When I return to Paciano that autumn, it's to personal news that dwarfs anything else that's going on in the world. The worst call I've ever received in my life. My brother has been diagnosed with a brain tumour. Drew is operated on almost immediately, and I'm at his side just about as quickly. When the doctors say he has six months to live, I call every high-level contact I can think of around the world, searching for a brain specialist who'll be able to fix it, to fix my closest friend for 63 years. Throughout my life, whenever I'm in serious trouble, it's always Drew I call. If it's medium trouble, like a divorce, he'll just tell me to fix it myself. But if it's serious, he'll move in, and when Drew moves in, he really takes care of it. Now my brother's the one in trouble, and I can't do a thing.

I've never felt so helpless.

My father's dead, my mother and sister are in a nursing home lost to Alzheimer's, and now I'm losing my brother, my best friend.

Drew dies on 22 February 1996 and I sink into a black hole that it will take me months to climb out of, not sure I'll ever make it all the way. It seems like the end of the family. Me the head of the family, that's a joke. After the funeral, Drew's wife, Myrna, gives me a copy of the picture that hangs on the wall at Buccaneer Bay – Drew and I as young boys in a little dugout canoe, me with a mischievous grin, Drew as always looking quite serious. But not even Buc Bay comforts me; every memory has my brother in it, or rather the absence of my brother.

When the walls close in on me during the months after Drew's death, I can't stop thinking about my own mortality. I don't mind so much that there's not a lot of time left but worry about what a mess will be left behind. I have trouble sleeping and wake up thinking about odd things. Greenpeace has signed my old boat back over to me, as a kind of retirement present, and I worry about the fact that I want to leave *Vega* to Chris when I go, but it's not yet in my will. My North American daughters don't talk to me anymore.

Christina and I seem to have almost as much trouble sorting out our divorced relationship as we did our married relationship.

But mostly when the house is quiet, I'm haunted by the fact that she and Julia don't yet know about George's birth. It's been almost five years now, and little George and I are getting closer and closer. He knows that he has sisters, including one fairly close to his age who also lives in Europe. Domitilla is ready to bring George and Julia together anytime, but I just don't know how Christina will deal with the knowledge that I've had another child without her. I fear it will mean losing Julia. But they've got to hear about my son from me before I go, and rationally I understand that the longer it's a secret, the harder it'll be to tell.

It wasn't supposed to happen this way. If life was fair, I'd be dead instead of Drew. He always bloody glowed with good health and clean living; married this fantastic woman, his one and only, and produced a totally stable family. I was supposed to go first. My breathing's getting worse and the doctors say my heart's in lousy shape, too, but I'm still alive, and I can hear my brother's voice in my head, telling me to bloody well get on with it.

By the spring of 1997 I've more or less rejoined the land of the living.

Brian Fitzgerald has had enough of the isolation of Paciano, and – I suspect – of being woken at 2 a.m. to get to work on my latest idea. I've now got a crazy Dane by the name of Michael Nielsen working with me full-time. He was raised an orphan, and at the age of 19 or so pretty much handed his life over to Greenpeace, and to me. Michael was one of the key people in our drive to open a Greenpeace office in the then Soviet Union, so you know he likes a challenge.

I've got my own foundation now, totally separate from Greenpeace, although we still work together sometimes and I represent Greenpeace at the Whaling Commission. I don't advertise it much, but most of the work on the Antarctic sanctuary, and on

Chernobyl, has been done by Fitzgerald and Leslie Busby and me, for the Third Millennium Foundation. And that's the banner under which Michael Nielsen and I go to Harare, Zimbabwe, for a meeting of the Convention on Trade in Endangered Species (CITES).

It's quite a scene. We have to stay at the big luxury hotel where the CITES meetings are being held, behind police guards, because it's too dangerous to stay anywhere else. Mugabe is just about to bring in his land-reform scheme – take the land from the whites and give it back to the blacks – and the air is electric with a sense of something big about to happen.

It's just about as tense inside the conference room. This is a crucial meeting. CITES faces enormous pressure from countries who want to turn it from a conservation convention into a wildlife trade convention. To put it simply, a handful of nations want to legitimize wiping out whole species for the sake of making a dollar.

This is the CITES conference that 'down-lists' elephants, agreeing to the resumption of ivory trade, most of it to Japan.

If Japan and Norway have their way, the whales will be next.

CITES makes the International Whaling Commission look simple, in terms of politics. There are almost a hundred and fifty countries represented and about two and a half thousand species listed as endangered. Every non-governmental organization is working to protect a favourite species or two, so the negotiations among the NGOs are just about as heavy as the negotiations among the delegate countries – you work to save my elephants, and I'll lobby for your whales. It's particularly complicated this time around because there's been a split within NGO ranks over the tuna boycott – whether any kind of compromise, any level of dolphin kill, is acceptable.

This is also the first CITES conference where secret ballots are commonly used, making it harder for us NGOs to direct our lobbying efforts, and making it easier for countries to vote with their pocketbooks, not their morals.

There are five resolutions on the table to down-list different species of whales. Greenpeace successfully concentrates on these, although they come close to blowing it with a very passionate speech that dumps all over the Norwegians and Japanese and hardens our opposition.

Michael and I focus on what *appears* to be a small resolution from Japan. But if it passes, it'll be like taking your finger out of the hole in the dyke – the whalers will come pouring through. As it stands, CITES can't act in contradiction to the IWC. So the commercial moratorium we've managed to establish at the International Whaling Commission guides CITES. Japan now proposes that CITES establish its own whaling policies, instead of following the IWC. It would make the Whaling Commission completely irrelevant – there goes the moratorium, and here comes full-scale commercial whaling. *Sayonara* to the whales.

We pull it off – this time. But I head home to Paciano worried about the fractures within the conservationist NGO community. If we don't pull together, twenty years of work to save the whales will come undone. We need a project, something everybody can pull together on, like the Antarctic sanctuary.

In my mind I run through all the remaining oceans, but keep coming back to the Caribbean. During the run-up to the vote on the Antarctic sanctuary, we'd gotten to know many of the Caribbean NGOs, and they'd asked not to be forgotten once they'd done their bit in getting the sanctuary through. I haven't forgotten them.

By November and olive-picking, we have the beginnings of a plan.

Harvest at the farm is always a very international affair. Friends from around the world come for two or three weeks to pick olives in exchange for a bed, good food and all the *vino rosso* they can drink. Chris Robinson comes in 1997, and in the evenings he sits outside and accompanies the church bells on his didgeridoo.

Every year there's one day when the men take off around the lake and drink too much, which is what Chris thinks is happening one sunny morning when I tell him we're heading out to get into trouble. Within a few hours it'll become clear just how much trouble I mean. We go to Sidney Holt's place outside Citta della Pieve, where Sidney pulls out maps of the Caribbean and begins to talk about the migration of the humpback whales. All very non-specific, but Chris can see this is going somewhere ... *he's* going somewhere. Once we actually say the words, it takes about two minutes for Chris to agree that a Caribbean campaign is a good idea, and about thirty more seconds, maybe less, to agree to another voyage on *Vega*, a public awareness tour of Caribbean nations.

The IWC holds its 1998 meeting in Antigua-Barbuda, the perfect location to test the Caribbean sanctuary idea on the other NGOs. At a small 'hard-core' meeting in my hotel room, we broach the subject with my closest allies – Cassandra Phillips from World Wildlife, Patti Forkan from the Humane Society of the USA, Vassilli Papastavrou from International Fund for Animal Welfare, and John Frizell from Greenpeace.

They're an easy sell. We take it to the daily meeting of all the NGOs, and the local NGOs give us the vehicle we need to make a difference in the Caribbean. There's an environmental protocol already on the books that just needs a big push. SPAW was designed to protect the Caribbean region, not just the whales, but all marine life! It stands for Specially Protected Areas and Wildlife, and is part of the 1983 Cartegena Convention. To go into force, the Protocol needs nine ratifications. It has five.

Now we have a plan, the kind I like, with a simple clear objective. Get those four ratifications.

By the time the IWC meets again in St George's, Grenada, in 1999, SPAW has been ratified by seven countries. Two more to go.

I'm pretty low physically in May of 1999 in Grenada, recovering from heart surgery some months before that's left me feeling pretty vulnerable. Late one night I'd fallen asleep in front of CNN and woken with an unmistakable pain across my chest. Heart attack. I'd been to the hospital earlier that day; they wanted to keep me in for tests but I wouldn't stay. They sent me home with a heart pill, just in case. But when the attack hit, for some reason I was almost blind and couldn't find the pill. I managed to crawl to the phone and dial Rowan's number next door. He rushed over and popped the pill in my mouth. Without him, there's not a chance I would have made it.

So by the time I'm back in action in Grenada, I know I should be taking it easy, but I don't want the Japanese to sense any weakness. One night Grenada's Prime Minister hosts a cocktail party for all the delegations and NGOs. It's in a big hall dominated by one wall on which is pinned a gigantic whale made out of balloons – an unintentional metaphor for the fragility of the environment. Rum and coke in hand, I make my way over to my old adversary, the head of the Japanese delegation. We have a hilarious conversation; he accuses me of being in the environmental business for the money! What money?!

At least it's clear that the Japanese don't have a clue that the main reason I'm here is to push SPAW. I make a very valuable new contact at that meeting, a man who has unique access to people in high places in the Caribbean. But he'll remain nameless, since his work isn't done yet, and he'll be more effective if they can't see him coming.

That summer, 1999, is a big one for me. I want to clean up SPAW. And, more, I have to clean up my personal life. I still feel like a teenager in some ways, eager to get in trouble, to push the limits. But my body is definitely telling me that I don't have for ever.

Julia is now 15. The little brother she doesn't yet know exists is seven. I finally tell Christina about George and Domi. And after many tears and accusations of betrayal, we arrange to meet, the five of us – two fantastic women, two fantastic children, and a very uncomfortable old man who is at the centre of it all and, for once, truly wishes he wasn't.

Christina flies with Julia from Stockholm to Paciano, for the first time in many years. Domi and George take the train up from Rome, a more routine excursion. Everybody's nervous. I'm terrified.

Julia and Christina arrive first, and together we three go to meet George and Domi at the little train station in Chiusi. Wise woman and fantastic organizer that she is, Domi suggests we take an excursion to the little island in the centre of Lago Trasimeno. Waiting for the ferry in the bar by the lake, George beings to play with little toys at the table. Julia has been very quiet, concerned about her mother, I think. But she joins George, the little brother born to her consciousness when he's already seven years old. And George – who's often quite shy of strangers – begins to talk. His first language is Italian, hers Swedish – like their mothers. So they speak to each other in English, a common tongue learned because their father is the only one in the room who has no ability with languages.

I am almost as proud as I am uncomfortable. Although I'm totally unsuited to fatherhood, these two beautiful and brilliant children are mine. And this time, I don't run away. To anyone who finds family life easy, and changing the world difficult, this probably sounds strange – but it's the hardest thing I've ever done.

Afterwards, George tells me that this is the best day of his life, and Julia is the most beautiful girl he's ever met. Julia writes and asks me to give George a big hug. I don't think anything in my life has been more satisfying, or a greater relief. Wish I'd discovered earlier that an obsession with saving a little bit of the world doesn't have to mean losing your own children.

It's one of the sweetest summers of my life, at least since my brother and I were boys in a dugout canoe on Buccaneer Bay.

A few days later I get a phone call telling me it looks like we have the last ratification to bring SPAW into force, to save the Caribbean Ocean. It's far from done, since only countries that ratify SPAW will enforce it. But we're on our way. If we can get Jamaica to ratify, that'll swing a big block of countries.

This is another big campaign, like saving Antarctica. And I can see clear, practical, small steps to winning it. It's simple. Seriously.

Think I'll have a go.

Epilogue

DAVID McTAGGART DIED on 23 March 2001 driving home along on a familiar stretch of highway near his olive farm at Paciano, Italy. It was late on a Friday afternoon, a lovely spring day. David had returned from the Caribbean just a few days earlier, and was high on the sweet smell of the next victory just around the corner. He felt very close to two crucial SPAW ratifications, Mexico and Jamaica, and thought one more trip in the summer of 2001 would likely 'nail it'. He had lunch with good friends about a forty-minute drive away from the farm, and then realized he had better head back to take the heart medication he'd forgotten that morning. David was perhaps ten minutes from home when he lost consciousness, drifted into the oncoming lane, and hit another vehicle. It's believed he died before the impact, which also killed an elderly Italian man and seriously injured his wife.

David would be desperately sorry he took anyone else with him, but *not* sorry that he himself didn't stick around into old age. During the 25 years that we've been friends, David talked with increasing frequency about his apprehensiveness around ageing. So much of David's strength was in his almost adolescent view of himself as invincible. His absolute belief, physically in his athlete's reflexes, and mentally in his extrasensory instinct, allowed him to walk through walls. He just didn't acknowledge them. It sounds like an exaggeration, but it's truly not: David simply didn't believe that any challenge was beyond him. That was the power, and the joy, of McTaggart in the environmental movement. He was proof of the phenomenal power of one individual, and it's impossible to exaggerate how convincing he could be in unleashing the power in others. During the months that I helped David with this book, many people laughingly told me of turning their lives upside down because David had a plan of which he'd convinced them they were an absolutely essential part. He entered lives as he entered rooms, like an electrical storm, charging the air around him, a very disturbing presence. Those of us frequently blessed with his company describe a common feeling – of sometimes wishing quite desperately that he'd leave, and missing him the second he did.

The Friday that he died, e-mail inboxes around the world filled up with grief as friends and colleagues sought one another out. Someone said it was as if all the air had left the room.

The next day Domitilla Senni left Rome for Umbria to help arrange the funeral. With Domi was George McTaggart, her nine-year-old son with David. Just outside Rome, they saw a rainbow, appearing to come down at Paciano, and as Domi turned off the main highway at Fabro there was another rainbow, a little one, also appearing to touch the earth near David's farm.

The funeral was in a little park along the Strada Serafini just outside the walls of Paciano. Between Domitilla and Brian Fitzgerald, they'd managed quite an accomplishment – no mention of God at a funeral service on a Sunday in Roman Catholic Italy. David would have been relieved, but not nearly as relieved as to see that four of his five children had come to say goodbye – one daughter, Tamra, was too ill to travel. During the last few years of his life, David talked often of his inadequacies as a father, especially with his eldest three children. His estrangement from them was a real sadness for him, one that he didn't know how to heal. What he says is true; for him changing the world was a much, much easier task than maintaining ordinary family relationships.

As the simple service began, friends and colleagues left the bar beside the park to gather on the grass beneath a little piazza. We looked up a long stone staircase to the rim of the terrace above, and gazing back at us was a poster-sized picture of McTaggart, chin on hand, looking both amused and world-weary, as if he'd prefer to be in the bar. Behind that picture was the coffin, and a few feet to our left of it stood a row of remarkable women, and one little boy: Drew's wife, Myrna, who anchored the family; David's grown daughters Lisa and Kerin; seventeen-year-old Julia with her mother, Christina; and young George beside Domitilla. The compartments of David's life sprang open upon his death, and those of us who knew his complicated family story wished he'd been there to see that it was fine, and to hear his eldest daughter Lisa's words of reconciliation: 'I grieve deeply that I was unable to find more tolerance in my heart before this. I hope and pray that David can hear me now and we can forgive ourselves.'

Many of David's old friends and colleagues were there, including most of the people you've met in these pages – Brice Lalonde, Remi Parmentier, Chris Robinson, John Frizell, Sidney Holt, Leslie Busby, Rowan Holloway and Annette Groenwold, David's girlfriend from Hoorn.

Perhaps this is a good time to mention that McTaggart was driven quite mad during the writing of this book by the impossibility of crediting everyone who'd played an important role in his life and work. Moving at the pace he did, David made so many important alliances, and attempts at describing all of them seemed to move us towards incomprehensibility. He was finally convinced that you would all understand his desire to keep it simple.

Typical of any gathering built around McTaggart, his funeral was translated, this time between English and Italian since so many local people attended. Bruno from his favourite pizzeria was there, and Anna from the restaurant, Marco from the bar, Luisa from the little café where David read his newspaper each day – she's put his table away for the time being, a quiet personal memorial.

McTaggart would have scoffed at all the fuss and the sentiment; he expressly wrote in his will that there would be a one hundred dollar (US) fine for sadness, but secretly he would have loved the attention.

Through it all, a restless wind blew and he seemed to be in it, pushing us along through our grief, since nothing ever went fast enough for him.

At the conclusion of the simple ceremony, we were all invited to climb the long stone staircase, pass under that bemused picture of McTaggart, and say goodbye at the coffin. Someone had filled big baskets with trimmings from the olive trees, so that everyone could take away a piece of Paciano. But instead, people chose to place the cuttings on the coffin, and it ended up covered in a soft green blanket from the land where David had finally found a home.

The music playing during the slow march of this sad procession was at David's request – Tom Waits' bluesy version of 'Waltzing Matilda', the tune most often blasting out of his car stereo, the song that took him back to Mururoa:

> And it's a battered old suitcase
> to a hotel some place,
> and a wound that will never heal.
> And no prima donna,
> the perfume is on
> an old shirt that is stained with blood
> and with whisky.
> We'll go waltzing Matilda …

Afterwards people gathered at a restaurant on the hill over-looking Paciano to drink and tell stories – McTaggart's favourite pastime, right after sticking the needle into the powerful and pompous. As at any wake, there was much laughter about the dearly departed's eccentricities; in David's case sharing a restaurant meal with him was a frequently re-told tale. As with everything, David was impatient; he couldn't stand how long it took to order, how indecisive people were, so he'd simply order for everybody, whatever he felt like. He did it all the time, no matter how strenuously people objected, and it speaks to what great company he was that he only dined alone by choice.

But there was more than memory on the wind that day. As always, David's clearest message came not in words, but in action. He worried that the environmental movement was fragmenting, people were losing the important lessons of the past – that success comes from working across national boundaries, working *together*. His death brought a powerful, international group of environmentalists together and the air buzzed with plans being made, plots being hatched, alliances rebuilt.

David McTaggart gathered around him a generation of young environmentalists, and fanned the fire in their bellies with the breath of his passion. He had an eye for the willing and the able, and the charisma to convince such people to leave ordinary life behind and 'have a go' at changing the world. This man who had such difficulty with ordinary family relations created a dynasty of committed campaigners for the natural world, colleagues and allies who carry on the good fight with much joy and hoisting of glasses, and with a sense of honouring David.

But they miss the man who could read shifting alliances at a glance, and who could persuade almost anyone to do almost anything.

In the weeks after McTaggart's death, dozens of people posted memories on the Greenpeace website. You could tell those who knew David well or had worked with him closely, because a word like 'exasperating' always appeared in close proximity to the word 'brilliant'.

Kieran Mulvaney wrote a couple of paragraphs that describe the McTaggart experience very well:

David was probably the single most exasperating, infuriating, obnoxious, obstinate man I ever met, and probably also the single most brilliant, charming, energetic, and charismatic ... As much as he sometimes seemed to regard details as an irritating irrelevance to be ignored or trampled over as appropriate, his overall strategic vision was outstanding, and his political antennae were remarkably acute.

Having David McTaggart in your life was like living in the path of a tornado. You knew the storm could blow along at any time, but there was never enough time to reach the storm cellar; before you knew it, your life had been turned upside down and inside out, and by the time you had caught your breath, he had moved on to something else. But it was an incredibly exhilarating ride.

David's friend and long-time administrative assistant, Jenny Stannard, talked about 'the collective dream that was David'.

In a sentence deceptive in its simplicity, Lena Aahlby summed up McTaggart's true value to Greenpeace, to the environmental movement, to modern history: 'He made millions of people realize that they could see a problem and act on it.'

But David would probably want to close with something like this, from Jon Hinck: 'My guess is that he would grow impatient with the remembrances, swear under his breath at us and then suggest, just a little more sweetly, that we get on with the goddam job.'

Helen Slinger

Index